ONE OF CUSTER'S WOLVERINES

ONE OF CUSTER'S WOLVERINES

The Civil War Letters of
Brevet Brigadier General James H. Kidd,
6th Michigan Cavalry

edited by

Eric J. Wittenberg

THE KENT STATE UNIVERSITY PRESS
Kent, Ohio, and London

© 2000 by Eric J. Wittenberg
Library of Congress Catalog Card Number 00-035635
ISBN 0-87338-670-1
Manufactured in the United States of America
04 03 02 01 00   5 4 3 2 1

Library of Congress Cataloging-in-Publication Data

Kidd, James Harvey, 1840–1913

    One of Custer's Wolverines : the Civil War Letters of Brevet
Brigadier General James H. Kidd, 6th Michigan Cavalry / edited
by Eric J. Wittenberg.

      p.   cm.

    Includes bibliographical references and index.

    ISBN 0-87338-670-1 (alk. paper) ∞

    1. Kidd, James Harvey, 1840–1913—Correspondence.
2. United States. Army. Michigan Cavalry Regiment, 6th
(1862–1865) 3. United States—History—Civil War,
1861–1865—Personal narratives. 4. Michigan—History—
Civil War, 1861–1865—Personal narratives. 5. United
States—History—Civil War, 1861–1865—Regimental
histories. 6. Michigan—History—Civil War, 1861–1865—
Regimental histories. 7. United States—History—Civil War,
1861–1865—Cavalry operations. 8. Soldiers—Michigan—
Correspondence. I. Wittenberg, Eric J., 1961– II. Title.

E514.6 6th .K44 2000

973.7'474—dc21   00-035635

British Library Cataloging-in-Publication data are available.

Frontispiece: Capt. James H. Kidd, age twenty-two years. This photograph was likely taken not long after he received his commission in the 6th Michigan Cavalry in fall 1862. Courtesy of the Bentley Historical Library, University of Michigan, Ann Arbor.

War must be carried on systematically, and to do it you must have men of character activated by principles of honor.
　　　　　　　　—*Gen. George Washington (1732–1799)*

If officers desire to have control over their commands, they must remain habitually with them, industriously attend to their instruction and comfort, and in battle lead them well.
　　　　　　　　—*Lt. Gen. Thomas J. "Stonewall" Jackson,*
　　　　　Letter of Instruction to Commanding Officers,
　　　　　　　　　　　　　　November 1861

In a great, momentous struggle . . . it is character that tells. I do not mean simply nor chiefly bravery. Many a man has that, who may become surprised or disconcerted at a sudden change in the posture of affairs. What I mean by character is a firm seasoned substance of soul. I mean such qualities or acquirements as intelligence, thoughtfulness, conscientiousness, rightmindedness, patience, fortitude, long-suffering and unconquerable resolve.
　　　　　　　　—*Maj. Gen. Joshua L. Chamberlain,*
　　　on the dedication of the 20th Maine Monument at Gettysburg,
　　　　　　　　　　　　　　October 3, 1893

The cavalry constitute the eyes and ears of the army. The safety of the entire command depends upon their vigilance and the faithfulness of their reports.
　　　　　　　　—*Lt. Gen. Daniel Harvey Hill to his troops,*
　　　　　　　　　　　　　　February 25, 1863

But foremost in the fight you'll see
Where'er the bravest dare be,
The sabres of thy cavalry
Michigan, my Michigan
    —From the Michigan Cavalry
        Brigade Monument on
    East Cavalry Field, Gettysburg

Contents

Editorial Notes and Acknowledgments

Rightly or wrongly, George Armstrong Custer has been a fixture in the collective American consciousness for almost a century and a half. As a result of the tragic end he met on the Little Big Horn in 1876, he is primarily remembered for his post–Civil War exploits. In recent years, however, historians have focused on Custer's pivotal role in winning the American Civil War. That attention, in turn, has brought to light the accomplishments of the command most closely associated with him, the Michigan Cavalry Brigade. Made up of four fine regiments of veteran volunteer cavalry, the Michigan Brigade fought hard throughout the war, gaining undying fame in the process. Custer's Wolverines, as they called themselves, left behind a sterling record of service, engaging in more than sixty battles and skirmishes during their career with the Army of the Potomac. By the end of the war, the Michigan Cavalry Brigade was, perhaps, the finest single cavalry brigade in service—for the Union or the Confederacy. It was certainly the most famous, perhaps as a result of the Custer connection.

James Harvey Kidd of the 6th Michigan Cavalry, who began the war as a twenty-one-year-old college student and ended it as a twenty-five-year-old colonel, was a fine example of the sort of men who followed Custer's lead. Not long after the end of the war, the young horse soldier received a brevet to brigadier general, a remarkable accomplishment for a man who was not a West Pointer. A newspaperman by trade and training, Kidd had a true gift for the written word, bringing a reporter's keen sense of observation to his writings. Throughout the war, Kidd wrote long, informational letters home to his parents and family. It is fortunate that those letters have been preserved and remain available to the modern historian. Kidd also wrote an outstanding memoir, *Personal Recollections of a Cavalryman in Custer's Michigan Brigade in the Civil War;* wrote a brief early biography of George Custer; and frequently lectured at various veterans' events.

I found Kidd's letters in the course of researching the June 1864 Battle of Trevilian Station, wherein Kidd's command played a major role. After reading several of the letters, I realized that this story needed to be told. My purpose here is twofold. First and foremost, the letters tell the story of a young man's participation in the greatest adventure of his life. Second, through the letters, Kidd's numerous postwar writings, and the words of others, I hope to portray some sense of the life of one of Custer's most loyal followers. This book is not intended to be a definitive biography of James H. Kidd. Instead, I have included all of Kidd's letters home describing his military service. The letters paint a picture of a close-knit family separated because of young James's sense of duty. Kidd's keen powers of observation and his ability to translate those observations into written words help us to understand the ordeals suffered by the men who fought and died during the American Civil War.

An appendix provides a complete itinerary of the actions, engagements, skirmishes, and raids of the 6th Michigan Cavalry, presented here for the first time. Many of Kidd's other writings about his experiences in the American Civil War will appear in the forthcoming companion volume to this book, *At Custer's Side: The Civil War Writings of Bvt. Brig. Gen. James H. Kidd.*

A number of the letters sent to Kidd by various family members in the years 1864 and 1865 survive, and, where appropriate, I have included excerpts of those letters in the narrative. Kidd's diary for a portion of 1864 and for most of the second half of 1865 also survives. No other work has utilized this insightful little tome, and I have used it to supplement the narrative, particularly in the section dealing with Kidd's unhappy service in the Far West during the months immediately following the Civil War. Finally, I have extracted some especially enlightening examples of Kidd's command style from the regimental order books of the 6th Michigan Cavalry.

In an effort to maintain the integrity of the originals, I have faithfully recounted Kidd's letters and diary, complete with his grammatical and spelling errors. Likewise, I have included relevant portions of the letters from his family just as they were written. I have done little to edit any of the letters other than to add some punctuation to make them more easily readable. Those few places have not been marked. There are also places where words are missing or Kidd's handwriting is illegible. In those places, the fact that something is missing is marked in brackets. In addition, there are several letters where Kidd wrote text and then crossed it out; however, those deletions remain easily legible. I have included these verbatim, but they also appear in brackets. All references to soldiers appearing in the notes were extracted from the regimental roster published by the state of Michigan unless otherwise noted. Any and all errors in transcription are solely mine, and I take responsibility for them. Further, any errors in annotating these letters or in writing the narrative are also mine. Finally, I accept all responsibility for the interpretation of the various writings set forth herein.

As with nearly every project of this nature, I am deeply indebted to the assistance of a number of people. I owe the largest debt of gratitude to Susannah Warner of Ann Arbor, Michigan. Susannah did a vast amount of legwork for me, including the duplication of the large collection of Kidd material held by the Bentley Historical Library at the University of Michigan in Ann Arbor. She also made a special trip to Kidd's hometown of Ionia, Michigan, to photograph his grave and obtain information about the family's life in Ionia—information that is available only there. Finally, she also obtained other information for me about Kidd's comrades in arms from the 6th Michigan to flesh out the framework built by his letters. I could not have completed this book without her assistance.

My other researcher, Steve L. Zerbe of Cherry Hill, New Jersey, was, as always, invaluable. Steve was instrumental in obtaining various materials for my use. My friend and fellow cavalry historian Edward G. Longacre, historian of the Michigan Cavalry Brigade, was kind enough to review the manuscript and to comment upon its accuracy. The archivists at the Bentley Historical Library in Ann Arbor granted me permission to publish these letters, to use the many items included in the James H. Kidd Papers, and to use the large collection of photos from the Kidd collection held there. Blake A. Magner prepared the excellent maps accompanying this volume. The archivists at the United States Army Military History Institute at the Carlisle Barracks, Pennsylvania, helped me identify both manuscript and photographic sources for this project.

Cathy Marinacci, of Springfield, Ohio, allowed me unlimited access to her collection of photographic images, including those of George Armstrong Custer and Philip H. Sheridan that grace these pages. Likewise, John R. Sickles of Merrillville, Indiana, freely shared his large collection of images of members of the Michigan Cavalry Brigade, including the photograph of Kidd's childhood best friend, Angelo E. Tower. And Doug Cubbison of White Star Consulting made a trip to Washington, D.C., for me to obtain important photographs and the materials from the regimental order books of the 6th Michigan Cavalry.

I am also grateful to a number of other friends and colleagues for their contributions to this project. Allan and Rita Losh of Cedar Falls, Iowa, were kind enough to allow me to use the unpublished 1864 diary of Lt. George W. Hill of the 7th Michigan Cavalry as a supplement to these letters. Don Allison of Bryan, Ohio, kindly shared a number of letters by J. Osborn Coburn of Company I of the 6th Michigan, as well as a photographic image of Coburn that has only appeared in one other publication. Don Allison also reviewed the manuscript for accuracy. Dave Finney of Howell, Michigan, also provided photographs and useful textual material to improve the quality of this work.

Dan Wambaugh of Flint, Michigan, spent hours poring through old newspapers, made several trips to the Michigan State Library, and obtained a number of other important items. Richard A. Sauers once again shared his indexes to the *National Tribune* and *Philadelphia Weekly Times* with me, greatly aiding my search for primary source material on the Wolverines.

As he always does willingly, my friend and mentor, Brian C. Pohanka, lent his time and efforts to making this a better book. Robert F. O'Neill Jr. of Stafford, Virginia, a native of Michigan, reviewed the manuscript and provided me with the benefit of his extensive knowledge of Federal cavalry operations and of the Michigan Cavalry Brigade in particular. Horace Mewborn, the authority on Mosby's command, gave me photos and other Mosby-related materials. My fellow cavalry historian, Dan Beattie, of Charlottesville, Virginia, who is the authority on the 1864 Kilpatrick/Dahlgren raid on Richmond, also provided the benefit of his expertise. Gregory J. W. Urwin, of Temple University, who is the leading authority on the Michigan Cavalry Brigade, reviewed the manuscript and wrote the excellent foreword that follows. Laurence D. Schiller of Northwestern University's history department carefully reviewed this manuscript, as did Michael P.

Gabriel of Kutztown University of Pennsylvania, and Lorle Porter of Muskingum College.

The good people at The Kent State University Press once again gave me a vote of confidence and provided me with a great deal of help in bringing this project to fruition. John T. Hubbell, the director of the press, gave my book a real vote of confidence early in the writing process. John also provided me with excellent guidance in improving the quality of this manuscript, and Joanna Hildebrand Craig once again shepherded my work through the seemingly endless publication process. Because this is the second book project that we have done together, we have once again succeeded in bringing this work to fruition.

Finally, I am, as ever, deeply indebted to my wonderful and most patient wife, Susan Skilken Wittenberg, for her endless patience with my love for Civil War cavalrymen and their exploits. As she has with all of my projects, Susan traveled with me and suffered with me as I struggled to complete this project. I owe all to my wife, Susan, for her support and assistance.

Foreword by Gregory J. W. Urwin

The Army of the Potomac was the largest field army to fight for the Union during the American Civil War. Many would argue that it was also the greatest. Despite a mixed won-lost record, the Army of the Potomac displayed incredible courage and tenacity in the war's biggest and bloodiest battles—the Seven Days, Second Bull Run, Antietam, Fredericksburg, Chancellorsville, Gettysburg, The Wilderness, Spotsylvania Court House, and Cold Harbor.

On those celebrated battlefields, some of the Army of the Potomac's brigades earned legendary reputations, usually at great cost to themselves. These elite formations included the Iron Brigade, the Irish Brigade, the Vermont Brigade, and the Pennsylvania Bucktails.

Shortly after the Army of the Potomac organized its cavalry into a free-standing corps in 1863, that corps produced a crack brigade of its own—the Michigan Cavalry Brigade. Under the charismatic leadership of a bold young brigadier general named George Armstrong Custer, those four remarkable regiments (the 1st, 5th, 6th, and 7th Michigan Cavalry) fought with an aggressive bravado normally associated with their Confederate foes. Maj. Gen. Philip H. Sheridan, the hard-driving, hot-tempered Irish bantam who took control of the Cavalry Corps in the spring of 1864, made Custer's "Wolverines" his chief troubleshooters. Sheridan once quipped that whenever the other elements of his corps found themselves in a tight spot, "they all wanted to see Custer and the Michigan Brigade." Such esteem brought the Wolverines a series of tough assignments, considerable glory, and heavy casualties. In fact, the brigade suffered more losses than any other Union mounted organization of equivalent size. Alarmed by her husband's many close brushes with death, Elizabeth Bacon Custer complained to him in a letter written in the autumn of 1864: "Why is it your Brigade has to do everything?"

Much of the Michigan Brigade's laudable history would have been forgotten if not for the patient efforts of one of its most prominent officers, James Harvey Kidd. Kidd began his involvement with the brigade in August 1862 as one of the original captains of the 6th Michigan Cavalry. He attained the colonelcy of the regiment by July 1, 1864. After Custer took charge of a division on September 26, Kidd served briefly as the Michigan Brigade's commander.

Following the war, Kidd worked for forty-three years as a journalist, but he devoted much of his spare time to memorializing the deeds and sacrifices of his beloved brigade. His 1909 book, *Personal Recollections of a Cavalryman in Custer's Michigan Brigade in the Civil War,* ranks as a classic, one of the richest and most reliable accounts of Union cavalry operations in the Eastern theater. It has been reprinted four times, most recently in 1997.

When Kidd wrote his book, he undoubtedly drew on the fifty-odd letters that he penned to his parents while he was in the Army of the Potomac. Those letters are housed at the Bentley Historical Library on the campus of the University of Michigan, where they have been consulted by a handful of historians. In many ways, Kidd's wartime letters are more lively and revealing than his book. Through them it is possible to watch a callow college student accept a position of leadership and mature into a seasoned and self-assured warrior. The letters also reveal that Kidd's dedication to the Union remained unshaken through three years of hardship and carnage.

Cavalry historian Eric J. Wittenberg deserves high praise for making Kidd's letters available to the reading public in this delightful and informative book. Instead of merely printing Kidd's letters with scholarly annotations, Wittenberg has woven his subject's observations into a fascinating narrative. The richly detailed character of Wittenberg's connecting passages demonstrates his mastery of a wide array of sources. His comments also make Kidd's own words all the more meaningful by placing them in context. This book is not just the Civil War as James Kidd experienced it. It is also an authoritative history of the Michigan Cavalry Brigade and mounted operations in the Eastern theater. This book will take its place alongside Kidd's *Personal Recollections of a Cavalryman in Custer's Michigan Brigade in the Civil War* and provide us with a fuller picture of the Army of the Potomac's most elite cavalry unit and the boy who became a man while riding with Custer.

List of Maps

Introduction

*To go [to war] . . . was to give up cherished plans and ambitions; to
abandon their studies and turn aside from the paths that had been
marked out for their future lives.*

THE KIDD FAMILY had its roots in upstate New York, where James M. Kidd,
James H. Kidd's father, was born in Orange County on November 13, 1813.
Along with his parents, seventeen-year-old James M. Kidd moved to the
wilderness of Michigan in 1830. Settling in Pontiac, he resided there for
six years. Leaving in 1836, James M. Kidd, then twenty-three and married
to Jane Stevenson Kidd, was one of the first settlers of Ionia County, in the
center of the state. In 1845, he purchased a sawmill and a tract of land on
the Flat River at a place that became known as Kiddville, just outside Ionia.
Ionia lies about 150 miles northwest of Detroit, approximately halfway
between the state capital at Lansing and Grand Rapids. In the 1830s, Ionia
was a town of about two thousand people, bustling and steadily growing.[1]

There, the Kidd family "lived and labored, enduring the toils and privations that were shared in common by the early settlers, and rejoicing
with their associates in every accession to the neighborhood and every
appearance of additional prosperity." An 1843 Ionia business directory indicates that James M. Kidd was a "manufacturer of fanning-mills, chairs,
bedsteads, etc." He was one of the first and most prominent merchants
of Ionia and served several terms as a city councilman and as mayor.[2]

The Kidds had seven children: James Harvey, Sarah, Catherine, William,
Willis, Frances, and Hampton. James Harvey, the eldest, was born in Ionia
on February 14, 1840. Except for his college years and his military service,

James—known to his friends as "Bob" to distinguish him from his father—
spent his entire life in Ionia, which held a dear place in his heart. In 1860,
young James was twenty, Sarah fifteen, Catherine fourteen, William eleven,
Willis ten, Frances four, and Hampton three. Their aged grandfather Stevenson also resided with the family, as did two servants.[3] Little information is
available on these siblings, although snippets about them appear in the various letters exchanged between Kidd and his family.

Kidd attended school and lived the normal life of a child in antebel-
lum Michigan. As he grew older, he spent his afternoons clerking at his
father's store, located at the corner of Main and Third Streets in down-
town Ionia.[4] In 1858, he enrolled in the state normal school and gradu-
ated from the Ypsilanti Union Seminary in 1860. Later that year, he
matriculated at the University of Michigan.[5] Kidd recalled his time at the
University very fondly.

> That noble institution was, even then, the pride of the Peninsula state.
> A superb corps of instructors, headed by Henry P. Tappan, the
> noblest Roman of them all, smoothed the pathway to learning which
> a thousand young men were trying to tread. These boys were full of
> life, vigor, ambition, and energy. They were from various parts of the
> country, though but few were from the Southern states. The atmo-
> sphere of the place was wholesome, and calculated to develop a robust,
> courageous manhood. The students were led to study the antique mod-
> els, and to emulate the heroic traits of character in the great men of
> modern times.

He continued:

> The faculty in the University of Michigan, in 1860, was a brilliant
> one, including the names of many who have had worldwide reputa-
> tion as scholars and savants. Andrew D. White, since president of Cor-
> nell University and distinguished in the diplomatic service of his
> country was professor of history. Henry P. Tappan, President of the
> University, or "Chancellor," as he was fond of being styled, after the
> manner of the Germans, was a magnificent specimen of manhood,
> intellectually and physically. Tall and majestic in appearance, he had
> a massive head and noble countenance, and intellect profound and
> brilliant. No wonder that he was worshipped, for he was god-like in
> form and in mind.[6]

The students closely followed an increasingly volatile political scene, attending political rallies and speeches. The coming of war was prominent in all of their minds.

Kidd enrolled in the university's classical course, intended to prepare its students for entry "into the Learned Professions." Admission requirements were steep. All candidates had to pass examinations in mathematics, English, Latin, and Greek, and had to be familiar with classical works, such as Caesar's *Commentaries*, the *Aeneid*, and Cicero's *Orations*.[7] Once admitted, freshmen took courses in Latin, Greek, algebra, and geometry. Sophomores studied Latin, Greek, trigonometry, history, rhetoric, and chemistry.[8] The academic year typically lasted from the beginning of October to the end of June. In 1862, Kidd's last year there, the university had a total of 615 students, most of whom were enrolled in the classical course.[9] For the privilege of learning, students paid an admission fee of ten dollars and an annual tuition of only five dollars.[10]

During his time at the university, Kidd was a member of the glee club. He carried his love of singing and music with him for the rest of his life. His fondest memories involved singing in a group with three friends, including a young man named Brewster, Gus Buhl of Detroit—who, as a member of the 1st Michigan Cavalry, would die in action in the Shenandoah Valley in the fall of 1864—and J. D. Town of Ypsilanti. Montgomery Bidwell of Tecumseh accompanied the singers on piano and guitar.

Kidd recalled the glee club traveling to Ann Arbor from Detroit via train, and "As college boys will do on such occasions, especially if they belong to the musical set, the time was spent in singing glees and college songs." Upon returning to Ann Arbor, they attended a temperance lecture, where the speaker, who had been on the train with them, specifically mentioned the melodic voices of some young male traveling companions, who never would have sounded as good had they used alcohol. Kidd recalled, "We were pretty well known in Ann Arbor, and the audience having seen us come in, all eyes turned in our direction to see how we took it. My recollection is that we endured the ordeal with becoming modesty."[11]

While attending the university, Kidd assisted the local correspondent for the *Detroit Free Press*. "Acquiring a liking for this line of work, he was seriously considering making that his vocation for life when the Civil War broke out." In fact, Kidd was offered a full-time position at a good salary with the *Free Press* before he decided to leave for the war.[12] After the war, his active military career ended, he returned to his chosen vocation as a newspaperman. The writing skills he developed while working with the *Free Press* served him well for the rest of his life, as demonstrated in the letters that are the subject of this book.

In a letter from November 1861, we get the first taste of his correspondence home. To his uncle, Richard Kidd, he wrote: "I am under a physician's care myself. I have been suffering from a severe attack of Diptheria. Have been constantly attended by a Doctor, and have been confined to my room. . . . I became more debilitated than ever before in a month. The Doctor however promises that I am now on the sure way to recovery."

Like college students of any era, "Bob" Kidd complained about the state of his finances: "You may perhaps think that my expenses promise to be unusually larger this year. . . . It takes a good deal to start out with at the beginning of the year, but after the 1st few weeks the expenses will be comparatively smaller. From the necessity of the case, I am compelled to ask you to send me some more money. Please send me if you can spare it $25, as soon as convenient."

Uncle Rich sent the twenty-five dollars a few days after receiving James's plaintive request.[13]

With the onset of hostilities, many of Kidd's friends went off to war. With the first call for troops in 1861, his roommate, William Channing Moore, enlisted. Moore survived the war but spent time in a prisoner of war camp. Others also heard the clarion call of war and answered its first sounding. Many, such as Norval E. Welch and Elon J. Farnsworth, found fame and glory, dying bravely in battle. Kidd waited until 1862 to enlist, when it became obvious that the war would not end quickly. Many years later he observed:

> But the students did not all go. Many remained then, only to go later. The prospect of danger, hardship, privation, was the least of the deterrent forces that held them back. To go meant much in most cases. It was to give up cherished plans and ambitions; to abandon their studies and turn aside from the paths that had been marked out for their future lives. Some had just entered that year upon the prescribed course of study; others were halfway through; and others still were soon to be graduated. It seemed hard to give it all up. But even these sacrifices were slight compared to those made by older men and heads of families.[14]

Kidd later suggested that Chancellor White believed the coming conflict would last as long as thirty years, which helps explain the reluctance of the university students to go off to war.[15] Many of those who remained joined the university's own militia unit, known as the Tappan Guards. There, Kidd learned William Hardee's *Rifle and Light Infantry Tactics*, trained in the art of war, and was appointed second lieutenant. When the 21st Michigan Infantry was organized shortly after the end of his sophomore year in 1862, Kidd was offered a lieutenancy in one of its companies. He declined the offer, wanting instead to serve in one of several new regiments of cavalry then being formed.

Michigan congressman Francis W. Kellogg came home from Washington, D.C., with authority from Secretary of War Edwin M. Stanton to recruit two new regiments of cavalry. In June 1862, during the previous call for volunteers, Kellogg had recruited and equipped the 4th and 5th Michigan Cavalries.[16] The two new regiments would be known as the 6th and 7th Michigan Cavalries. When the 5th Michigan was formed, Kidd heard that it was to be called "Copeland's Mounted Rifles," named for the commanding officer, Col. Joseph T. Copeland, a prominent attorney.[17] Kidd knew about the good service done by the Regiment of Mounted Rifles in the Mexican War and was intrigued by the idea of serving in such a regiment. Along with several of his friends, Kidd attempted to enlist in the 5th Michigan Cavalry as a private but arrived in Detroit after the regiment's companies had been filled.[18]

Young James Kidd was a man blessed with keen powers of observation and a gift for description. He was a popular fellow, well liked by those who met him. His natural leadership skills, which developed during his formative years, served him well for the rest of his life. As a consequence, other brave young men followed his lead.

At age twenty-two in the summer of 1862, James stood 5 feet, 9 inches tall, and weighed about 140 pounds. He had a dark complexion, brown eyes, and black hair.[19] He also had a baby face. Wartime photos show a slight young man, possessed of angular, almost sharp, features, with a wild shock of hair, and little facial hair. In his memoirs, recalling his fear of being rejected from the cavalry as being too boyish-looking, Kidd wryly commented: "One of [Kidd's friends] called me into his private office and inquired if I could not manage to raise a beard somehow. I am not sure that he did not suggest a false mustache as a temporary expedient. I told him that it would have to be with smooth face or not at all. It would be out of the question to make a decent show in a year's time and with careful nursing."[20]

He eventually succeeded in raising a beard, which made him look a bit older than his actual years. Years later, the following description of "Bob" Kidd was given:

> He did not wear his heart upon his sleeve, nor did he open the gates of friendship to a stranger. But when he proved a man, found him worthy and appreciative; then he gave him confidence and friendship. He was never too busy to pay one courtesy. He would stop his work to visit with a friend at any time. He would put himself to inconvenience for one whom he gave his confidence. . . . I noticed that he was a man of generous judgments of others even when they might be opponents or open enemies. It was not easy for him to say a bitter thing. Often his opinions of others were more generous than was deserved. If ever he misjudged unfavorably, or spoke with bitterness, this was balanced over by the many times when he said kindly things about his injurers and rated his friends more highly than was just.[21]

This popular, brave, bright young man was about to set off on his greatest adventure, an adventure that shaped and molded the rest of his life.

The Organization of the 6th Michigan Cavalry

I am ready to obey orders, and only hope that I may not prove inadequate to the difficult task I have undertaken.

WHEN PRESIDENT ABRAHAM LINCOLN called for 300,000 additional volunteers "to bring this unnecessary and injurious civil war to a speedy and satisfactory conclusion" in the summer of 1862, Michigan had one mounted regiment, the 1st Michigan Cavalry. Commanded by Col. Thornton F. Brodhead, a Mexican War veteran, the 1st Michigan performed fine service in 1862 against Confederate major general Thomas J. "Stonewall" Jackson in the Shenandoah Valley and under the command of Brig. Gen. John Buford during the Second Bull Run campaign. The regiment took heavy casualties in a saber-swinging melee with Confederate cavalry at Lewis Ford on the afternoon of August 30, 1862, an engagement that unfortunately cost Brodhead his life. The 2d and 3d Michigan Cavalry were formed in late 1861, and the 4th Michigan Cavalry was formed in 1862. These units served in the West.[1] Michigan was to raise three new mounted regiments in response to Lincoln's call, with the 5th Michigan Cavalry being the first. "Early in August Col. Joseph T. Copeland obtained authority from the War Department to raise a regiment for the cavalry service. . . . On the 14th day of August 1862, the colonel very quietly went about the work of enlistment. From all parts of the lower peninsula the response came, full, hearty, and quick."[2] When Kidd's attempts to join the 5th Michigan were rebuffed, he and his friends returned to Ann Arbor "with heavy hearts at the lost opportunity."[3] The boys did not have long to wait for another opportunity.

Using his influence as a community leader, James M. Kidd asked several friends to intervene on his son's behalf with Congressman Kellogg. "Bob" Kidd's excitement about his prospects comes through in the following letter:

Ionia Mich
Aug 28, 1862

Dear Father

Mr. Lovell retd last night. Messrs. Jno. J. Fox & Avery[4] were at Detroit and pushed my matter along. Kellogg agreed that a company should be raised here and that I should have Lieutenant if not Captain. He wants to see the candidates and say *himself* who shall be Captain.

Mr. Lovell will go down tomorrow and wants you to go down. I can get quite a no. of boys right here in town.

Yours affectionately,
J. H. Kidd

OBVIOUSLY, THE EFFORTS of Mr. Kidd's friends succeeded, because the following letter was sent out by Kellogg's office that same day:

Headquarters of 6th Reg't
of Mich. Cavalry
G. Rapids, August 28th/62

To Capt. James H. Kidd

You are hereby authorized to raise a company of Mounted Riflemen for this Reg't on condition that you raise them within fifteen days from this date and report with them at the Rendezvous in this City.

F. W. Kellogg
Col. Commanding

The time is intended for recruiting this company up to Tuesday of next week-Sept 16th.

F.W. Kellogg

IN HIS MEMOIRS, Kidd commented, "My surprise and gratification can better be imagined than described. To say that I was delighted would be putting it mildly."[5]

To keep his tentative commission as captain, Kidd had to recruit at least seventy-eight men to fill the company. The first recruit was his life-long friend Angelo E. Tower, whose name appeared often in letters that Kidd sent home. Kidd described his task:

> The method of obtaining enlistments was to hold war meetings in schoolhouses. The recruiting officer accompanied by a good speaker would attend an evening meeting which had been duly advertised. The latter did the talking, the former was ready with blanks to obtain signatures and administer the oath. These meetings were generally well attended but sometimes it was difficult to induce anybody to volunteer. Once, two of us rode sixteen miles and after a fine, patriotic address of an hour, were about to return without results, when one stalwart young man arose and announced his willingness to "jine the cavalry." His name was Solomon Mangus and he proved to be a most excellent soldier.[6]

By September 15, 1862, Kidd had succeeded in filling quota. The unit was designated Company E, 6th Michigan Cavalry, and Kidd's commission as captain became permanent. His new recruits in tow, the newly minted captain arrived at the regiment's meeting place at Grand Rapids. An early history of the Michigan Cavalry Brigade noted that the new regiment "was rapidly filled, and mustered into service on the October 15, 1862, its rolls carrying the names of 1,229 officers and men."[7]

The new troopers "were all in citizens' clothes, and equipped with neither uniforms nor arms. . . . No two were dressed alike. They were hungry and wet. Few had overcoats, none ponchos or blankets."[8] Kidd's men fell in with the other nine companies of raw recruits at Grand Rapids, where Kidd met his fellow officers, men whose hardships he would share for the next three years.

The commanding officer was Lt. Col. George Gray,

> a lawyer of brilliant parts, a good type of the witty, educated Irishman, a leader at the bar of Western Michigan who had no equal before a jury. He had much reputation as an after-dinner speaker, and his polished sentences and keen sallies of wit were greatly enjoyed on occasions where such gifts were in request. Though generally one of the most suave of men, he had an irascible temper at times. The flavor of his wit was tart and sometimes not altogether palatable to those who had to take it. In discipline he was something of a martinet.[9]

Another officer commented that Gray "is very popular among the soldiers."[10] Gray's appointment was not without political intrigue: Representative Kellogg persuaded another officer, William D. Mann, to accept command of the newly formed 7th Michigan Cavalry so that Gray could be appointed to command the 6th Michigan.[11] Gray was shortly promoted to colonel of the regiment, and Maj. Russell A. Alger[12] was transferred from the 2d Michigan Cavalry to assume the post of lieutenant colonel.

Shortly after reporting for duty, Kidd wrote his first letter home as a soldier.

Ionia Mich
Sept 25, 1862

Dear Father

I came up from the Rapids night before last but expecting you out yesterday I did not write. The thing is now without doubt all right. Col. Gray Tuesday afternoon read at a meeting of Officers the names of Captains assigned to the "6th regiment Mich Cavalry." The following is the list:

(1)	Thompson	(2)	Torry
(3)	Drew	(4)	Deane
(5)	Weber	(6)	Andrews
(7)	Kidd	(8)	Armstrong
(9)	Pratt	(10)	Royce
(11)	Hyser	(12)	Wise[13]

The remaining Captains 6 or 8 in number were assigned to the "7th regt Mich Cavalry" to be formed immediately at Grand Rapids.

The Junior 2nd Lieutenants are *not* to be mustered out as was talked. I do not think you need suffer any apprehensions for me longer. I am assigned to the regiment although I have not got any *commission* yet. We expect to be mustered in the last of next week. Kellogg has gone to Washington for 10 days. A petition was sent to the Governor by the commissioned officers of the regiment to appoint Lieut. Col. Gray Colonel. It may or may not work. I prefer a regular army officer although I signed the petition. If you get a good chance to buy a *good* horse I think you are now safe in buying. I am obliged to return today and don't know when I should be at home again.

Very truly
Yr. affect. Son
James H. Kidd

THE INEXPERIENCED HORSE SOLDIERS spent their days learning their new trade, investing countless hours drilling, and mastering the skills necessary to perform their anticipated duties with the army. Kidd noted, "I was arrayed in Union blue, with shining brass buttons, bright yellow facings, and the shoulder straps of a captain of cavalry. No boy in his first trousers ever felt happier or prouder."[14] The camp bustled with activity. J. Osborn Coburn of Company I observed, "Camp Kellogg is . . . 'all noise and confusion'—no, not confusion—for everything seems to move along quite smoothly, and in tolerable order." He continued,

> It is a new thing to [the boys], and I fear that as its newness wears away, and the camp rules are more vigorously enforced, they will see less fun in it, and begin to realize that they are soldiers, and not citizens. How the change, when fully felt, will relish, is yet to be learned. I think there are none but have come determined to do their duty, and conduct themselves as becomes "American Soldiers." To fight the battles of their country mindfully, and when peace is again restored, to return home to their families and friends, as good but wiser men when they left.[15]

In the meantime, Kidd learned the ways of army bureaucracy.

Grand Rapids
October 14, 1862

Dear Father

I wrote yesterday in answer to yours but did not get to the post office to mail my letter. The cot which you sent was received and makes a very comfortable bed. Lt. Col. Smith[16] came out here Friday and Saturday and mustered in the regiment. I mustered 99 men and 4 officers. I have been very busy the last few days in making out trip locates etc. We shall now go to work at our muster rolls and I expect to get ready this week, so that I can spend next week in visiting. Col. Gray issued an order last night that all the officers of the regiment should be fully equipped with horses, sword, sash, etc in 12 days, or by the 25th of October. I have received my letter "E." I am on the right of the 3rd Battalion.[17] This is a good position one that suits me much. Capt Pratt is Co. M at the bottom of the heap.[18]

He says that some figuring has been done. He not having participated in that sort of thing has come out at the little end of the horn. I have heard of no presentations to come off and cannot say when the Girls must come down. My company is crazy for furloughs and a good many of them will be gone for some time. Please write often. You tell me not to be slow to make my wants known. I am in want of nothing just now except money of which can you send me a supply when convenient.

Affectionately,
James H. Kidd

As KIDD MENTIONED, the regiment was formally mustered during the second week of October. Coburn described the process:

> An entire company is called into line, upon the left of the officer, when the name of each commencing with the Captain, and following in order of rank, is called, who pass as their names are called by the mustering officer, forming in another line to his right. A few horses are provided, and each in the order above mentioned is required to mount, trot about forty paces, and walk back. The entire company is then sworn. This completes the mustering in. But, it of course is followed up by three cheers for the Colonel and three for everybody else.[19]

Kidd's Company E was now officially in the Federal service, and its training began in earnest. A few members of the 6th Michigan sneaked away from their training long enough to go home and cast their ballots on election day.[20]

As their training progressed, the men acquired mounts. Interestingly, each company was mounted on horses of one color. For instance, the men of Company A rode bays; Company B, browns; Company C, grays; and so on.[21]

On the bright, moonlit night of December 10, 1862, the newly mounted 6th Michigan Cavalry left Grand Rapids and marched to the local train station to catch a train to Washington, D.C. They carried no weapons. Kidd recorded, "On to Detroit, Toledo, Pittsburg, Harrisburg, Baltimore, quickly whirled. Flowers, music, words of cheer, everywhere. 'God bless you, boys,' was the common form of salutation. 'Three cheers for the old flag,' and 'Three cheers for "Abe Lincoln,"' were sentiments offered amidst the wildest enthusiasm, to which the twelve hundred Michigan throats responded with an energy that bespoke their sincerity."[22] Arriving in Washington, D.C., the Michiganders heard the booming of the guns at Fredericksburg, where the Army of the Potomac was desperately engaged.

The 6th Michigan pitched camp on Meridian Hill, in the northwest quadrant of the city. When Congressman Kellogg came out to visit, he invited some of the officers to accompany him on a call to the White House. Kidd was fortunate enough to be among the select group. His first sight of Lincoln was stirring: "There was no mistaking the tall, gaunt figure, the thin, care-worn face, the slovenly gait, as he entered the room. In appearance he was almost as unique as his place in history is unexampled. But spare, haggard and bent as he looked, he was yet a strikingly handsome man, for there was on his brow the stamp of greatness."[23]

The officers were introduced one by one, and the president greeted each in turn. Kellogg then stated, "Mr. President, these are the officers of a regiment of cavalry who have just come from my state of Michigan. They are 'Wolverines' and are on the track of 'Jeb' Stuart, whom they propose to pursue and capture if there is any virtue in a name." Lincoln's legendary sense of humor kicked in. "Gentlemen," said Lincoln, "I can assure you that it would give me much greater pleasure to see 'Jeb Stuart' in captivity than it has given me to see you." On that note, the president took his leave of the awe-struck officers.[24]

Upon the arrival of the other new regiment, the 7th Michigan, the units were formed into a single brigade. As a result of concentrated lobbying by Michigan's congressional delegation, command of the newly formed brigade went to Brig. Gen. Joseph T. Copeland, who armed the new regiment "after much personal effort and expense."[25] By mid-January, most of the regiment was armed with a combination of sabers, pistols, newly developed Spencer repeating rifles, and single-shot breech-loading Burnside carbines. The rapid-firing breech-loading weapons proved decisive on more than one field of battle.

With this powerful new ordnance, both the 5th and 6th Michigan were intended to do most of their fighting dismounted—much like classic dragoons—while the 1st and 7th Michigan were expected to fight mounted most of the time, using sabers and pistols in close combat. One regular horse soldier observed that the "Spencer . . . did . . . excellent service and gave an immense advantage to the troops armed with it. The brigade could throw in a tremendous fire when necessary, with great effect upon the enemy, who was naturally very often deceived in his estimate of the force opposed to him, judging from the unintermitting, incessant rattle along the line that he was contending with at least a division."[26] The newly formed brigade was assigned to the division of Gen. Silas Casey and attached to the defenses of Washington.[27]

> Camp near Meridian Hill
> Washington, D.C.
> December 27, 1862

Dear Father

Your very welcome letter of the 22d instant came to hand today and found me busy at work arranging for the conveniences comfort and healthfulness of the company quarters in our new camp. We have removed from the ground occupied by us on our 1st arrival in Washington which was low and the very *home* of disease and death to a location which is high pleasant and healthful. One can inhale a breath of air here without fear of pestilential damps and miasmic vapors. We are just outside the city on Meridian Hill overlooking Washington. Our camp has not yet received a name but may be christened "Camp Gray." All letters addressed to me as usual at Washington will be received. I have been provided with what are called the "A" tent for the men. Each tent holding 4 men. We have dug ditches entirely around the camp as well as by each side of the streets and entirely around each tent. This will keep our ground and the inside of the tents perfectly dry in rainy weather. The probability now is that we shall remain in camp here until spring and we are making every possible arrangement to promote our comfort and health. We are soon to have stables for the horses, and floors and stoves for the company tents. I find that men will exercise but little forethought or care for their welfare unless forced to do it by the strictest kind of military discipline.

> Monday Jan. 5

I commenced this letter as the date indicates several days ago but failed to finish it. Since that time we have become firmly settled in our new camp and have commenced daily squadron and battalion drills. Our horses are in excellent condition. Col Alger told me the other day that I had the best looking lot of horses in the regiment, that they showed evidences of the best care, but I can only merit such a compliment by *compelling* the men to take care of them. I am becoming every day more and more a believer in the strictest form of discipline. Men won't "do" if left to themselves. Isaac Hart and the two Brown[28] boys who worked for Mrs. Webster are among the very best men that I have got in my company. *Such men are scarce* in the army. Hart has been sick, not seriously. They are always well and always on hand. I am *perfectly* well, haven't seen a sick day since I left Grand Rapids. In fact I think I never felt so well in my life. Lieut. Soule[29] has been confined to his room ever since he has been in Washington. I have no confidence in his physical ability to endure a campaign in the field even if he were to recover from his present attack. The officers of the regiment visited the President, Gen Halleck, Gen Meigs, Secretaries Stanton and Welles[30] soon after our arrival and last week we paid our respects to Gen Casey[31] who has command I believe of all the reserve forces in and around Washington. "Copeland's" Regiment[32] it is understood has received marching orders to go to Fairfax. How soon we may be ordered off, no one can say. Our preparations are ample enough for a winter's stay in this city, but not our wishes or any convenience but the interests of the Government and the behests of the powers that be must be our authority and our *call*. I for one do not hesitate to say that I *prefer* to remain here, but come what may I am ready to obey orders, and only hope that I may not prove inadequate to the difficult task I have undertaken.

Our regiment is a fine one and undoubtedly could do good service in the field and there is where we *ought* to be. I hope we shall receive our arms soon. We have now sabres and 10 revolvers to a company and expect either to get the Spencer revolving rifle or the Ballard repeating rifle,[33] which just loads at the breach and is a very fine arm.

January 8, 1863

I have kept to work at this long enough to finish it and will tonight bring it to a close by assuring of my continued good health and promising to write hereafter as often as once a week to some member of the family.

Your affectionate son,
James H. Kidd

WEARY OF DRILLING and the monotony of camp life, Kidd and his colleagues itched for action. Maj. Noah H. Ferry, of the 5th Michigan, whose brother, Senator Thomas Ferry, was an influential Michigan politician, wrote, "I want to fight."[34] Another trooper of the 5th commented, "We have everything ready to leave here . . . [at] a minute['s] warning and go to the front lines near the enemy."[35] Although bad weather delayed their march to the front, the long-awaited orders to march finally arrived at the end of January.[36]

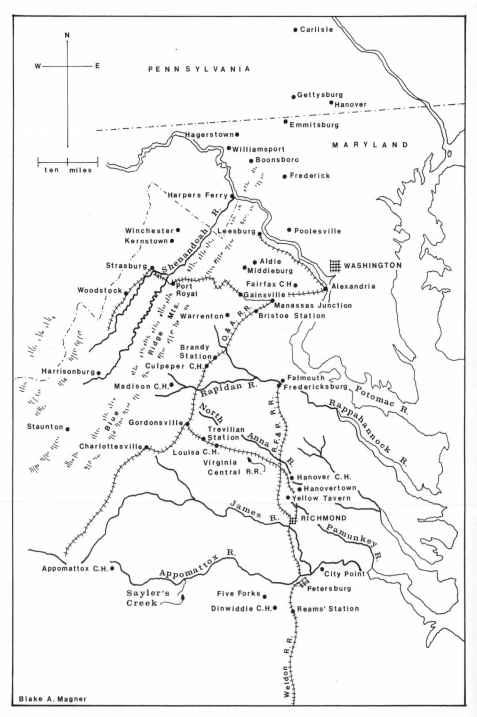

Theater Map of Operations by the 6th Michigan Cavalry.

2

In Pursuit of Mosby's Raiders

I came near running into a "hornets nest" of rebels.

THE 6TH MICHIGAN began the new year the way it ended the old, anxiously awaiting its first taste of action in the field. J. Osborn Coburn described conditions in the regiment's camp on New Year's Day 1863:

> The tattoo is sounding, and the pale moon is lighting the soldiers' way to his quarters, to answer his name at the roll call. The bands are finishing their last piece of music for the night, and the air is cool and bracing. Many of the soldiers feel as happy as though in the "old house at home," though without a coat, while many wend their way slowly and sadly to their tents, their day's duty over, there to lie down wrapped in their blankets, to pass perhaps a sleepless night, in thinking of their destitute families at home, and themselves powerless to aid them.[1]

Whiling away the cold winter days on Meridian Hill, Kidd wrote to his Uncle Rich in mid-January.

Headquarters 6th Mich Cavalry
Camp Gray near Washington
January 18th, 1863

Dear Uncle Rich

Yours by Mrs. Kennedy was received. I was very glad indeed to hear from you the more so as I did not expect to receive a letter from you until

I had first written myself. You was of course notified of my safe arrival at Washington through my letters to Father, and also from Mr. Farrer. The first two weeks of our residence here was rather unsettled but after considerable delay we pitched upon a satisfactory place for a camp and have now become comfortably if not permanently settled. Many conflicting rumors were afloat as to our ultimate plans and destinations. These have been finally settled & set at rest. Our regiment is brigaded with the 5th Mich Cavl'y under General Copeland who has received his commission and assigned to Gen Casey's division. Gen Casey is in command of the reserve forces in & around Washington and it is asserted that our Headquarters will be Washington, & this on apparently good authority. The 5th was understood to have received marching orders, but they were countermanded as I believe through the influence of Congressman Kellogg. That regiment has received nearly if not quite all of its quota of arms. Sabres, revolvers, and the "Spencer Rifle." Yesterday (Monday my letter not having been finished on Sunday) the 5th and 6th were reviewed on Capitol Hill by Gen Casey.

The payment of the amt. due the regiment came near suffering another delay. The pay rolls were made out from Oct 31st to Dec 31st and assigned to a Paymaster who had not yet entered upon the discharge of his duties and the prospect was that several weeks would elapse before we would receive a cent, but Mr. Kellogg took the matter into *his* hands and made such representation of our necessities refusing to take "no" for an answer that he succeeded in getting our pay up to Oct 31st with the promise that the balance should be paid within 10 days. Judging from what I have seen, I have made up my mind that Mr. Kellogg is the very best man our part of the country could have sent to Congress. The amt. of influence he evidently has with the departments surprised me. Any favor he asks for regiments from Michigan seems to be granted with pleasure.

For the comfort this regiment is now enjoying you can chiefly thank him. He is energetic and untiring and looks closely after the interests of his constituents. This tribute to his worth is not a *hired* newspaper eulogizing but a confidential expression of my honest sentiment. Between myself and Mr. Kellogg there has never been any *particular* cordiality and so far from anything it may say being instigated by him. He never could be aware that I entertain such an opinion of him. I hope that as long as I am in the army Francis W. Kellogg may be in Congress. Mr. Kennedy[2] has been rather unfortunate in his collections in connexion with this regiment. The Paymaster refused to acknowledge his claims or to take the trouble to pay them at the paytable leaving him to collect of the men or lose it. Numbers of the men refused to pay the amt. due him, and have left him $1600 short to await another pay day.

I am glad to say that my company has with one exception settled their matters to his satisfaction. One or two companies hearing of the stand taken by the Paymaster repudiated his claims almost in toto. The men in my company are most of them well. R. S. Compton has been sick but not seriously. Charles Axtell is progressing firmly with his band.[3] He gives good satisfaction to those officers who have to pay his salary and that is saying a good deal. Capt Pratt is working into his new profession admirably. He is becoming *"acclimated"* and will make an excellent Captain. Angelo is my *"right Bower."* Lieut Soule is still unfit for duty having been sick ever since the day of his arrival.[4] Lieut Craw notwithstanding his *greedy* desire for a Captaincy, and his earnest and most unsuccessful effort to gain popularity with the men is proving himself of great service to me.[5] We have had no snow here but the most changeable weather I have ever seen. One day is warm and sunny as a day in May the next cold as November the next rainy. Today it is raining and the wind blows causing us to be confined to our tents. For the first time in Washington I am at *leisure* with nothing to do except to attend to matters that have before been neglected. It would give me more pleasure than you could believe to hear from you often. Please write when convenient.

Yours very truly
James H. Kidd

As THE WAR unfolded, Kidd frequently sent money home. His letters on the subject indicate that his absence created financial hardship for his parents, and that he tried hard to make a contribution from far away. Logistical problems often caused paydays to be infrequent, creating great hardship for the men in the ranks.

Headqrs 6th Mich Cavalry
Washington D.C. Jany 20/63

Dear Father

I send you today by express $100. Mr Kennedy promised to take it but he went before I saw him & I could not send it in that way. I should like to send more but cannot until we get all of my pay. I may sell my horse but do not like to part with him. I could ride a company horse but you know what an attachment one forms for a good horse which is perfectly safe as mine is. He will stand until I get on & tell him to go. He learns faster that the men.

If you are in need of money immediately let me know & I will sell him. Col Gray wants him. It has been very rainy here of late. The mud is so deep as to render *"navigation"* almost impossible. *I am well.*

Affectionately yours
James H. Kidd

THIS LETTER ALSO points out the shortage of good cavalry horses. Government-issue horses were often largely untrained and had to be saddle broken and then trained to serve as cavalry mounts. A good horse was always in demand.

HeadQrs 6th Mich Cavly
Washington Feby 11/63

Dear Father

Enclosed you will find a draft on New York for $180. Please dispose of it as soon as possible. I would like to have you pay Uncle Edward the $30 he lent me. I wrote to him a few days since, and presume he has rec'd it and this. I am well but have not time to write a long letter today. The package of papers on 2nd, also the letters from yourself and Uncle Rich from Chicago and the one from you at Detroit. I hope to write you again in a day or two. Sarah's last letter came to hand. Love to all.

Yr. affectionate son
James H. Kidd

AFTER BEING TRAPPED in their camps by a series of snowstorms, the Michiganders finally received orders to march. The 5th Michigan received its on February 1, and orders for Companies I and M followed a few days later on February 6. The two companies went looking for a network of civilians that was smuggling medical supplies and other war goods to the Confederates. Two other companies joined the Michigan soldiers later.[6]

Kidd finally saw active service for the first time on February 26, when the two regiments of Copeland's demi-brigade were ordered to go on an expedition into Virginia. When the orders came, Kidd was in Washington, enjoying the sights. He returned to camp around 10:00 P.M., surprised to find his men scurrying about to get ready to march, cooking rations and packing supplies for the field. Thinking ahead, Kidd packed some food, sugar, coffee, and matches, supplies that served him well in the coming days. But the men of the 6th Michigan met no Confederates other than a few guerrillas. Their first expedition into the field was of little consequence.[7] With characteristic candor, Kidd accurately recounted the hardships faced by cavalry troopers on the march.

Washington D.C.
March 6, 1863

Dear Mother

If you have heard of our unexpected trip into Virginia you are very anxious to hear of my whereabouts and condition. As to the 1st, I am in Washington resting after the fatigue of a tedious march and as to the latter I am better than I was when I left, which is saying a great deal, for my health has never been better than since I came here. I felt a little out of sorts the morning I left, but was not *sick* and have been perfectly well up to that time. After a long rest in camp unvaried except by the daily routine of camp duties and drill in fair weather which we had but little of. We were ordered off unexpectedly in the night no one knew whither.

Marching all day from 2 o'clock in the morning till dark at night in a drenching rain, we encamped at Centreville, and tried to sleep without fire, or covering, the rain lasting all night. This was the 1st day of our *1st* experience and strange as it may seem I *enjoyed* it. Before starting I filled my haversack with some of the nice ham you and Emma sent. Hard crackers & above and some of the nice tea and coffee which was in the box. The little bag of coffee you sent was a real God-send. For not expecting tobacco I should have had some prepared. (hereafter I shall be *always* ready to leave at a moment's notice) I had a little tin cup, and some sugar and every time we halted, I made haste to build a fire, if dry wood enough could be found, then filled my cup, with water sometimes dirty from some streams & putting in a handful of the coffee made a drink, which was more invigorating & more palatable than I ever supposed any beverage could be. Hot coffee for a soldier wet & cold is better than medicine, and it is strange that anybody should advocate whiskey as a beverage when they have tried the effects of this simple proposition, a tin cup a canteen of water & a few matches suffice. I can do without anything to eat but can not dispense with coffee.

Many of our men were without food for two days. I was myself once so hungry after having marched from 4 o'clock in the morning till after 8 o'clk at night & our march not having yet ended then I ate a piece of *clear* fat ham, now with more relish than I ever ate an orange. But in spite of the hardships I actually enjoyed this trip, and felt perfectly well during the whole thing. When I began to feel cold & hungry, a cup of coffee made with my own hands set me all right again and 3 minutes was time enough to make it. But my men did not *all* stand it so well, several of them are sick, though most of the men reported sick in my company were sick in camp before we left. I now report 34 sick men. Most of them *slightly* so. My orderly Sergeant was H. Robinson[8] of Muir, a splendid fellow died of typhoid fever the day before we left. His body was embalmed and sent home. Levant Barnhart[9] is now my orderly. My horses are all used up. Out of 80 horses I only report 22 fit for duty. Such raids under the command of such men as Sir Percy Wyndham[10] will do more for the rebels than for us.

At Falmouth I saw Wm. Barden. He had received a commission as 2nd Lieut only the night before and was of course feeling rightly elated. I also saw Frank Wilson[11] son of Geo W. Wilson of Ionia.

Gen Hooker[12] was there and seems to be bringing order out of chaos. Our return occupied two days and was unmarked by any events of importance.

Saturday, March 21, 1863

I commenced this letter intending to send it off by the same mail or soon after the one I sent Father but before I had finished it we had again received marching orders. This time we were not ordered off on so short notice but were ordered at dark to be ready at daylight. We left here Wednesday morning March 11th and were gone a week. Our march only took us to Fairfax Court House. We were joined by the 5th and evidently started out for a long tramp but for some unknown reason we were stopped there, and kept in expectations for a week when we were abruptly ordered back to Washington. You have seen an account of the gallant exploits of Gen Averill's Cavalry on the Blackwater.[13] This was probably the work set apart for us but for some reason it was thought advisable to change the plan. Some say the streams were swollen so we could not cross. Some think a sufficient force failed to co-operate with us, and other stories are rife as to why *we* could not measure our strength with the celebrated Stewart.[14]

Col Wyndham has been ordered to report to Gen Hooker, and we shall therefore no longer be under his command.

Gen Stahel[15] formerly of Blenkers Division Sigel's Corps[16] is now in command of all of the cavalry in and around Washington. I rec'd a letter from Father today for which give him my thanks. I have received two (unanswered) letters from Kate. Tell her they gave me very great pleasure & I will answer them as soon as possible. I have also recd a letter from Uncle Rich for which I am very grateful. Please let him read my letters to you as I am unable to write to him personally very often. Give my love to all of his Family. Uncle Ed has not replied to the letter I wrote him. Willie's letter was received.[17] Thanks to him. Love to all.

Affectionately your son
J. H. Kidd

P.S. I forgot to state that your letter came duly to hand.

THIS LETTER ACCURATELY portrays the command problems faced by the cavalry forces assigned to the Eastern theater. For the first year and a half of the war, these cavalry forces were poorly utilized, often serving in small detachments assigned to menial tasks. When Maj. Gen. Joseph Hooker took command of the Army of the Potomac in January 1863, he formed a cohesive Cavalry Corps. In addition, there was also Stahel's independent division of cavalry assigned to the defenses of Washington, D.C. While not formally a part of the Cavalry Corps, Stahel's force often worked in concert with it. The first commander of the cavalry forces assigned to the defenses of Washington was a rakish twenty-nine-year-old English soldier of fortune named Sir Percy Wyndham, of the 1st New Jersey Cavalry. Years later, Kidd recalled,

> This officer was an Englishman, an alleged lord. But lord or son of a lord, his capacity as a cavalry officer was not great. He had been entrusted with one or two independent commands and was regarded as a dashing officer. . . . He seemed bent on killing as many horses as possible, not to mention the men. The fact was the newspapers were in the habit of reporting that Colonel or General so-and-so had made a forced march of so many hours, and it is probable that "Sir Percy" was in search of some more of that kind of cheap renown.[18]

One Confederate trooper noticed that Wyndham, who was adorned with a spectacular mustache nearly two feet wide, was "a stalwart man . . . who strode along with the nonchalant air of one who had wooed Dame Fortune too long to be cast down by her frowns."[19] Lt. Sam Harris, of the 5th Michigan Cavalry, called Wyndham "a big bag of wind."[20] Another Federal officer, remembering his first encounter with Wyndham, compared him to a bouquet of flowers, noting, "You poor little lillies, you! You haven't the first chance with the glorious magnificence of this beauty. He's only been in Camp for two hours, and he now appears in his third suit of clothes!"[21]

Wyndham quickly grew frustrated with the activities of the Rebel partisans. Their leader, Capt. John Singleton Mosby, became a focus of the Federal cavalry for the balance of the war. A twenty-nine-year-old lawyer, Mosby's reputation grew larger than life. Small in stature, he was memorable nonetheless. One observer, meeting Mosby for the first time, commented, "I was . . . somewhat surprised when one of my companions pointed to a rather slender, but wiry looking young man of medium height, with light keen eyes and pleasant expression."[22] This rather nondescript young man nevertheless struck fear in the hearts of professional soldiers.

Late in 1862, after good service as a staff officer, Mosby obtained permission to form a partisan unit, patterned after the exploits of the Revolutionary War hero Francis Marion, the "Swamp Fox." In September 1863, Mosby described his style of warfare: "The military value of the species of warfare I have waged is not measured by the number of prisoners and material of war captured from the enemy, but by the heavy detail it has already compelled him to make, and which I hope to make him increase, in order to guard his communications, and to that extent diminishing his aggressive strength."[23]

Recruiting men of northern Virginia, Mosby built a fearsome partisan force that began active operations during the winter months of early 1863. Lt. Robert Wallace of the 5th Michigan, captured by some of Mosby's raiders in April, recalled, "I was surprised to find that they were nearly all bright looking, intelligent, young fellows, sons of the country round about. They were a better class than is usually found in the ranks of either army."[24] It did not take long for this force to make its presence felt and for it to attract the attention of the Northern high command, which expended huge amounts of resources trying to hunt it down. It failed.

In early February, Wyndham was so aggravated by Mosby's activities that he threatened to send civilians to Old Capitol Prison as punishment for helping Mosby.[25] The failure of this threat to curtail the activities of the guerrillas led to a failed excursion that Kidd described. Wyndham blamed the Wolverines for the failure, writing, "My forage having given out, the Michigan cavalry not having brought any with them, and being a short distance from Falmouth, I thought it advisable to go there to supply my command."[26] Trying to justify his failure, Wyndham complained, "Had Stuart crossed the river, this movement would have been very successful, in conjunction with the cavalry of General Stoneman."[27]

Colonel Gray's report indicated that conditions were less than ideal for mounted operations: "The road, after leaving Warrenton, was in the worst possible condition. A very heavy snow, which had fallen previous to our march was disappearing, saturating the ground. Frequent rains contributed to make the roads bad and the march laborious."[28] Gray vented his frustration in his report to General Copeland:

> [I]n consequence of the extraordinary condition of the roads and the rapidity of the march from Bull Run to the camp near the Wolf Run Shoals, the brigade has sustained great loss. Not only were many of the men and horses compelled to be left behind, to come up when they hereafter can, but also many horses were left dead by the way. It will be many days before large numbers of the horses which reached camp can be used, and several, I fear, are rendered wholly unfit for future service. Not having any knowledge of the object of the expedition, I am, of course, unable to say whether or not it was accomplished. We did not see the enemy, and our march from his supposed direction was generally at least as rapid as toward him. A few stragglers were captured, and some horses taken, but what disposition was made of either I have not learned.[29]

As a consequence of his fruitless expedition, Wyndham was relieved and later assigned to command a brigade that included his 1st New Jersey.

After Wyndham's removal, Brig. Gen. Julius Stahel assumed command of the 3,600-man independent division of cavalry assigned to the defenses of Washington. Stahel was born in Hungary and was a veteran of the Hungarian war for independence. He arrived in the United States in 1859 and, in 1861, recruited the 8th New York Infantry (German Rifles), which he commanded at First Manassas. Serving with distinction in the infantry corps of Maj. Gen. Franz Sigel, Stahel was promoted to brigadier general in November 1862. Shortly after taking command of the cavalry division, he was promoted to major general.[30] Kidd left the following description:

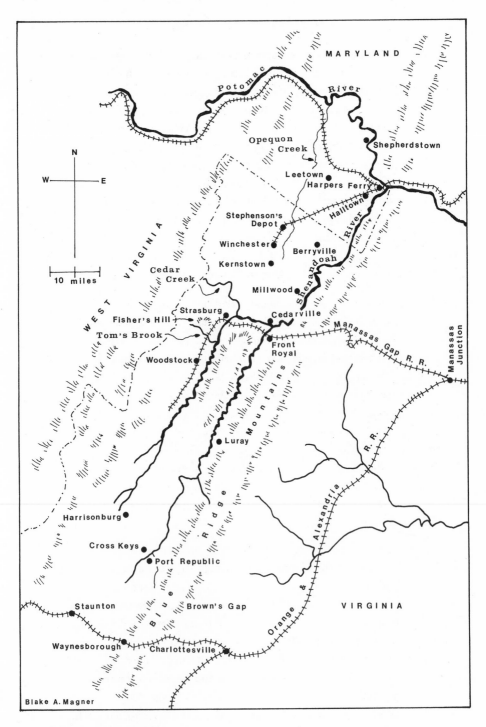

The Shenandoah Valley.

Stahel was . . . a "dapper little Dutchman," as everyone called him. His appearance was that of a natty little staff officer, or even a brigadier general by brevet. He affected the foreign style of seat on horseback, and it was "as good as a show" to see him dash along the flank of the column at a rattling pace, rising in his stirrups as he rode. . . . He took great pride in his messing arrangements and gave eloquent "spreads" to invited guests at his headquarters. . . . His staff were all foreigners, and would have been "dudes," only there were no "dudes" in those days. Dudes were a type of genus homo evolved at a later period. They were dandies and no mistake, but in that respect had no advantage over him, for he could vie in style with the best of them.[31]

A modern historian rendered the following verdict on Stahel's skills as a cavalry leader: "Though a lackluster field leader, the thirty-seven year old Stahel occasionally relayed credible intelligence about enemy movements outside his departmental confines."[32]

Kidd gave a very amusing account of the same expedition in a letter to his father. In it, he painted a humorous portrait of life in the field, with a small item like a bag of coffee playing a major role in the unfolding drama. The account shows how much the little things meant to a soldier in the field. This incident left such a strong impression on his mind that Kidd recounted this tale almost verbatim in his memoirs, written almost fifty years later.

Head Qrs 6th Mich Cavalry
Washington, DC March 6, 1863

Dear Father

I have received three letters from you since I last wrote, viz. one from Chicago, one from Detroit, and one acknowledging the receipt of the draft I sent and informing me that you had sent a box. I am very thankful for your letters and also for the box of provisions, which was very acceptable. The little bag of coffee which Ma sent has been of inestimable value to me and I shall show in the course of this letter. Our regiment has just returned from a "raid" into Virginia which for hardships and barrenness of results will lie with any similar expeditions that ever attempted to bag the Rebel General Stewart[33] or any other *fox*. On Wednesday night of last week I had been down to the city on business and pleasure and returned to camp at 12 o'clock at night completely tired out and nearly sick. I stopped two or three times to rest and with no little self congratulations arrived in sight of camp thinking of the pleasant sleep I was to have, but what was my surprise and chagrin to find the camp in commotion and everything in bustle and stir. Rations were cooking and knapsacks packing blankets swelling. Horses saddling preparations for a speedy departure, every where going on. The regiment had recd marching orders, and was to leave in two hours. I immediately set to work to expedite matters and exactly at 2 o'clock Company "E" was in line, with cooked rations (as was supposed) ready for "Dixie." None of us knew our destination nor did we inquire. I have learned one thing. *Never ask questions. Obey orders.* At 2 1/4 o'clock Thursday morning we left camp. We had hardly made our exit from the sally-port when it began to rain and rained with but little interruptions till the next (Friday) morning.

We marched till day break when we halted a few miles from Washington and were joined by the 5th Michigan Cavalry. When we resumed the march and at dusk that night reached Centreville passing through Alexandria.

The men slept out in the rain all night, or rather stood out for sleep was impossible. No wood could be procured and consequently no fires or hot coffee could be made. I was fortunate enough this first night to get a tent to sleep in and a fire to dry my feet, which with my clothes were completely soaked.

The next morning at 4 o'clock, we were again out on the march, having been joined by the N.Y. 5th Cavalry the Virginia 1st[34] and Pennsylvania 18th making in all about 2000 cavalry, all under the command (Col. Gray *2nd* in command) of Colonel *Sir Percy Wyndham* an English *lord* who has been in our service for some time and who has gained considerable *undeserved* notoriety. That day we marched beyond Warrenton, at which place we all supposed we were to have a fight, but although there were undoubtedly rebels there apparently no effort was made to capture them.

The next day being out of forage & rations and Fredericksburg (Falmouth) being the nearest point at which they could be procured to Falmouth we went, and Saturday night we camped in sight of Burnside's great battle-field.[35] No rations could be procured that night, and we went to bed on the ground without fire or food, in the rain. All night it rained, and the next (Sunday) morning we found ourselves in pools of water, our blankets wet through. Many of the men had eaten nothing for two days, having failed to provide themselves sufficiently before leaving Washing-

ton. Sunday morning we had rations of bread meat and coffee and managed to *steal* wood enough to cook a little coffee. Sunday we rested and
got our horses shod most of them having lost their shoes in the Virginia
mud. So little like Sunday did it seem that I did know or did not *think* of
it until nearly night. Monday morning at 4^1/2 o'clock, we started by the
nearest route, via Aquia Creek, Stafford CH, Fairfax CH &c to Washington where we arrived Tuesday night at 8 o'clock.

That this expedition accomplished nothing worthy of note is certain
that it might have accomplished much if it had been properly conducted
in my opinion equally true. It was a big *raid* on Government horses, and
men's health and that is about all. We lost a great no. of horses. I lost 4
from my company alone. One man, the Bugler of my company, whose
horse gave out, was left behind and probably taken prisoner. I sent 4 sick
men by rail from Falmouth and two by ambulance from Fairfax. I was out
6 days & five nights and was under cover once the first night. Thursday,
Thursday night, Friday, Saturday night & Monday night & Tuesday it
rained. Most of the time we went without wood nights. When I left I was
tired out and nearly sick when I got back I felt better than I have for some
time. I did not even take a slight cold. I will give further particular in other
letters. Love to all.

Affectionately

J H Kidd

THE NEXT NIGHT, seeking retribution, Mosby went after Wyndham personally because the "English officer's capture would help prevent any retaliation on the elders of Middleburg for allegedly supporting the raiders'
activities. Wyndham also had insulted the Confederate raiders by calling
them horse thieves, to which Mosby had replied that it might be true, but
all the horses had soldiers armed with pistols and carbines mounted on
them." Tipped off by a deserter from the 5th New York Cavalry, Mosby
led a raid far behind Union lines aiming for Wyndham's headquarters and
capturing the Englishman's uniforms and several of his staff officers. Wyndham had gone to Washington for the evening, thus avoiding the humili-
ation of being taken by Mosby's men. Another contingent commanded by
Mosby himself also captured Brig. Gen. Edwin H. Stoughton, commander
of the 2d Vermont Brigade, who was picketing along Cub Run and at Wolf
Shoals. Accompanied only by a detail of one hundred men and isolated from
the remaining regiments of his brigade, Stoughton made an easy target.[36]

Because of Mosby's increased activity, Federal efforts to capture him intensified. Partly in response, what became known as the Michigan Cavalry Brigade came together as a cohesive unit for the first time during March 1863. On March 11, the 6th Michigan left the defenses of Washington for good. The 5th, 6th, and 7th Michigan served together for the first time in the Loudoun Valley of Virginia. They made a good team. The 5th and 6th Michigan, equipped with their Spencer rifles, were intended to do most of their fighting on foot, while the 7th Michigan was "generally employed as a saber regiment but was able to fight skillfully afoot."[37] General Copeland noted, "The latter part of March . . . my Brigade was ordered to Fairfax C. H. where it was assigned to outpost and picket duty, and continued to perform that inglorious though important duty."[38]

The Michigan Brigade came together for an expedition to run down Mosby's partisans, who controlled a major portion of northern Virginia known as "Mosby's Confederacy."[39] One of Mosby's biographers described the terrain:

The strip of country spreading toward the Blue Ridge from the Potomac at Washington, the area from Dranesville and Leesburg to Warrenton, was ideal ground for cavalry fighting. It was made up of beautiful vistas, bare rolling hills, little clumps of trees. Stone and rail fences girdled occasional wheat fields and orchards, sprinkled about expansive pasture lands. Villages were small, far apart. In the western part of this stretch is a valley, small compared to the Valley of Virginia. It is bordered on the east by the Bull Run and Catoctin mountains and across the state from the Potomac to the southwest. This range rises to above 2,000 feet and is broken at intervals by gaps through which roads lead to the main valley. There is Snicker's Gap, opening the way to Winchester; Ashby's Gap; Manassas Gap, where the Manassas Gap railroad from Manassas Junction to Strasburg and other valley points tops the wall; still farther south, Chester Gap, around which the hills drop to afford passage to Front Royal, and finally, Thornton's Gap, making way for the road from Culpeper west. Through this country Mosby had determined to operate. It was rich and pastoral and would afford his command a not too difficult subsistence. But more important, the towering Blue Ridge and the lower-lying Bull Run range, within easy gallop of each other, would enable him to find quick cover when hard pushed by the enemy.[40]

Kidd found time to write home just before taking the field.

Vienna Va March 30, 1863

Dear Mother and Father

Last Tuesday our regiment was ordered off from Washington. We encamped 5 miles from Washington, supposing we would remain there or go to Fairfax the next day. At 8 o'clock next (Wednesday) morning having unloaded our baggage wagons. I had pitched my tent, set up my stove & commenced to cook a *nice* breakfast when I was ordered "to report with my whole command to Col. Alger[41] immediately." The 4 largest squadrons[42] in the Regt had been ordered off under his command. These were companies C D E & L. We went that day to Vienna our present location. We found the place guarded by about 150 men Cavalry & Infantry. Col Alger informed us on our arrival that intelligence had been recd by Gen Stahel commanding our division that this place was to be attacked that night & we had been sent to defend it. I was officer of the day & spent the whole night on horseback, posting and visiting our pickets but the enemy failed to come. The next day I went out on a scout & also on Friday I arrested several secessionists but discovered no trace of an enemy. We have since been re-enforced by two regiments of NY Infantry & a NY Battery. Col Gray with 5 companies left Fairfax this morning on a scout. There is a large cavalry force at that place. The 5th 6th and 7th Mich. & other regts.[43] Tonight we were informed that Stonewall Jackson is 16 miles distant with his whole command moving in this direction. At 12 o'clock we leave to reconnoiter. I have thought best to tell you the whole facts in this case. I shall inform you whenever possible of our whereabouts. The time has come for us to *work*. Pray that I may do my duty manfully in a manner worthy of you and of the men under my command.

Our detachment will be employed principally in scouting probably. I have great confidence in Col Alger. I write this sitting on the ground beside a camp fire which I have just been ordered to extinguish. Love to all. God bless you. Goodbye.

Yr. affectionate son
James H Kidd

ELEMENTS OF STAHEL's command almost captured Mosby on the night of April 1. Not expecting Mosby to go on the offensive in response, six companies of the 1st Vermont Cavalry were defeated by Mosby's bold counterattack.[44] The next day, as a result of the attack on the Vermonters, the 6th Michigan searched for the elusive Gray Ghost, but failed to find either Mosby or his men.[45] Another expedition set out on April 3. General Copeland, commanding the Michigan units, took them into the Loudoun Valley, into the heart of Mosby's Confederacy.[46] Although the Federal troops saw many signs of Mosby's activities, few of his men were spotted during the course of the four day expedition.

> Head Qrs Copeland's Cavalry
> Brigade
> Stahel's Division
> Fairfax CH April 7, 1863

Dear Father

The last time I wrote I was at Vienna. We were expecting an attack from nobody knew whom. All sorts of rumors floating about Stonewall Jackson, Fitzhugh Lee[47] and others. We went out as I told you we expected to but discovered "nary secesh." The next day our detachment was ordered back to this place. When we start our day when "boots and saddles" announced our departure again. We went in force and at 12 o'clock at night reached Aldie near Bull Run Mountain. Then we encamped or rather *stopped*. We had no tents and no fires and now on picket till morning when we resumed the march at daylight. We went to Middleburg and charged into the town finding no enemy *"as usual."* There we stopped and foraged finding plenty of rebel corn, hay, chickens, sheep, etc. Some men . . . while patroling the road beyond Middleburg met three men in citizens clothes one with a red overcoat on, and charged on them firing at the same time. Several shots were exchanged, these "citizens" showing their colors in the shape of revolvers. One of our men was killed & one of theirs when 4 more joined them and the remaining man was shot in 4 places viz in both arms. These are the kinds of men that Mosby commands. Citizens expect they can attack a weak or defenseless or careless force when they are the terror-inspiring band of Capt Mosby. Our boys killed one rebel and wounded another so that we would be even if one of our men were not worth a dozen of these miserable "bushwhackers." We are in the saddle constantly. If it were not for the weather we could endure this but it either rains or snows incessantly. Saturday and Sunday we were out in a pelting snow storm that drove away every thought of the most *sorry* kind of comfort. The mud is worse than ever. While such weather continues it is impossible for cavalry to accomplish much but kill horses and men. Now we are in camp I hope I shall be able to write some letters before we leave again. It takes one day for sleep after we have been out night and day for a week. It is strange how men will endure. They are healthier in the field than in the camp. I shall endeavor to write to Uncle Rich & others. Love to all. Write.

Yr affectionate son
James H Kidd

THE WOLVERINES SPENT several days searching for Mosby and his men, but failed miserably. One correspondent of the Michigan Brigade reported, "Next morning the force proceeded to Middleburg Armory, then about sunrise, but found no enemy, the patrols and pickets completely surrounding the place, so that if any unfortunate rebel was there his chance of escape was small." Colonel Gray's patrol encountered several of Mosby's men on the road, one of whom wore a Federal cap. Gray's men charged the few Rebel troopers, wounding a captain of Mosby's command, while one of the Wolverines was killed. The correspondent continued, "The rebels with characteristic chivalry stripped the dead body of the Union soldier, taking his arms, uniform, boots, and cap before our men came up." He concluded, "The General being satisfied that there was no larger force to be found and that Mosby had escaped, turned homeward with his command."[48]

One officer of the 5th Michigan wrote home to express the frustration that he and his comrades felt: "Had I been on trial in Michigan for whipping a lame idiot and stealing his dinner, I should not have been more mortified and ashamed that I was coming home yesterday."[49] Another, more concerted effort began a few days later on the 11th, and evoked similar frustration. One local resident described the scope of the search for the Gray Ghost: "The country is again filled with Yanks. Now in every direction we look we see squads riding over the fields stealing every horse have had four different squads here have searched the stable and brought out the old gray mare."[50] In the meantime, the Army of the Potomac prepared to begin the spring campaign known today as the Chancellorsville campaign.

On April 18, Kidd wrote an interesting letter in which he gave his father advice on politics. This letter highlights a major challenge faced by a Union army operating among a hostile populace.

Head Qrs Cavalry Detachment
Freedom Hill Va[51] April 18, 1863

Dear Father

I am here on picket duty. I wrote Uncle Rich once since we came here. This locality is two miles from Vienna near the Alexandria & Leesburg Turnpike.

The following is a rough sketch of the line picketed by our detachment under command of Lt Col Alger. I will however make a sketch and enclose it to you. This picketing is very pleasant duty, though dangerous and fatiguing. My company has been on every other day. 24 hours on and 36 off. We are hereafter to be on duty 48 hours. I have not allowed myself any sleep when officer of the day have been most of the time in the saddle.

Yesterday while riding through the lines with Lieuts Craw & Soule[52] I came near running into a "hornets nest" of rebels. I had crossed "difficult run"[53] which is beyond our pickets and took it into my head to explore a road which I had never been on. Spurring our horses into a gallop we went tearing along for several miles without finding any end to the road. I finally concluded to inquire where the road led & was informed by a woman that we were going to Drainesville where Mosby's whole force was said to be. Some of his men are known to be. She gave the distances to that place as 5 miles. I afterwards ascertained from a Union man that it was only 3. At the rate we were going, 10 minutes would have brought us there. I went on ½ a mile to a cross road leading to a ford across difficult and made my way back to our lines. I have no desire to meet any great no. of Mosby's men singled-handed and besides that had no business outside the Pickets. But a man on a horse grows explorative. We discovered tracks of 3 Rebel patrols who had been there the night before. The difficulty is they always know where we are what we are doing, and how many there are of us. We know comparatively nothing of them and have to find them in their own haunts. Everybody here is rebel. To my surprise little children surround us as our children would an Indian or an orangutan. By *proper treatment* I sometimes manage to work myself into the good graces of the secesh ladies but the men are unsusceptible as logs of wood. In this immediate vicinity there are several (3 or 4) men who are undoubted Union men besides them many who pretend Unionism but are ready to take the other side any time. This is a most beautiful country, and inhabited by enterprising Northern men would make a *garden*. That portion of Virginia between Washington & Bull Run which has been marched over repeatedly by Union and Rebel armies is desolated it is true but that does not imply the whole of northern Virginia.[54]

The country between Fairfax and Middleburg and the Blue Ridge is as fine as any I ever saw.[55] One feature I noticed beyond Aldie the fences are all stone and when a large farm is fenced entirely in this way it looks well. I enjoy myself very much in making explorations in sections that I have not before visited and in making the acquaintance of the people. The towns are dull spiritless places. There is but little of northern business enterprise. One good result of this war will be to supplant the stolid wooden men who inhabit the south by decent enterprising "*Damned Yankees.*" I am quite well. Your last was recd last night. I am right glad to hear of your success in business. Glad on your acct and for Mother and the other children. I hope to come home some day to see you in the enjoyment of prosperity and independence. If you keep on with your business as you have done you must succeed. It cannot be otherwise. Do not allow yourself to become involved in politics. Above all do not lend your countenance to the contemptible Copperhead treason that is disgracing, not the Democratic party, but to the country. Keep clear of politics entirely is my advise. Let your platform be the Union and the Constitution. The old slavery question is settled.[56] The only question now is loyalty or treason. And eternal infamy will fasten upon the names of those north and south of whatever political party shall in any manner aid or encourage the treason which is striving to destroy this government. Give my love to all. Compliments to J B Hutchinson if you see him, also to Mr Hull Mr Rogers and Mr Ball. Tell Uncle Ed he has not returned my letter. Why does he not do it.

Yr affectionate son

James H Kidd

Address as usual to Washington

JHK

AT THE END of April, Stahel took his command in search of the troublesome Mosby. Stahel and his troops spent the next several weeks jousting with Mosby along the course of the Orange & Alexandria Railroad, which runs to the south and east of the Bull Run Mountains, the eastern border of the Loudoun Valley of Virginia. Repeated Federal efforts to corral him failed.

Just before taking off after Mosby again at the beginning of June, Kidd found time to relate his personal experiences during the pursuit. In this letter, Kidd also predicted the coming Confederate invasion of the North, but he placed too much confidence in the ability of the Federal pickets to spot the Confederate advance.

> Head Qrs. Detroit Cavalry
> Outposts
> Camp Meeting Hill Virginia
> June 1st 1863

Dear Mother and Father

The date of my last is so far back that I have forgotten it and your last letter I have lost, so that I cannot apologize for not acknowledging the recpt of the one or for the long time since I wrote, as the time may have been long or short for all I know. I could however have written but little particularly interesting, for we are *still* in "status quo" not having been relieved. The last week I have been having the easiest work that has fallen to my lot in my life military. Col Alger very kindly permitted me to be off duty one trip, which gave me six days for pleasure & recuperation.

This time, I have improved in reading, writing and riding with two very pleasant young ladies who live near our camp. I suppose you will be shocked to hear that I have not discarded all notions of society & civilization and that I have not become utterly *savage & bloodthirsty*, that the scout by day and the vigilant watch by night, may be varied by an occasional flirtation (or something more serious) while off duty, but boys are boys although soldiers, and Virginia girls are very like Michigan girls though most are horribly "*secesh*" by the way thinking hangs a tale.

I went last week outside our lines with a scout of 20 men to Drainesville[57] the most rebel town in all the "*Old Dominion.*" There lives a certain "Maggie Day," young and beautiful the daughter of a sergeant in the Rebel army. She has been accustomed to relating his secession sentiments publicly & unhesitatingly. She is particularly "*heavy*" in her abuse of Union officers. She had a fine horse well broken to the saddle, which horse I took *of course*. "You miserable Lincoln horse thief" said she. "Thank you" said I. "I hope he carries you into the mouth of the rebel cannon." "Michigan men always go there when they can," said I.

"Mosby will have you," said she. "I am his holly hock," said I. "I shall see him before tomorrow night" said she. "Give him my compliments" said I "& tell him I will meet him for an intense charge of sabre & pistol compliments at your place anytime." This is the type of secesh ladies down here. They are death on Yankees.

Reports are rife of a projected invasion by Stewart on Washington or Alexandria alternate in spasms of fear.[58] The Rebels have gone through our lines twice *without our knowledge*. Chain Bridge has been torn up (by the frightened Washingtonians) and Alexandria has had all the niggers out digging rifle pits, etc. We have been gobbled up repeatedly and awful danger has surrounded us (according to Washington authority) utterly without our knowledge. That Lee will attempt a raid into the north is possible perhaps probable, but when he comes we shall probably hear of it before he wakes up Lincoln to demand that the White House be "turned over" to Jeff Davis, besides having an efficient and perfect line of pickets. Scouts are daily out on our front, so that the idea of the Rebel army reaching Washington without our knowledge is preposterous.

Lee may make a rapid march up through the "Shenandoah Valley" a la Jackson and thence into Pennsylvania or Maryland, but nothing would please the Union army better than to have him make the attempt.[59] Gov Blair visited us a few days ago. I had the pleasure of riding to Washington with him. Saturday night I had dinner with Gen Stahel. Gen Stahel & staff are Hungarians and not as you would suppose Germans. Gen Stahel was adj gen to Gen Kossuth in Hungary. Angelo (Lt) Tower has been quite sick for some days. He is now recovering slowly. I consider him entirely out of danger though quite weak. I wrote a line to his Father yesterday stating the facts. Hoping to hear from you soon, I remain

Yr affectionate son
James H Kidd

I enclose a draft of $100, and will send another $100 in another letter. JHK

Head Qrs Detroit Cavalry
Outposts
"Camp Meeting" Hill Va
June 1st 1863

Dear Father

I have already written to you today inclosing a draft for $100. Thinking it safe I have enclosed another $100 draft in another letter.

Very truly
J H Kidd

Mosby's Confederacy.

Blake A. Magner

N
W — E

ten miles

MARYLAND

VIRGINIA

Potomac River

WASHINGTON

Alexandria

Fairfax C.H.

Centreville

Manassas Junction

Edward's Ferry

Dranesville

Aldie

Leesburg

Middleburg

Bull Run Mountains

Manassas Gap R. R.

Warrenton

Orange & Alexandria R. R.

Culpeper C. H.

Harpers Ferry

Snicker's Gap

Ashby's Gap

Manassas Gap

Chester Gap

Thornton's Gap

Winchester

Front Royal

Strasburg

Shenandoah River

Blue Ridge Mountains

MICHIGAN GOVERNOR AUSTIN BLAIR's visit brought changes for the 6th Michigan. In his memoirs, Kidd noted,

> Early in June a thing happened that brought a feeling of gloom into the little camp. Colonel Norvell of the Fifth having resigned, the officers of that regiment united in a petition to the governor to appoint an outsider to the vacancy. Governor Blair selected Lieutenant Colonel Alger. Indeed, that was probably part of his business on the occasion of his recent visit. Colonel Alger was ordered to report immediately for duty with his new command, and left, taking with him the hearty congratulations and good wishes of all his comrades of the Sixth. But their regret at losing him was profound. They did not know how to spare him. It gave him more rank and a larger field of usefulness. Major Thaddeus Foote assumed command of the detachment.[60]

A few days later, orders came to break camp and move north, to picket the line of the Potomac River. On June 6, Stahel received orders from headquarters of the Department of Washington: "There is little doubt that Lee has moved his army from Hooker's front. His object is not known. Push a strong reconnaissance into the Shenandoah Valley at once, to acquire any information which may be had of the enemy's whereabouts or intentions."[61] Stahel left on June 7 at 3:00 A.M., taking sixteen to seventeen hundred men and a battery of guns with him.[62]

On June 11, Capt. Charles Deane led a squadron of the 6th Michigan on a reconnaissance along the Maryland side of the Potomac River, departing from their base at Seneca Mill. Mosby's command crossed the river at Rowser's Ford, advanced along the towpath of the Chesapeake and Ohio Canal, and boldly attacked Deane's camp, driving the Wolverines back toward Poolesville. After burning Deane's camp, Mosby and his men melted away, causing more frustration for the nearly four hundred Federal troopers sent to find him. Coburn recounted, "Our boys behaved well, and have been highly complimented for the pluck they showed in this, their 'first fight.' They are in good spirits, and would not hesitate to display still greater valor, if possible, whenever an opportunity is given them."[63] Stahel's men spent a month trying to destroy Mosby. They failed but fought well. One observer noted that the efforts to destroy Mosby "were very trying."[64] A few days later, Mosby suggested that Confederate cavalry use the now-abandoned Rowser's Ford to cross into Maryland as they marched toward Gettysburg.

Later in June, Robert E. Lee's Army of Northern Virginia moved north into the Loudoun Valley, its advance screened by the active and efficient cavalry of Jeb Stuart. As the army traveled, word filtered north of a great cavalry battle on June 9, fought near Brandy Station in Culpeper County, wherein the Yankee troopers caught Stuart's men by surprise and gave them a long, hard day of combat. On June 14, Confederate infantry under Lt. Gen. Richard S. Ewell captured the Federal garrison at Winchester, which indicated that Lee's army was on the move north. On June 16, Maj. Gen. Joseph Hooker, commanding the Army of the Potomac, wrote to President Lincoln: "[N]early all of the cavalry of the Army of the Potomac should at once be sent into Maryland by the most direct route. General Stahel has an abundance to perform all cavalry duty south of the Potomac."[65]

Maj. Gen. Alfred Pleasonton, commanding the Army of the Potomac's Cavalry Corps, did not like foreigners and was determined to rid himself of them. Writing to his political patron, Representative John F. Farnsworth, formerly commander of the 8th Illinois Cavalry, Pleasonton commented, "I have no faith in foreigners saving our government or country." He continued, "Stahel has not shown himself a cavalry man." Pleasonton wrote to Farnsworth that "the cavalry [should be] consolidated and Stahel left out for God's sake do it."[66]

On June 17, the Wolverines heard the horse artillery of Union brigadier general David M. Gregg's cavalry division booming near Aldie, Virginia, as it fought with the Confederate cavalry forces assigned to guard the mountain passes to the Loudoun Valley. Stahel's men broke camp; believing that they were going east toward the sound of battle at Aldie, the Wolverines instead headed north.[67] The next day, Stahel's cavalry reconnoitered toward Warrenton and Culpeper. Stuart dispatched Brig. Gen. Wade Hampton's cavalry brigade to meet the threat; Hampton drove Stahel back to Fairfax Court House.[68] On the 20th, Sgt. Edwin B. Bigelow of the 5th Michigan noted in his diary, "Were in camp all day waiting orders to march but received none. Heard that the main body of Lee's Army were marching on Washington."[69] The war was about to come to Stahel and his command along the banks of the Potomac River.

3

Campaigning with the Army of the Potomac

GETTYSBURG AND AFTER

*They stood facing each other when charge was sounded and they met
hand to hand.*

LEE'S ARMY MOVED into Pennsylvania, living off the rich northern countryside. Hooker cautiously followed, trying to ascertain the Rebel leader's
intentions. On June 25, the Michigan Brigade crossed the Potomac River
at Edwards Ferry, where Goose Creek empties into the river, and marched
into Maryland and on across the Mason-Dixon line. The 6th Michigan
brought up the Federal rear.

Emmitsburg Md

June 28, 1863

Dear Father

I wrote to Mother a little more than a week ago stating that we were
off from Fairfax and off from picket duty.

We are now *temporarily* attached Hooker's army. Gen French commands
the 1st Army Corps.[1] Gen Reynolds the left grand division of "the Army
of the Potomac"[2] and Gen Stahel now reports to Gen Reynolds in the 1st
Corps.

Today is Sunday. One week ago today we left Fairfax the same day of
the cavalry fight at Aldie.[3] We heard the cannonading and supposed we
were off for that fight, receiving orders when it was first heard, but instead
of going there our division went off on a reconnaissance to Warrenton and
the Rappahannock. We were within a short distance of Fredericksburg and

stopped at Bealeton Station and reconnoitered to Kelley's Ford where Pleasonton[4] had his first fight with Stewart, but no enemy was discovered. We
returned by the most direct route, going to the right of Warrenton via
Gainesville to Fairfax CH reaching there Wednesday having had a hard
but pleasant trip. The rains which had previously fallen held the dust so
that Cavalry march with little inconvenience. Our trains failed to keep up
so that we were without forage or rations a large portion of the time. Our
horses were fed but once during the three days we travelled all day and far
into the night. Much of the country has been rendered desolate by the passage of troops, but in the vicinity of Warrenton & Gainesville we found a
rich country. The road was lined with huge cherry trees loaded with ripe
cherries and the boys enjoyed a fine treat in the absence of the usual rations
of "Hard Tack" and pork. We went out expecting a fight and returned disappointed, whether happily or fortuitously you can infer. We had one day's
rest in Fairfax and then were off again at 2 o'clock Friday morning "to horse"
summoned us to be ready for a start. Our whole division accompanied by
our baggage train, forage & rations were off. Fairfax was deserted for an
indefinite period. The 6th in rear as rear guard moved very slowly. The
train was in front and caused great delay. The road was constantly blocked
with wagons that at Vienna the Regt stooped to feed not being able to move
while *"waiting for the wagons."* Here Capt Weber (Co B)[5] & myself obtained
permission, and went to our old camp at "Camp Meeting Hill" intending
to overtake the regiment at noon. After a hasty visit with our *very dear* friends
in that vicinity, we took the shortest route to Drainesville. A little apprehensive about being *"gobbled"* we were much grateful to find 10 men from
the Mich 1st who were going across to join the Division. Hurrying on we
passed through Drainesville at 11 o'clock and overtook the 5th Mich Cavalry there, and ascertained for the 1st time that we were up with the advance
and our regiment was still in rear. Unsaddling our horses we settled ourselves for a comfortable smoke and for 6 hours sat waiting. Mile after mile
of baggage wagons and artillery went rolling by and still no sign of the old
6th. Finally at 6 in the evening we mounted and went on to a farm house,
and ordered supper, to which we had not paid our regards when by the aid
of my glass I discovered the advance of the 6th in the distance. At a fast
walk, we closed up in column of four on the "guidons"[6] flying "our" regiment brought up the rear of the column which was 7 hours passing a given
point. We finished our supper, and overtook our companies much to the
gratification of our *boys* who were fearful that they had lost their Captains

having seen nothing of us since morning. It was now dark and a drenching raid had set in although the moon prevented it from being *very* dark.
That night we marched to "Edwards Ferry"[7] and passed our baggage trains.
The Potomac here, is ⅔ds of a mile wide, and the current rapid. Each company in crossing was carried downstream somewhat so that our companies
in the rear came near running into deep water. The water comes to the
top of my thigh boots, but we crossed without accident and after losing
our way several times moved out through Poolesville MD at 2 o'clock Friday morning. Slept in the rain without food and were off again in the morning at day light. Passed the 1st Army Corps going in the direction of
"Harper's Ferry." Arrived that night at "Frederick City" MD. A description of this place and vicinity I will attempt to give in my next. Splendid
country wheat 40 bushels to the acre perfect gardens. 1200 inhabitants
Union. Demonstration strong pretty girls, best bread. I even saw empty
camps. Sympathy encouragement, gloriously *loyal* Eden-like enchanting
Maryland. Yesterday we reached this place and have seen no secesh here
yet. I shall write again soon. Am sleeping on the ground every night. On
duty all day in the saddle often, half of the night. I am well fortunately
hopeful and happy such demonstrations of sympathy & encouragement
met here make us feel strong and willing to suffer. I have 65 men with me
one of the largest companies in the Div. Col Gray is sick in Washington.
Major Foote and Brown[8] are the only Field officers with us. Love to all.

Yr affectionate son
J H Kidd

THE JOYOUS RECEPTION afforded by the Marylanders stayed with Kidd
for many years. When he wrote his memoirs, he commented, "But more
pleasing still, were the evidences of loyalty which greeted us on every hand,
as we entered the village. The stars and stripes floated above many buildings, while from porch and window, from old and young, came manifes-
tations of welcome. The men received us with cheers, the women with
smiles and waving of handkerchiefs. That night we were permitted to go
into camp and enjoy a good rest, in the midst of plenty and among friends."[9]
After the bleak Virginia countryside, stripped of provisions by the armies
that occupied it, the plenty of Maryland was a welcome sight.

On June 27, the Wolverines marched into Pennsylvania and entered
the town of Gettysburg, which the Confederate infantry and cavalry had
visited on June 26. Terrified locals reported that cavalry under command

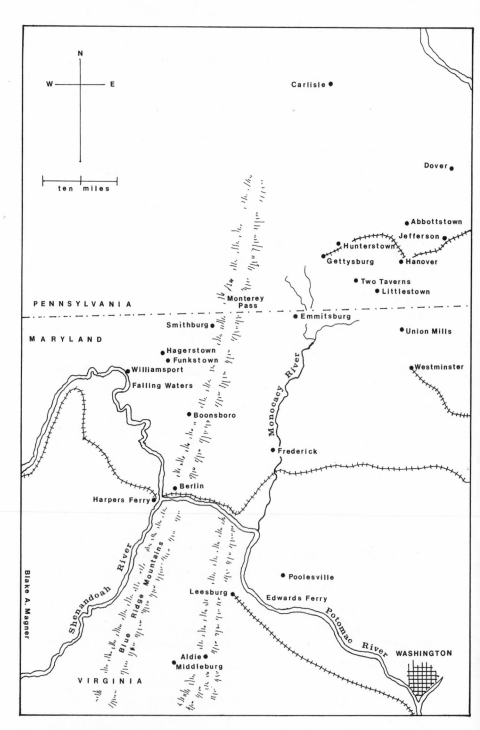

Theater Map of Operations of the Gettysburg Campaign.

of Brig. Gen. Albert G. Jenkins "rode into Gettysburg . . . shouting and yelling like so many savages from the wilds of the Rocky Mountains; firing their pistols, not caring whether they killed, or maimed man, woman, or child; and rushing from stable to stable in search of horses."[10] Pickets were sent out to watch for Confederates. A prominent local businessman, David McConaughy, left a detailed note for Copeland, describing the disposition of the Confederate infantry in great detail.[11]

That night, at his request, Joseph Hooker was relieved as commander of the Army of the Potomac, and Maj. Gen. George Gordon Meade took his place. Word filtered down that Stahel and Copeland had also been relieved, replaced by two recently appointed brigadier generals. Copeland vigorously protested, riding off to see Pleasonton, who informed him "that he had only taken the Cavalry of Genl Stahel under his command with the understanding that he should have the assignment of the commanding officers, and that he had selected officers known to himself and who affiliated with him, and that while he intended no disrespect nor reflection on me, he must insist on giving the command to those best known to himself." Copeland fired off a scathing letter to army headquarters arguing his case, to no avail.[12]

Division command passed to Brig. Gen. Judson Kilpatrick, of the 2d New York Cavalry. Kilpatrick was a controversial character with a reputation as being "flamboyant, reckless, tempestuous, and even licentious."[13] A brother officer recalled that, when Kilpatrick arrived at West Point, "his ambition was simply boundless, and from his intimates he did not disguise his faith that . . . he would become governor of New Jersey and ultimately president of the United States."[14] Capt. Charles Francis Adams of the 1st Massachusetts Cavalry complained, "Kilpatrick is a brave, injudicious boy, much given to blowing and surely will come to grief."[15] Col. Theodore Lyman, a volunteer aide at Army of the Potomac headquarters, observed during the fall of 1863 that Kilpatrick was "a frothy braggart without brains" and that "it is hard to look at him without laughing."[16] Another horse soldier observed, "Kilpatrick is the most vain, conceited, egotistical little popinjay I ever saw. He is a very ungraceful rider, looking more like a monkey than a man on horseback."[17] The new brigadier received orders to put his troopers "in condition for instant service."[18]

Command of the Michigan Brigade fell to a newly appointed twenty-three-year-old brigadier general named George Armstrong Custer, promoted that day from brevet captain.[19] Aggressive, daring, and ambitious, the young horse soldier caught the eye of the Federal high command as a result of his daredevil antics leading a mounted charge against a large force of Rebel cavalry at the Battle of Aldie on June 17. The new brigade commander joined the 7th Michigan at Abbottstown late on the afternoon of June 29 but did not see the 5th or 6th Michigan until the 30th.[20] On the 29th, the Wolverines spent the day scouting east of Gettysburg, fanning out toward Hanover, twenty-four miles east. On the morning of the 29th, Kilpatrick's command passed by Sugarloaf Mountain, near Frederick, where they encountered Maj. Gen. John F. Reynolds, who commanded the left wing of the Army of the Potomac. Copeland briefly consulted with Reynolds's and told him what the Wolverines had found upon entering Gettysburg. Reynolds pointed to the heights beyond nearby Emmitsburg and shouted, "Boys, you must get those heights quick, there are rebels ahead." Lt. Samuel Harris of the 5th Michigan recalled that Reynolds's words "worked like a charm on the weary and fagged out boys," who turned to march back toward Pennsylvania.[21]

On the morning of the 30th, Kilpatrick's division engaged three brigades of Confederate cavalry in Hanover. That morning, the 5th and 6th Michigan got their first glimpse of their new brigade commander. Kidd never forgot the sight:

> Looking at him closely, this is what I saw: An officer superbly mounted who sat his charger as if to the manor born. Tall, lithe, active, muscular, straight as an Indian and as quick in his movements, he had the fair complexion of a school girl. He was clad in a suit of black velvet, elaborately trimmed with gold lace, which ran down the outer seam of his trousers, and almost covered the sleeves of his cavalry jacket. The wide collar of a blue navy shirt was turned down over the collar of his velvet jacket, and a necktie of brilliant crimson was tied in a graceful knot at the throat, the lower ends falling carelessly in front. The double rows of buttons on his breast were arranged in groups of twos, indicating the rank of brigadier general. A soft, black hat with wide brim adorned with a gilt cord, and rosette encircling a gold star, was worn turned down on one side giving him a rakish air. His golden hair fell in graceful luxuriance nearly or quite to his shoulders, and his upper lip was garnished with a blonde mustache. A sword and belt, gilt spurs and top boots completed his unique outfit.[22]

Clad in this outlandish getup, Custer personally led his new brigade in a headlong mounted charge through the streets of the town, helping to defeat Stuart's vaunted troopers. Kilpatrick reported that "the conduct of the Sixth Michigan . . . is deserving of the highest praise." He continued, "For the first time our troops had met the foe in close contact; but they were on their own free soil; fair hands, regardless of the dangerous strife, waved them on, and bright, tearful eyes looked pleadingly out from every window. . . . The foe turned and fled. He had for the first and last time polluted with his presence the loyal town of Hanover."[23]

After defeating Stuart, Kilpatrick turned north and west of the town, finally arriving at Gettysburg late in the day on July 2. The Confederate cavalry, which had swung as far north as Carlisle after leaving Hanover, was marching toward the fighting at Gettysburg. Kilpatrick, marching across country, ran into the rearguard of the Rebel column just outside the small town of Hunterstown. Spotting the end of the column, which consisted of Brig. Gen. Wade Hampton's brigade and some artillery, Custer decided to attack, with the 6th Michigan in the van. Kidd recorded, "When nearing the village of Hunterstown, on a road flanked by fences, the advance encountered a heavy force of Confederate cavalry. A mounted line was formed across the road, while there were dismounted skirmishers behind the fences on either side."[24] Capt. Henry E. Thompson's Company A led the charge, clearing the road of Rebel pickets. The other three squadrons dismounted and laid down a heavy supporting fire with their Spencers. The brisk fire allowed Lt. Alexander C. M. Pennington to bring his battery of horse artillery onto the field and open fire on the Rebel positions.[25] According to Kidd, "The enemy attempted a charge in pursuit, but the dismounted men on the right of the road kept up such a fusillade with their Spencer carbines, aided by the rapid discharges of Pennington's battery, that he was driven back in great confusion."[26]

Custer personally led Company A's mounted charge at Hunterstown, had his horse shot out from under him, and barely escaped capture when a trooper of the 1st Michigan Cavalry named Norvill Churchill, who had left the ranks of his regiment to ride with Custer, rescued him from the soldiers of Hampton's brigade.[27] Hampton himself engaged in a duel with Private James C. Parsons of Co. I of the 6th Michigan. When Parsons's Spencer jammed after several rounds, Hampton chivalrously waited for the trooper to clear his weapon before wounding Parsons with a revolver shot.[28] After the gray-clad troopers counterattacked and the Wolverines were driven back, Thompson's squadron left behind two killed and twenty-five wounded, including Thompson. Lt. Stephen H. Ballard was taken prisoner.[29]

After the encounter at Hunterstown, the Wolverines continued their march toward Gettysburg, turning south and passing near the important landmark of Two Taverns, a few miles south of the fighting. Kidd had painful memories of this march:

> I . . . remember well the weary night march, which lasted until the first streaks of dawn had begun to appear in the east. It was then, and not till then, that Custer's men were permitted to stretch their limbs upon the ground and catch a brief rest. . . . The manner in which the Sixth Michigan Cavalry "spent the night" is pretty indelibly photographed upon the memory of every survivor who served with it in the Gettysburg campaign. . . . [T]hey had hardly been given a moment for rest, and had been in motion for the most part by night as well as by day.[30]

Finally given a chance to unsaddle and rest for a few minutes, the Wolverines picketed the critical crossroads of the Hanover and Low Dutch Roads, three miles east of Gettysburg. There they met their destiny on the afternoon of July 3, an encounter described in great detail by Kidd in a letter to his parents. Custer personally led two mounted charges by his men, his cry, "Come on you Wolverines," echoing in their ears.

Boonsboro, Maryland
July 9, 1863

Dear Father and Mother

Yesterday I attempted to write you a letter but was obliged to stop just as I had made a commencement. It is almost impossible to write or do anything as they do in civilized life. I have no conveniences for writing but a roll of paper etc. in my saddle bags. Have no clothes but what are on my back. No tent and no blankets. Nights I have a poncho blanket under me, my overcoat over me, rainy or dry weather sometimes with water, sometimes with some rails laid on the ground to keep me up out of the water. Oftentimes we are not even permitted to have this imperfect rest but are kept on the march all night.

You may know of our doings by the account of Gen Kilpatrick's command[31] which you will see in the paper.

In my last you left me just entering upon my first fight. We skirmished with Stewart's cavalry that day and drove them the next day west of Abbotsburg and Berlin[32] at which later place we arrived an hour too late to intercept Stewart's cavalry. The next day we went to the vicinity of Gettysburg where the great battle had commenced between Meade and Lee. At dark that night we arrived at Hunterstown where we encountered a force of Stewart's cavalry with a battery. We silenced the battery and drove out the cavalry but not without loss. Lt. Shipman, Co. D, Capt Thompson, Co. A, were wounded. Sgt. Cox Co. C killed[33] besides others that I cannot enumerate. The 6th was ordered to support our battery and while in rear of it was exposed to a galling fire of shell from the rebel battery. Leaving we marched all night, and next morning arrived upon the field of Gettysburg, the third and decisive day of the fight. Early in the morning our cavalry division were posted to support the right wing of our army. Skirmishing soon commenced between the cavalry on the rebel left, and us. The 6th supported the battery. Our position was about a mile and a half from the point where the issue of the day was decided. When after an hour of silence that unexampled cannonading which broke the rebel army commenced again. Our cavalry skirmishing culminated in a hard fight. The Michigan 7th led by Gen Custer made the 1st charge and were, after fighting bravely, repulsed and driven beyond their former ground. On came the rebel cavalry, yelling like demons, right toward the battery we were supporting apparently sweeping everything before them.

Before they reached the wood to which our men had retreated a column of cavalry advanced to meet them moving straight toward them. They halted and formed in line of battle. For an instant the rebels halted forming. An instant they stood facing each other when charge was sounded and they met hand to hand. For one instant the brave rebels stood then broke and fled in confusion. The Michigan 1st Cavalry had whipped more than their number in a hand to hand fight, and as the rebels retreated across the open field our battery made dreadful havoc in their ranks.

Two charges were made by each side and skirmishing was kept up all day. After dark when fighting had ceased and the enemy had entirely disappeared we were ordered to retire to our former position, arriving there at midnight, when we learned the result of the battle at the center and on the left. Lee was most completely discomfited, *whipped*. The next day, the 4th of July, Gen Kilpatrick announced that we were to go to the "Enemy's right and rear" to be separated from the army for some time, to execute which we immediately set out with rations for three days.

At dark that night we reached a gap in the mountains[34] defended by a battery and a force of cavalry. The battery was captured and we drove the cavalry which was guarding a wagon train, burned the train and took, during the night, 1860 prisoners. The fighting had been done in the night. We were deployed as skirmishers through a thick wood, so dark that we could see nothing, seeing the Rebs only by the flash of their guns. This was a night never to be forgotten. Imagine a mountain with a turnpike road running down with considerable descent. Our cavalry on the summit, a long train of wagons reaching for miles. A shell from our battery sent roaring down, would go crashing through breaking wagons, killing horses. At last a regiment of our cavalry the 1st Virginia,[35] formed in column of fours on the top of the mountain. The order "draw sabres" was given. "Use sabres alone, I will cut down the first man who fires a shot," said the colonel. "Charge." Away they went. Yelling, striving only to go fast and faster. For several miles they charged and then returned. They had overtaken the head of the train and it was captured. Then imagine it so dark that you can only hear, not see, and a heavy rain falling, and you have a pretty accurate idea of the night fight in the mountains of Pennsylvania. We arrived at Smithsburg at daylight, burned the train, and sent off our prisoners.

We had now reached the "enemy's rear" and that afternoon had a skirmish with the advance guard of Lee's advancing army. As one division of cavalry could not resist the whole army, we were contented to worry the advance, and then returned to Boonsboro, traveling nearly all night again. Resting till noon we advanced to Funkstown where we had a fight with a force of Stewart's cavalry, capturing Col Davis, the identical Virginian who hung John Brown, and who led the charge against us at Gettysburg on the 3rd. Still further at Hagerstown we had another skirmish driving the rebels. Thence we went to Williamsport where the rebels had a large train of ammunition and baggage wagons.

This is the only point where they could cross, and to this point he was then advancing as we knew. Unexpectedly, as I believe we encountered resistance from a whole corps of the rebels being supported by heavy batteries. After skirmishing with them for half an hour with considerable loss, we were attacked in the rear by the advance of Lee's army coming up. It was now dark, and under cover of the night we got out of it by a circuitous route to Boonsboro. Our loss in killed and wounded were heavy. Aaron C. Jewett, of Ann Arbor, acting adjutant of the regiment was killed by a shell. My company was exposed to a galling fire from the batteries for some minutes before getting into position to fight but, strange to say, not a man was injured. Yesterday after writing to you, I was into a fight in less than ten minutes. We fought all the afternoon and drove the rebels 3 miles when darkness cut off the pursuit. Last night Meade's infantry came up and we are back with our army again and shall not probably so incessantly engaged. Our cavalry is doing noble work. In fact of late we have done the most of the fighting. I can't say that I like it, but under the present state of things and our present cavalry commander can't say we'll avoid it. I have had several narrow escapes but have not been hurt and have not had a man of my company injured.

I forgot to say that Major Ferry[36] of Grand Haven was killed at Gettysburg. The Rebel army is used up, demoralized. I have talked with rebel prisoners and they are almost unanimous in saying that they are heartily tired of this *"useless"* war. The Col Davis whom I spoke of before said so. "Don't you like to see the Stars and Stripes sometimes," said one officer. "It revives old memories" said he "but the thing is not 'flags' but to end up this useless war as soon as possible," and this from a Virginian and the "man who hung John Brown." Hundreds of men come out of the woods and give themselves up voluntarily saying that they are heartily tired of it. Rebellion is about "played out."

> Love to all as ever.
> Yr affectionate son
> J H Kidd

KIDD'S LETTER IS ONE of the best accounts of the furious midnight fight in the Monterey Pass. He had no way of knowing that only a scratch force of Confederates had impeded Kilpatrick's progress. One company of the 1st Maryland Cavalry (Confederate), approximately twenty men commanded by Capt. G. M. Emack, held off the Yankee troopers for several hours until the breakthrough finally came. One gray-clad trooper described it best: "The night was hideous in the extreme."[37]

The next morning, Kilpatrick's division tangled with Stuart's troopers at Smithsburg, Maryland. The Wolverines then moved on to Hagerstown, where they had to fight their way through the streets of the town. Driven from Hagerstown, Kilpatrick marched to nearby Williamsport, where his command joined Brig. Gen. John Buford's division in fighting there. On the 7th, the Wolverines got a much-needed day of rest, near Boonsboro. The next day, the combined forces of Buford and Kilpatrick again fought Stuart's troopers near Boonsboro, prompting one Wolverine to write, "This is the eighth fight that we have had with the Rebs and have whipped them everry [*sic*] time."[38]

Kilpatrick's men got another day to rest and refit on the 9th, then spent two days picketing near Funkstown, waiting for the arrival of the Union infantry and pursuing Lee's army, which was trapped along the flooded banks of the Potomac River. Recognizing his plight, Lee's engineers laid out a formidable defensive line. Hermann Schuricht, one of Jenkins's officers, noted that, once the news of Maj. Gen. Ulysses S. Grant's dramatic victory at Vicksburg reached the North, combined with rumors of a large Federal concentration near Winchester, it caused panic in the Confederate ranks. The butternut cavalry waited in line of battle for a day and a half, "ready for action." There they waited for an attack that never came.[39]

Finally, on the 14th, Kilpatrick learned that Lee's army was crossing the river on pontoon bridges near Falling Waters, Maryland, and ordered an immediate attack. Kidd noted Kilpatrick's attributes: "He had begun to be a terror to foes, and there was a well-grounded fear he might become a menace to friends as well. He was brave to rashness, capricious, ambitious, reckless in rushing into scrapes, and generally of expedients in getting out, though at times he seemed to lose his head entirely when beset by perils which he, himself, had invited. He was prodigal of human life, though to do him justice he rarely spared himself."[40]

This character flaw would not serve Kilpatrick well as the 3rd Division went into battle on the 14th. Kidd then described Kilpatrick's zeal to catch the Rebel rear guard: "The march from Williamsport to Falling Waters was a wild ride. For the whole distance the horses were spurred to a gallop. Kilpatrick was afraid he would not get there in time to overtake the enemy, so he spared neither man nor beast. The road was soft and miry, and the horses sank almost to their knees in the sticky mud. For this reason the column straggled, and it was not possible to keep a single troop closed up in sets of fours. At such a rapid rate the column plunged through the muddy roads."[41]

Kilpatrick's eagerness to pitch into the fray prevented him from coordinating his assault with Buford's division, which was coming up to join the attack. Instead of launching a coordinated attack that likely would have bagged an entire Rebel division, Kilpatrick could not wait. He ordered the charge.

As the Gettysburg Campaign began, frustrated with his regiment's role in doing most of its fighting dismounted, Maj. Peter A. Weber turned to Kidd and said, "I want a chance to make one saber charge."[42] He got his chance at Falling Waters, leading his squadron in a charge into the Confederate rear guard near the pontoon bridge, which cost him his own life along with those of his adjutant and twenty-eight other Wolverines. The death of Weber, considered "the best officer in the regiment," was a real loss for the 6th. In his after-action report, Col. Gray noted, "Another brigade, drawn up in line in rear of the first, opened a murderous fire upon the gallant little band . . . and the survivors were forced to withdraw, leaving the bodies of many of their gallant and lamented comrades within the Rebel works, a witness of their noble and heroic daring."[43] Another Yankee officer observed, "Kilpatrick charged the fort and lost several men and horses; whereas, if he had waited twenty minutes, General Buford would have swung his command between the fort and the river, thereby capturing all the enemy left behind without the loss of a man."[44]

Despite this failure, nearly fifteen hundred Confederates were captured, as well as two pieces of artillery and two battle flags. Kidd took a bullet through his foot.[45] His memoirs describe the circumstances.

My troop was the fourth from the rear of the regiment, and consequently several preceded it on the line. When I reached the fence, along the side of the field next to the woods, I found Lieutenant A. E. Tower . . . at the gap giving orders. He directed me to take my command across the field, and form on the right of that next preceding. I had ridden so rapidly that only a few men had kept up the pace, and the remainder were strung out for some distance back. But taking those that were up, and asking the adjutant to tell the others to follow, I dashed into the field, and soon found that we were targets for the enemy on the hill, who made the air vibrant with the whiz of bullets. It was hot, but we made our way across without being hit, and reached the place where the regiment was trying to form, under fire of musketry from the hill, and getting badly cut up. Reining up my horse, I gave the order, "Dismount, to fight on foot" and, glancing back, saw my men coming in single file, reaching to the fence—probably an eighth of a mile—and the rear had not yet left the woods. The two leading sets of fours which alone were closed up obeyed the order and, dismounting to direct the alignment, I stepped in front of my horse, still holding the bridle rein in my right hand, when a minie bullet from the hill in front with a vicious thud went through my right foot, making what the surgeon in Washington afterwards said was the "prettiest wound I ever saw."[46]

Unable to walk, Kidd was taken to a field hospital, where he spent several unpleasant and painful days. He was then taken in by a local family, which did its best to make him and a wounded officer of the 1st Michigan Cavalry comfortable.

In his next letter home, written from his sickbed in Maryland, Kidd gave a remarkable analysis of the severe casualties taken by the officer corps of the 6th Michigan over the course of the Gettysburg campaign, which ended at Falling Waters.

Hagerstown MD

July 16th 1863

Dear Parents

[For four toilsome & eventful weeks I have not heard from home. I wrote once from Emmitsburg and once from Boonsboro but do not know that you received my letters.] The Rebels have at last disappeared from Maryland [and Meade had neither "bagged" nor annihilated them]. For several days we waited expecting another great battle to begin but it did not. On Sunday July 13th our division occupied Hagerstown, driving out the Rebel Cavalry with but little resistance. The fact is the rebels have got a perfect terror of Kilpatrick's Cavalry and since Gettysburg Stewart's *redoubtable* cavalry have always fled without a fight at our approach. Day before yesterday reconnoitered to Williamsport and found Lee's army at that point all across, having forded the river without loss. One portion was crossing at a point lower down called "Falling Waters," and Heath's Division of Infantry[47] was still on this side as rear guard. Whether we went as fast as our horses could carry us through mud nearly a foot deep. Arriving there we found the Infantry entrenched on a high hill behind earthworks. The Mich 6th, the only Regt which had yet arrived was ordered by Gen Kilpatrick to charge upon the entrenchments. The charge was gallantly led by Major Weber formerly Capt Weber who had been promoted only the day before. He charge was unsuccessful [as might have been foreseen] and our regiment returned terribly cut up to the woods. Here they dismounted, and with our seven shooting rifles, support coming up soon, whipped the rebels capturing 1000 prisoners & 2 pieces of artillery and leaving the ground literally covered with Rebel dead and wounded. In the 1st charge Major Weber was killed, shot through the head. Capt Royce Co D killed. Lt Bolza Co B killed. Lt Potter Co C wounded or prisoner.[48] Lt Kellogg Co H wounded & missing. Lt Crawford Co F leg amputated.[49] I was myself in the early part of the action wounded in the foot by a minie ball which passed entirely through fracturing the bone. I am now in a private house, with the best of accommodations. I shall endeavor to get to Washington within two or three days. Srgt Burkhart[50] is with me. Surgeons say it will be months before I am fit for service again but think that with good care my foot can be saved. 22 were killed in our regiment besides a large number of wounded most of them badly many of them mortally. I am thankful to get off so well only one man besides myself was wounded in Company E. Since our campaign commenced our regiment has been extremely unfortunate with line officers.

[Co A   Capt Thompson - wounded
          Lt. Birge[51] - Sick at Washington
          Lt Ballard[52] - Prisoner
Co B   Capt (Major) Weber - Killed
          Lt Powers[53] - Prisoner
          Lt Bolza -
Co C   Lt Potter - Wounded & prisoner
Co D   Capt Royce - Killed
          Lt Shipman - Badly wounded
          Lt Royce - Badly wounded
Co E   Myself - Wounded
Co F   Capt Hyser[54] - Sick
          Lt Crawford - Wounded, leg amputated
Co G   Officers all on staff
Co H   Capt Wise[55] - Sick
          Lt Jewett, actg adj - Killed
          Lt Kellogg - Wounded
Co I   Not with the regiment
Co K   Capt[56] - Sick
          1st Lt[57] - On staff
Co L   Capt[58] - Sick
Co M   Not with Regt.]

Companies B F D & L have suffered most. I have had only one man wounded during our whole campaign and my men have not been backward either. Mere luck I suppose. Gen Kilpatrick is called here Gen *"Kill-Cavalry"* which is about as appropriate as his real name. Lt Angelo Tower is now with the regiment and acting adjutant to Col Gray. [I hear rumors that our division is to be relieved from duty for three weeks. I hope so. The men and horses are worn out. If Meade had followed the enemy as closely as we have Lee's army must have been annihilated, for it is unquestionable that they were demoralized out of rations & out of ammunition.]

I have no doubt that when I reach Washington I could get a furlough to go home but I should have to depend upon strangers as it is impossible for me to walk, even with crutches. I want to get home if possible but may be obliged to wait until my foot begins to heal.

> [With love to all
> I am ever
> Yr affectionate son]
> James H Kidd

KIDD ALSO LAMENTED the passing of his former school chum from the University of Michigan, Brig. Gen. Elon J. Farnsworth, who took command of Kilpatrick's First Brigade on June 28. Farnsworth personally led the decisive charge at Hanover and died leading a heroic but futile charge against Confederate infantry at Gettysburg after the repulse of Pickett's Charge, late on the afternoon of July 3, 1863. Kidd noted,

> I knew [Farnsworth] before the war when he was a student at the University of Michigan, and a more intrepid spirit than he possessed never resided within the breast of man. It was but a day, it might be said, that he had worn his new honors. He was proud, ambitious, spirited, loyal, brave, true as steel to his country and his convictions of duty, and to his own manhood.
>
> The Cavalry Corps had lost an officer whose place was hard to fill. Had he lived, the brave young Illinoisan might have been another Custer. He had all the qualities needed to make a great career—youth, health, a noble physique, courage, patriotism, ambition, ability and rank. He was poised, like Custer, and had discretion as well as dash. They were a noble pair, and nobly did they justify the confidence reposed in them. One lived to court death on scores of battle fields, winning imperishable laurels in them all; the other was cut down in the very beginning of his brilliant career, but his name will forever be associated with what is destined to be in history the most memorable battle of the war, and one from which is dated the beginning of the downfall of the Confederate cause, and the complete restoration of the Union. Farnsworth

will not be forgotten as long as a grateful people remember the name and the glory of Gettysburg.[59]

Ironically, this turned out not to be true. After a week, the wounded officers traveled to Washington, D.C., where Kidd recuperated and passed long, lonely hours.

Washington DC
Friday July 24, 1863

Dear Father

I wrote you once since I came here but have recd no letters from you. I forgot to say you must leave off the 6th Michigan Cavly address. Capt J H Kidd at Washington House Washington DC. If you put on the name of regt, the letters will be sent on & I will not receive them.

I am doing well. My health is excellent, but I am obliged to be very quiet, not leaving my rooms at all. It will not be safe for me to attempt a journey home at present. I have written you several times of late and in my letters gave full particulars of our campaigns under Kilpatrick. I do not know whether you recd my letters or not. I have not heard from you in more than a month not since I left Fairfax (by letter). I saw Capt Vinton[60] yesterday he saw you at Ionia. I sent you $200 June 1st nearly two months ago & I do not even know whether you recd that or not, it is of considerable importance for me to know for there were two drafts & if lost should have been repeated.

Tell Mr. Tower that Angelo was quite well when I left the regt and is now.

As I had not drawn my pay & had not sufficient money, Col Kellogg got $100 and very kindly loaned it to me. Expenses here in Washington are enormous. I shall get my pay when the rolls are in or when I get a leave of absence which I can get whenever I am ready to go home.

If Lee's army had been properly disposed of in Maryland my chances for serving the country in a military way would be very slim but as it is, Rebellion "aint dead yet." Love to all.

Yr affectionate son
J H Kidd
Don't forget the address

IT TOOK ABOUT three weeks for Kidd to gain sufficient strength to go home to recuperate. Leaving Washington by train, he stopped for a couple of days near Altoona, Pennsylvania, enjoying fresh mountain air, passed on to Pittsburgh, and then went on to Michigan. Reaching his family in Ionia, he had some quiet time to rest. When his certificate of disability expired, a local physician, who noted that it would be several more weeks before Kidd would be ready to rejoin his regiment, extended it. In the meantime, he was promoted to major, taking the lamented Weber's place.

The war did not wait for Kidd's recovery. On July 24, a substantial fight took place at Battle Mountain, near Newby's Cross Roads, where Col. Gray, supported by Pennington's battery, had a crisp skirmish with charging Rebel cavalry.[61] The Michigan Brigade quickly was earning the reputation of being one of the hardest fighting of all of the cavalry units, both blue and gray. A sergeant of the 5th Michigan wrote home in late July, "We are in a fight all most every day and will be till Lee surrenders or gets back to Richmond, which I think is impossible for we are in front of him. . . . We are put in all of the worst places on account of [our] seven shooters. The rebs call us the seven devils for they say we can load in the morning and fight all day."[62] Lt. S. H. Ballard of the 6th wrote, "The command perfectly idolized Custer. The old Michigan Brigade adored its Brigadier, and all felt as if he weighed about a ton."[63] Custer returned the sentiment, saying of the Michigan Brigade, "I would not exchange it for any other brigade in the Army."[64] The morale of the Wolverines was high as the armies returned to their original positions along the banks of the Rappahannock, continually fighting throughout the balance of the summer.

On August 1, a major cavalry battle took place at Brandy Station, and more combat occurred as the armies continued to probe each other's positions, looking for weak spots. In late September, the Michigan Brigade moved toward Madison Court House and crossed the Rapidan River. There, it encountered a substantial force of cavalry and, badly outnumbered, withdrew to a position along the Robinson River, where the brigade picketed, covering the army's advance toward Bristoe Station.[65] The withdrawal disheartened many of the blue-clad horse soldiers. One of Kilpatrick's officers complained, "Greatly to my mortification, this army is going to fall back to the Potomac. . . . It is very disheartening to the cavalry, who have done so much hard work and fighting since Gettysburg, to have to turn back."[66]

Kidd's good friend, Capt. Hank Thompson, sent a gossipy letter to his wounded friend, hoping to catch Kidd up on the pertinent news.

Capt J H Kidd
Washington House
Washington DC
Culpeper C.H. Va Sept 30, 1863

Dear Major "Bob"

For the sake of a poor "fellow critter," if nothing else, do come back to the regiment. I joined on the 8th of September, made the first campaign in an ambulance, reported for duty on the [Rapidan], went into camp at Stevensburg a few days, "on or about" the 29th set out on an expedition via Madison C.H. & across the [Rapidan] & back (quite lively) & the next day after returning moved out to relieve Gregg's cavalry[67] which was picketing the Robinson's River. Col. Gray gave out with a lame back on our way out at Madison C.H. on that road, & has gone to Washington.[68] Last Monday morning, everything being quiet at the front, I reported for medical treatment to Dr Armstrong, Div. Hosp. Surgeon here & have been taking Tincture of Iodine & Quinine, and having my arm worked at ever since. I hope to be strong again soon—my arm is the greatest bother— not worth a straw. Moreover, there are no field officers, except myself, now with the Regt. Major Drew[69] is on Brig. Staff, & no one has been appointed in Foote's place. There is but one Captain on duty (Birge), & but three Lieuts that have been mustered. Barnhart, Pendill & Henshaw[70] have their commissions & can be mustered as soon as their discharge papers are made out & properly signed. That is being done in the meantime they are acting Lts. Seager[71] could not muster in Co "B" to which he was assigned, on account of lack of men. He went home this morning. I am looking anxiously for somebody to "turn up." Quite a number of our best officers are prisoners, you know, & Powers[72] has been paroled, has been ordered to duty notwithstanding the parole, but has done nothing as yet, being somewhat doubtful about the propriety and safety of taking up arms until after properly exchanged. Throop and Cory[73] are skylarking around among the hospitals getting their resignations through. It looks as though there had been a sort of tornado in the regiment, & certain limbs &c lie about in all directions. Capt Hyser is here in the hospital really disabled. He can't get home, not get to Washington & is heartily sick, about. Now, if you are well, come to me & we will try to fag through the fall campaign. Next winter if we sit still a while, the regiment can be together, filled up, officers will return though now in prison & the vacancies can be filled &

the regiment drilled & disciplined into something of its former "shape and comeliness." If you are *not well*, don't come too soon & I will try to get through alone. I came too soon by a month, but with the rest I am getting now, hope to get along. Pardon great length. Write at once.

> Very respectfully
> Your most obedient servant
> H. E. Thompson
> alias "Hank"

KIDD PASSED HIS RECUPERATION quietly and, on October 1, started from home to rejoin his regiment. He wrote, "My wound was healed, so that crutches had been laid aside and a stout stick substituted. I was too lame to march on foot, but thought there would be no trouble about resuming my place in the saddle." A group of his friends saw him to the train station in Ionia, as the newly promoted major set about returning to service. While en route to Washington, he stopped at Ann Arbor to visit old friends. While there, he witnessed a demonstration wherein students burned in effigy the new chancellor of the university. Henry P. Tappan, chancellor during Kidd's years at the University, had been driven from office, in part because of his political views. Kidd commented, "The removal of Doctor Tappan was resented as a work of petty partisan and personal malice, by the community generally, but especially by the students, who were loyal partisans of the deposed chancellor." The students then marched to the chancellor's residence and stoned the house with a sympathetic Kidd looking on.[74]

On October 11, his lengthy recuperation finally over, Kidd arrived in Washington and boarded a "ramshackle" train of the Orange and Alexandria Railroad and took passage to Bealton Station, north of the Rappahannock River. There, Kidd found a retreating army and a regiment whose ranks had been reduced by hard marching and harder fighting.[75] His regiment was already on the march, with the combined forces of Kilpatrick and Buford advancing across the Rapidan toward Madison Court House. On October 11, Buford's command encountered Rebel cavalry and was driven back across the Rapidan toward Brandy Station, where the two columns converged. A third battle of Brandy Station occurred, with the familiar ground around Fleetwood Hill changing hands several times in the fray. A trooper of the 7th Michigan recorded, "Although thrown into confusion our Chief of Cavalry, Alfred Pleasonton, sits his horse like a centaur and gives his orders as though on dress parade. Kilpatrick is swearing a blue streak."[76]

At one point, Pleasonton personally led a desperate charge, with Kilpatrick and Custer riding at his side. Kilpatrick later remembered, "Custer, with hat off, laced jacket, yellow hair dancing in wild confusion over his head and shoulders, carrying his own battle-flag, rode a perfect picture of manly strength and courage, at the head of his Michigan brigade." Kilpatrick continued, "As our column closed in compact order and three thousand bright, sharp sabres leaped from their scabbards and danced in the sunlight."[77]

The Confederate forces swung aside and trapped the charging column, with the Wolverines taking heavy casualties in the process. Pleasonton regrouped his command, and the two sides fought to a standstill. Custer personally led a charge, yelling, "Boys of Michigan, there are some people between us and home. I'm going home! Who else goes?" His cheering Wolverines drew sabers and followed, prompting Custer to observe, "It required but a glance at the countenances of the men to enable me to read the settled determination with which they undertook the task before them."[78]

After four charges by the Wolverines and a day of hard fighting, the two sides withdrew, with Kilpatrick overheard stating to Pleasonton, "Alf, it's a pretty hard job to capture a division of cavalry."[79] Fifty years later, Kidd commented that the fight at Brandy Station "was a brilliant passage at arms, in which neither side obtained a decisive advantage."[80]

Kidd had missed the battle but rejoined his command the next day and enjoyed his first personal interview with his brigade commander, Custer. Several days later, commanding the regiment for the first time, Kidd led a reconnaissance toward Gainesville to ascertain "the position and strength of the enemy." Custer praised Kidd's performance, writing that the "reconnaissance was entirely satisfactory and showed the enemy to be in considerable force at that point."[81]

On the 18th, Kilpatrick moved his entire division toward Warrenton, with the Wolverines marching on a side road paralleling the Warrenton Turnpike. They encountered the enemy along the road and drove them toward Gainesville, where Kilpatrick called a halt, intending to fight. Early the next day, a staff officer approached Kilpatrick and said,

"A fine day, General." The rash Kilpatrick responded, "Yes, a fine day for a fight," and ordered the attack.[82]

In accordance with Kilpatrick's orders, Custer sent the Wolverines forward, where they were soon engaged along a line from Gainesville to Buckland. The Confederates held their main line of resistance along a stream called Broad Run.[83] After commanding his regiment in pitched battle for the first time, Kidd described the Union defeat known to history as the Buckland Races.

> Head Quarters 6th M C
> 2nd Brigade 3rd Div CC
> Gainesville Oct. 26, 1863

Dear Father & Mother

When you saw me last I was making coffee and had just ceased skirmishing. We had crossed "Broad Run" a stream which at that time was unfordable and could be crossed only by a single bridge or by swimming. The enemy as I think I told you had given up a splendid position to our advance a position which they could have held against two times their number whereas as the sequel proved they greatly outnumbered us. The 1st Brigade went on towards Warrenton and our brigade remained on the bank near the bridge making coffee feeding our horses at ease and unsuspicious of danger but it seems that General Stewart who was in command left his strong position to allow us across intending when we had placed sufficient distance between ourselves and the chance of retreat. While making strong show of resistance in our front to have Fitz Hugh Lees cavalry attack our rear. This ruse partially succeeded. An accidental circumstance interfered with in some measure with his plan. Gen Custer was ordered by Gen Kilpatrick to push on towards Warrenton after the 1st Brigade which passed us at Buckland Mills where we halted. Gen Custer declined to go on until his men had had dinner they having had nothing to eat since the day before. This delay saved us. Fitz Hugh Lee[84] evidently waited for us to move on until Gen Kilpatrick obtained some inkling of his presence upon our flank when he ordered Gen Custer's brigade back across the run at the same time sending orders to Gen Davis[85] commanding the 1st Brigade to return. Gen Custer ordered me to move 500 yards to the left and remain there while the column was passing out. At that time I am satisfied that he was entirely unaware of the presence of an enemy in our immediate neighborhood. I moved the regiment through a field till I came to a fence and intended to go on to the woods beyond the next field but not thinking it worth while to remove the fences I commenced to form the regiment in "columns of battalions" where I was. I had found one battalion with the left flank towards the woods and was forming the other in its rear when the enemy concealed in the woods opened fire upon us. The balls whizzed through and over us strange to say injuring no one. I was astonished, and for a moment supposed they were our own men as Gen Custer had told me that the 7th Michigan were near there but they were more to the right. A second volley satisfied me and in two minutes I had dismounted the regiment, the deployed the skirmishers along the fence facing the woods and sent the horses back to our former position under cover of a hill. I reported to Gen Custer who on hearing firing was as much surprised as myself he immediately placed the battery in position in our rear, by which time the rebels opened fire from a masked battery, right in front of us. They however directed their attention to our battery and to the rear of our battery. Five minutes after a heavy force of mounted Infantry dismounted made its appearance to the front and left and coming down upon our left flank while the 7th Mich Cavly had been driven in upon our right. Our battery immediately limbered up when I had informed Gen Custer of this new danger and went for the bridge on the run, while all the mounted regiments all retired slowly. Gen Custer ordered me to mount my men who when they received the order fell back at a walk firing as they retired and mounted and got out of the way in good order. After we had all got safely over the bridge the rebels planted a battery and shelled the road while a force of cavalry which had crossed below came in upon what had been our left but was then our right flank. At Haymarket we met our Infantry and was out of danger. The 1st Brigade was cut off also the 5th Michigan and made their escape by turning off to the right and swimming the stream. Col Alger lost a whole battalion over 50 men with Major Clark Capt Lee[86] and his adjutant. I lost 5 men wounded one sniping. This was a most beautiful trap for our division and came within one of succeeding. Dinner saved us. The following is a rough sketch of our position. Having escaped we came to the place where we have since been. The N.Y. Herald gives Col Alger all the credit and made a charge. No charges were made and the particulars of the fight were given to the Herald correspondent by Col Alger himself. "*Such is life.*" Mum, this I know. If you see any letters in the Free Press from the 6th you may suspect from whom they came. Love to all.

Yours affectionately
J H Kidd

THE BRIGADE OF Brig. Gen. Henry E. Davies joined the Wolverines, and the two units fought their way to safety at the cost of 150 casualties.[87] The defeat was a great embarrassment to the Federal cavalry; Maj. Henry B. McClellan, Stuart's adjutant, crowed, "Kilpatrick's men ran in a manner worthy of the occasion. For nearly five miles the chase was continued without a pause. Naturally the panic-stricken crowd of fugitives, among whom all order was cast aside, made faster time than did the pursuing brigades. . . . I may safely claim that during the war there occurred no more complete rout of any body of cavalry."[88] Custer himself lost his tent, desk, and personal papers, and commented that it had been "the most disastrous [day] this Division ever passed through."[89] Kidd recalled, "Custer on the whole, was very fortunate and had reason to congratulate himself on escaping with so little damage."[90] After the debacle, Kilpatrick did his best to make light of the disaster, inviting all officers of the division to his headquarters for an attempt at merrymaking. Kidd wryly commented, "There were milk-punch and music, both of very good quality, but the punch, palatable as it undeniably was, did not serve to take away the bad taste left by the affair, especially among the officers of [Davies's] Brigade."[91]

The Army of the Potomac took position along the banks of the Rapidan as Meade prepared for his Mine Run campaign. Kidd found time to write home on Halloween:

Head Quarters 6th Mich Cav
2nd Brigade 3rd Div CC
Gainesville, Va Oct 31, 63

Dear Father

Yesterday I wrote to Sarah. Today we are mustered for pay at $1^{1}/_{2}$ o'clock and are ordered to be ready to move immediately. We had secured a most beautiful camping ground and fitted it up in nice style. Set up our tents, and made ourselves comfortable as possible. We have occupied this place just 24 hours, and now we are ordered to leave. "Such is (army) life." Whence we go I am not aware. Wherever we go and, whatever befalls us, I will let you know.

In regard to pay, I am not yet mustered as major nor can I be until the comdg officer of the Regt is officially informed that Col (Major) Foote has resigned and that such resignation is accepted. Major Drew whose commission is dated more than two months after mine was allowed to muster in in my absence although I ought to have been mustered in first. The no. of men in the regiment, as shown by the rolls, does not allow more than two Majors and while Col Foote holds his position I cannot get mustered. I shall be unable to get any pay either as a captain or major this pay day, as my name cannot appear on the rolls. I got my pay in Washington up to Aug 31, and shall have money enough to last me two months if I do not get any but I would like to have sent some money home. I have not been very well since I came back but am getting on slowly. My foot troubles me very little, it is about well. You have heard all the news from here through the papers that I could tell and more.

My previous letters to you have told you of my self. I cannot add more. Hoping to hear from you often as I have not yet done. With love to all I remain

Yr affectionate son
James H Kidd

THE WOLVERINES PROBED at Lee's positions along Mine Run, clearing the way for the army's advance. They held Morton's Ford on the Rapidan, and Kidd, along with the 6th Michigan, marched upstream to guard other fords and the Federal left flank. As he prepared to march, Kidd scribbled a hasty request for personal items to his friend Angelo Tower, who had received a furlough to Ionia.

Head Quarters 6th M C
Stevensburg VA Nov 17, 1863

Dear Father

I write in haste this time. I have just learned that Angelo is going home.

I merely write to tell you what I want you to send me by him. Please put in a box

40 or 50 lbs Butter
1/2 Bushel dried Fruit

2 Pr Socks
2 Towels (Fine)
A knife, fork, spoon, plate, cup & saucer.

Enclosed I send you paymaster's check for $200.

Yrs as ever
J H Kidd

MAJ. GEN. GOUVERNEUR K. WARREN, temporarily commanding the Second Corps, detected a trap set by the wily Lee and aborted a planned general attack by the entire Army of the Potomac.[92] Instead, the army pulled back, its withdrawal covered by the Cavalry Corps, which stayed in position for another six days. Finally receiving orders to withdraw, the cavalry fell back toward Brandy Station and went into winter camp. Kidd, to his great displeasure, was detailed to a court-martial panel then sitting at Gen. Davies's headquarters. Kidd made an unsuccessful attempt to evade the duty.

Headquarters 6th Mich
Cavalry, Dec. 6, 1863

Captain

I am detailed by order of Gen Kilpatrick, as a member of the General Court Martial now in session at HdQrs 1st Brigade.

I would respectfully ask to be relieved from that Court-Martial for the following reasons:

1st, I am the only Field Officer with the command,
2nd I am in command of the Regiment,
3rd We are in picket,
4th There are only six other officers on duty in the regt.

Very respectfully
Yr obt servant
J. H. Kidd
Maj Comdg 6th Mich Cavalry
To
Capt. L. G. Estes
A.A.G.

As THEY RESTED, wounded men returned to the regiment, and prisoners came back after being exchanged. Kidd noted that, before the October fight at Brandy Station, his regiment had less than 100 men and officers fit and present for duty; by mid-December, the total had risen to 250.[93] As a busy year drew to a close, Kidd described the regiment's winter surroundings and routine.

Head Qrs 6th Mich Cavly
Dec. 24, 1863

Dear Father

Yours have all been received. I have not written for several days for I have been too busy. I am alone in command, and have had a heavy press of business, more than usual, making out all sorts of official "red tape" documents. And in addition we are ordered to go into winter quarters and are trying to make ourselves comfortable.

I have had 7 teams of six mules each drawing timber, men cutting logs tearing down old houses to get the lumber and nails, and brick chimneys to get the brick. We are putting up log huts and in a day or two shall be ready to live quite comfortably.

I have had put up for Head Qrs a log house 12 feet square, with one window and a huge "fire-place" in it, and tonight feel more like a civilized being than for a long time I have permitted to do. The men work night as well as day, and quite a village is growing up, with well laid out streets, uniformly built. Each house provided with a chimney which indicates the comfort of a fire place within. We are picketing and are out to the Rapidan for ½ the time 3 days out of 6. This is Stevensburg[94] (3 miles back from the line) where our Head Qrs are. Our labors are to be lightened. The Infantry have come to our rescue & will do ½ the work. Officers are going home on leave many of them. I don't know that I shall be able to go home this winter. So many officers are absent on picket and on orders that those who are here have slim chance.

I am making efforts to have some of the absentees ordered back, and hope to succeed. I recd a letter from Rich yesterday in which he says that he would have visited us had he known certainly that we could be found. He was in Washington.

I am very much disappointed that he did not come. It would have given me a "*heap*" of pleasure to see him here.

I could have shown him plenty of Rebels without the least danger to him. I think he would have enjoyed a visit to the front vastly. I recd a letter from Ma a few days ago. Also one from Kate & one from Sarah, but I cannot possibly write (more than to tell you I am well) just at present. In a few days I shall have it easier.

C H Patten Quartermaster of our Regiment[95] has gone home to Grand Rapids on a 15 Day leave. He said he would bring my box. If you write to him you can ascertain when he will pass Ionia on his return and it can be put aboard the same train. Mark it CH Patten, QM 6th Mich Cavalry Washington D.C. Love to all

> Yr affectionate son
> J H Kidd

LATER, IN A REPORT to the Adjutant General of Michigan, Kidd noted: "Except a skirmish with Wade Hampton's Division of cavalry at Stevensburg in the early part of November, and three or four demonstrations upon the enemy's lines on the Rapidan at Raccoon, Somerville and Morton's Fords, no active duty was assigned to the regiment from November 1 until the expiration of the year 1863."[96]

Kidd's first full year of campaigning ended. It was an exciting one. He faced combat for the first time, received a serious wound, and ended up with regimental command because of heavy losses among the regiment's officer cadre. The year 1864 promised more excitement for the young cavalryman.

4

Grant's Overland Campaign

I expect a tremendous struggle the coming campaign with what result I cannot predict.

THE MICHIGAN BRIGADE went into winter camp near Stevensburg. The men lived in temporary structures consisting of logs surmounted by tents and outfitted with doors, chimneys, and fireplaces. While not luxurious in any sense, these were pleasant enough quarters, despite the freezing cold winter. Some officers, like Kidd, were gifted singers, and they often entertained the men in their cabins, enjoying a mixture called "milk punch," which consisted of condensed milk and commissary whiskey. The Wolverines constructed a brigade theater, giving amateur plays accompanied by the brigade's band. Lt. Robert C. Wallace of the 5th Michigan observed, "Friendships were there formed that winter that will last until the end, and nowhere else than in the army during war can men become so well acquainted and know each other so thoroughly."[1] Lt. George W. Hill of the 7th Michigan noted in his diary, "I shall remember my stay in Stevensburg a long, long time, the pleasant times I had there and all the good things we had to eat."[2]

The men of the 6th Michigan took their turn picketing along the Rapidan, the dividing line between the two armies. There was an unspoken agreement between the two foes that the winter would be a time of relative peace, with the pickets even conversing, visiting, and trading with each other. A member of the 5th Michigan noted that the troopers had "the finest times in the world talking with the 'Rebs.' We trade spurs and coffee and all such things. They are good friends now but when they come to fight they are as bad as ever."[3] Kidd observed, "Life in winter quarters was at best dull and it relieved the monotony to go on picket."[4] He often broke the monotony by riding the lines and acquainting himself with the Virginia families living along the river.

In addition, the men of the Michigan Brigade spent the winter learning new drills. Instead of using the single rank formations traditionally relied upon by Brig. Gen. Philip St. George Cooke's cavalry tactics manual, the troopers switched to double rank tactics, which had to be learned by all of the Union cavalry regiments. Kidd pointed out that "there was little time for rest or recreation. Long and tiresome drills and 'schools of instruction' made up the daily routine." New recruits had to be incorporated into the ranks of the regiment, so extensive drilling was necessary anyway.[5] In January, his friend, Lt. Col. Henry Thompson, presented Kidd with a diary. On the 14th, Kidd made his first entry: "Reader: You ask why commence at this date? Why have you not chronicled the events since Jan'y 1st. A 'diary' I have scarcely ever kept, and did not propose so to do now. But Lt. Barnhart has just handed me this book with 'Lt. Col. Thompson's compliments.'"

Kidd managed to keep the diary for only a couple of weeks; in 1865, he picked up the same diary and started writing in it again. Despite such negligence, some interesting insights emerge. For instance, on January 15, he proudly wrote, "I quit smoking today at noon. Made a resolution not to smoke for a month nor drink." He lasted two days, complaining on the 17th, "Find that total abstinence from smoking has not a salutary effect on the temper. Can't be good natured if I try." The next day, he wryly commented, "Smoked two cigars. To quit abruptly might end my life."[6]

Hd Qrs 6th Mich Cavalry
Jany 18, 1864

Dear Mother and Father

I owe you both a letter and will answer them both at once on a sheet of Official size for I have no other.

I suppose I should be very prompt now in answering your letters for I have plenty of time; in winter quarters, and not now in command, (as I was recently); and I shall endeavor to write often; indeed I think I have done so hitherto, since my return from home.

Your box, I suppose, must be in Washington by this time and I shall try to get it this week when Mr. Patten[7] goes to W. I wish you could visit me here and the expense for you would not be much greater than for me to come there, although I should not see you all which I want to do. We all of course look with great pleasure upon the prospect of going home. But fifteen days with scares give us a taste, what with going and coming, the probably delays incident upon the journey thither. We are rather discouraged at the idea of attempting it at all. If I could get twenty days, I should make up my mind to come at all hazards, and if Gen. Custer could say. I doubt not I could, but Gen. Meade is very particular and will not consider an application for more than 15 days. However, I *may* come home about the middle of February, if I can get leave.

I am for the first time since my return at liberty to do something besides work. I have for two or three days read considerably and take great comfort in it. Kate's letter is recd also one from Emma Rich and one from Sarah I believe since I wrote her.

Today, we have been favored with one of Virginia's characteristic rains, and tonight the mud is sufficiently deep to impede navigation. This Virginia mud is horrible, just like our red & blue clay, only worse. It sticks to you with a tenacity that only the most vigorous kicks can overcome, and once fast if you bring your boots out with you you are fortunate.

Many civilians are visiting the army. I have noticed several ladies. I saw an Infantry officer the other day going out to visit the picket line with his wife, both on horseback. Gen Custer is to go home in a few days to get married. The fortunate young lady is a resident I understand of Monroe.[8] She will accompany him on his return.

Mrs Col Alger is to visit the army soon, also several other ladies, wives of officers of this brigade. I suppose I shall wish myself *not* a single man. Hoping to hear from you, with love to all, I remain

Your affectionate son
J H Kidd

NOT LONG AFTER, Kidd asked for and obtained permission to go home to Ionia for a visit. After a brief respite from the winter's drudgery, Kidd returned to his unit, which was preparing to take the field for a dangerous winter raid deep into enemy territory.

Sometime in January, Kilpatrick had devised a plan to take a picked force of cavalry to free the large contingent of Union officers being held as prisoners in Richmond's notorious Libby Prison, as well as enlisted men held at the nearby Belle Isle prison camp. General Custer led a diversionary raid toward Albemarle County, Virginia, and, as a consequence, did not command the Michigan Brigade during what became known as the Kilpatrick/Dahlgren Raid.

One element of the force was commanded by Kilpatrick himself, and the other column of five hundred handpicked men was commanded by a dashing one-legged cavalryman named Col. Ulric Dahlgren, an officer "who had established a reputation for extraordinary daring and dash." Col. Edward Sawyer of the 1st Vermont Cavalry, whose fine regiment had joined the Michigan Brigade some months earlier, commanded the brigade, and Kidd commanded the detachment from the 6th Michigan Cavalry.[9] Kidd described the raid, which commenced on February 29, in the following letter.

> Hd Qrs 6th Mich Cavalry
> Yorktown, Va
> Tuesday, March 8, 1864

Dear Father & Mother

You have been informed by the newspapers of the late movements of Kilpatrick's Division of Cavalry and know more about it than I could tell you.

We left Stevensburg Sunday night, Feby 29th at 6 o'clock. Marching incessantly day & night we reached this place Saturday night. Longstreet[10] was reported to be advancing on Suffolk[11] and 1500 picked men from this Division were sent by transports to Norfolk and Portsmouth, when we found it a false alarm and returned to this place.

On this trip I visited Fortress Monroe[12] and have my first *real* experience of travel by water. It was pretty much of a pleasure trip & I enjoyed it much. Our raid on Richmond was a big thing if you can *only see* it. We went in sight of the City, threw in a few shells, skirmished a little and then vamoosed.

That night we encountered [encamped] within three miles of Richmond and owing to the inefficiency or callousness of the pickets were attacked in our camp while asleep by the enemy. Some regiments lost heavily. I lost one man only who I am afraid was killed by a shell as they threw several into our camp. It was very dark and we were around our camp fires giving the enemy every advantage. Not knowing their position or numbers and not having an efficient Brigade Comd'r (Gen Custer having been

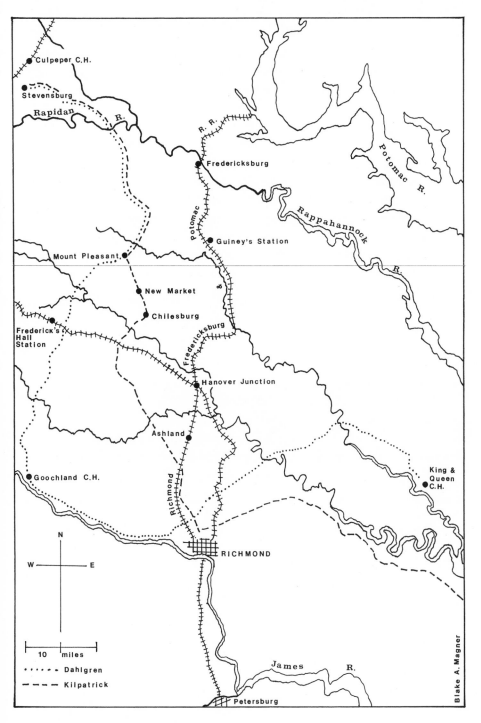

The Kilpatrick/Dahlgren Raid.

taken away before we left Stevensburg)[13] we, acting on our "own hook" those regiments that attempted to fight dismounted were driven back and their horses taken from the trees to which they were tied.

I although waked from a sound sleep by firing almost inside of our camp, had presence of mind enough to mount my men the first thing and get them in line. Afterwards I recd orders to move off & did so without loss. The 7th Michigan and 1st Vermont lost most. Everybody pretty much was "wonderfully and fearfully" *demoralized*.

I could tell you ten thousand things, but it will satisfy you for the present to know that I am alive and well. We shall probably go back to the Army of the Potomac by water. Today, we hear that Col Dahlgreen, who led a separate detachment of 500 men in the raid on Richmond has been murdered by citizens. If this be true Gen K will be revenged on them for he has started out with 1500 men to ascertain the facts in regard to that unfortunate party. If true that citizens have murdered any portion of Col Dahlgreen's command he proposes to burn every house in the neighborhood where it was done.

I do not know how soon we shall leave this. I hope very soon. I am tired of this kind of business. Fighting in the front is preferable ten times over. Hoping this may find you well I am

Affectionately

Your son

J H Kidd, Major

I enclose an ambrotype taken since I came here.

KIDD WAS CORRECT about Dahlgren's demise. Troopers of the 9th Virginia Cavalry and home guard units killed him in an ambush. Finding documents that allegedly revealed a plan to kill Confederate president Jefferson Davis and his cabinet, the outraged local civilians desecrated his corpse. Kidd correctly observed that Dahlgren "deserved a better fate."[14]

Kidd pointed out that the march to the outskirts of Richmond was "at a fast walk," meaning that the column got strung out; the trailing elements often had to gallop just to keep pace. He continued, "There was an air of undue haste—a precipitancy and rush not at all assuring."[15] By 11:00 A.M. on March 1, his column was within a mile of Richmond, engaged in small skirmishes with increasingly stiff resistance by the Confederate home guard. Kilpatrick was heard to say, "They have too many of those damned guns; they keep opening on us all the time."[16] According to Stephen Z. Starr,

This is Kidd's own caption for this photograph: "Taken in Yorktown Virginia, in February 1864, the day of the arrival from the Kilpatrick raid on Richmond, at which time I was commanding the 6th Mich. Calvary with the rank of major. Was promoted to colonel the May following. Age 24. J. H. K." Courtesy of the Bentley Historical Library, University of Michigan, Ann Arbor.

A photo of Colonel Kidd taken in early spring 1865, just a few weeks before the end of the Civil War. In it, he is proudly wearing his Custer Badge, which was given to select members of the Michigan Calvary Brigade by George A. Custer himself. Courtesy of the Bentley Historical Library.

Lt. Col. Henry E. Thompson of Company A. Thompson, Kidd's good friend, eventually achieved the rank of lieutenant colonel, before disability forced his resignation. Kidd succeeded Thompson in command of the regiment. Courtesy of the United States Army Military History Institute (USAMHI), Carlisle, Pennsylvania.

Four officers of the 6th Michigan Cavalry, taken in early 1863. The officer seated on the left is believed to be Kidd's childhood best friend, Capt. Angelo E. Tower. The seated officer with the mustache is Lt. Charles Bolza, who was killed in action leading a mounted charge at Falling Waters, Maryland, July 14, 1863. Courtesy John R. Sickles, Merrillville, Indiana.

Maj. Peter A. Weber, killed in action leading a mounted charge at Falling Waters, Maryland on July 14, 1863. His loss was deeply felt by the regiment. Courtesy of John R. Sickles.

Capt. Manning D. Birge of Company A. When Kidd was promoted to colonel, Birge was promoted to major. Courtesy of John R. Sickles.

Capt. John Torrey of Company L. Courtesy of John R. Sickles.

Capt. James H. Kellogg was the son of the regiment's political patron, Representative Francis W. Kellogg. Courtesy of John R. Sickles.

Capt. Angelo E. Tower of Company E. Kidd's childhood best friend was the first soldier Kidd recruited into his newly formed company. Courtesy of John R. Sickles.

Capt. Benjamin F. "Frank" Rockafellow of Company M. Rockafellow was Kidd's close friend and his tent-mate during the Powder River Indian Expedition in the spring of 1865. Courtesy of the Colorado Historical Society, Denver, No. F-779.

Lt. Luther Kanouse of Company D. Kanouse would attend Kidd's funeral in 1913. Courtesy of USAMHI.

Lt. Charles E. Bolza of Company B. Courtesy of John R. Sickles, Merrillville, Indiana.

Sgt. J. Osborn Coburn of Company E. Courtesy of Don Allison, Bryan, Ohio.

Pvt. Edwin E. Harmon of Company K. Harmon's uniform and equipment are typical of an enlisted member of the 6th Michigan Cavalry. Courtesy of John R. Sickles.

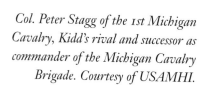

Col. Peter Stagg of the 1st Michigan Cavalry, Kidd's rival and successor as commander of the Michigan Cavalry Brigade. Courtesy of USAMHI.

Col. Charles H. Town of the 1st Michigan Cavalry. Although he was slowly dying of tuberculosis at the time, Town led the mounted saber charge of his regiment at the Battle of Gettysburg. Courtesy of USAMHI.

Col. Russell A. Alger, first lieutenant colonel of the 6th Michigan Cavalry, then transferred to the command of the 5th Michigan Cavalry. He later served as secretary of war in the McKinley administration. Courtesy of USAMHI.

Maj. Luther S. Trowbridge of the 5th Michigan Cavalry. A fine soldier, Trowbridge was eventually brevetted brigadier general of the volunteers. Courtesy of USAMHI.

Maj. Gen. Alfred Pleasonton, commander of the Army of the Potomac's Cavalry Corps from June 1863 through March 1864. Pleasonton deserves credit for recognizing the talent of good young cavalry officers such as George A. Custer, Wesley Merritt, and Elon J. Farnsworth. Courtesy of the National Archives.

Maj. Gen. Philip H. Sheridan, commander of the Army of the Potomac's Cavalry Corps and commanding general of the Army of the Shenandoah in 1864 and 1865. The Cavalry Corps reached the zenith of its power under Sheridan's able hand. Courtesy of Cathy Marinacci, Springfield, Ohio.

Maj. Gen. Alfred T. A. Torbert, commander of the 1st Cavalry Division of the Army of the Potomac and chief cavalry for the Army of the Shenandoah. Kidd and Torbert disliked each other; their animosity led to Kidd's relief as commander of the Michigan Cavalry Brigade in October 1864. Courtesy of USAMHI.

Col. Percy Wyndham, first commander of the cavalry forces assigned to the defenses of Washington D.C. One officer of the 5th Michigan called him "a big bag of wind." Courtesy of the National Archives.

Brig. Gen. Julius Stahel, who succeeded Wyndham as commander of the cavalry forces assigned to Washington D.C. Kidd described the Hungarian-born Stahel as "a dapper little Dutchman." Courtesy of the National Archives.

Brig. Gen. Joseph T. Copeland, first commander of the Michigan Cavalry Brigade. Copeland, a prominent attorney, was unceremoniously relieved of command in favor of Brig. Gen. George A. Custer on the eve of the Battle of Gettysburg. Courtesy of USAMHI.

Brig. Gen. Judson Kilpatrick, also known as "Kill-Cavalry," the first commander of the 3d Division, Cavalry Corps, Army of the Potomac. "A frothy braggart without brains," Kilpatrick was vain, licentious, reckless, and personally ambitious to a fault. Courtesy of the National Archives.

This photo, taken in the Shenandoah Valley in August 1864, in front of Sheridan's tent, with his headquarters guidon displayed prominently, depicts Sheridan and his cavalry commanders. From left: Brig. Gen. Wesley Merritt, Brig. Gen. David McMurtrie Gregg, Maj. Gen. Philip H. Sheridan, Brig. Gen. Henry E. Davis, Brig. Gen. James Harrison Wilson, and Brig. Gen. Alfred T. A. Torbert. Courtesy of USAMHI.

Maj. Gen. Wesley Merritt, who commanded the 1st Cavalry Division of both the Army of the Potomac and the Army of the Shenandoah in 1864 and 1865. Merritt, one of the so-called boy generals, was promoted from captain to brigadier general on June 28, 1863, along with George A. Custer and Elon J. Farnsworth. Courtesy of the National Archives.

Maj. Gen. George A. Custer, the officer most closely associated with the Michigan Cavalry Brigade. Kidd plainly and unabashedly idolized Custer, as did most of the rest of the men who served under him. Courtesy of Cathy Marinacci.

Brig. Gen. Elon J. Farnsworth, Kidd's friend and classmate at the University of Michigan and commander of the other brigade in Kilpatrick's 3d Division. Farnsworth died leading a brave and futile charge late in the afternoon of the last day of the Battle of Gettysburg. Courtesy of the National Archives.

Maj. Gen. Grenville Dodge was the commander of the Department of Missouri and of the Federal forces in Missouri and Kansas. Dodge was the architect of the Powder River Indian Expedition. Courtesy of USAMHI.

Brig. Gen. Patrick E. Conner, shown here as a major general, was the commander of the Powder River Indian Expedition. Rnowned as an Indian Fighter, he left the army in disgrace after the failure of that expedition. Courtesy of the Library of Congress.

Maj. Gen. James Ewell Brown "J. E. B." Stuart, the famed Confederate cavalry chieftain, mortally wounded by a member of the Michigan Cavalry Brigade at the Battle of Yellow Tavern on May 11, 1864. Courtesy of the National Archives.

Lt. Gen. Wade Hampton, Stuart's successor as commander of the Confederate cavalry. Hampton thrashed Sheridan at the bloody Battle of Trevilian Station in June 1864. Courtesy of the National Archives.

Maj. Gen. Fitzhugh Lee, senior division commander under Hampton and Stuart. Courtesy of the National Archives.

Maj. Gen. Thomas Lafayette Rosser, the so-called Savior of the Shenandoah Valley. Rosser, who had been Custer's close friend at West Point, tangled with the Wolverines a number of times during 1864, including during the harsh fights at Trevilian Station and Tom's Brook. Courtesy of the Library of Congress.

Maj. Gen. Lunsford Lumax, Rosser's co-commander of the Confederate forces in the Shenandoah Valley in fall 1864. Courtesy of USAMHI.

At an encampment of the Michigan National Guard in the 1880s, Kidd, by then a brigadier general in the National Guard, is seated at the far left of this photograph. Seated immediately to his left is his wife, Florence, and their son Frederick McConnell Kidd stands between them. Courtesy of the Bentley Historical Library.

Col. John Singleton Mosby, the famed "Gray Ghost of the Confederacy." Mosby was the nemesis of the Federal cavalry, which devoted great effort to unsuccessful attempts to bring him to bay. Courtesy of Horace C. Mewborn, Springfield, Virginia.

Kidd's son Fred's original caption for this photograph: "This picture was taken after the Civil War at an encampment of the Michigan State Troops and shows James H. Kidd holding the horse 'Billy' he rode during the Civil War and brought home." Courtesy of the Bentley Historical Library.

James H. Kidd in the full dress uniform of a brigadier general of the Michigan National Guard, taken in the 1890s. Note the Custer Badge worn in the center of his uniform. Courtesy of the Bentley Historical Library.

James H. Kidd in a photo taken not long before his death, when he was in his early seventies. Courtesy of the Bentley Historical Library.

The Michigan Cavalry Brigade monument on the East Cavalry Field at Gettysburg. Kidd gave the dedication address for this monument in 1888, a proud moment for the veteran cavalryman. Photo by author.

"So far as one can tell from the rather uncertain language of his report, Kilpatrick simply lost control; he was face to face with a tactical situation for which he was unable to find a solution."[17] So he drew back. Largely as a consequence of Kilpatrick's timidity at the critical moment, his column failed to reach Libby Prison.

The blue-clad troopers retreated to safety after a heavy skirmish with Wade Hampton's cavalry near Hanover Court House. The cold, wet, tired, and miserable Wolverines made their way back to the main Union lines, their expedition an utter failure and their spirits low. The eight-day raid took a heavy toll in men and horseflesh, which did not have adequate time to recuperate before the beginning of the spring campaign season.

Col. Charles S. Wainwright, commander of the First Army Corps' artillery battalion sniffed, "These raids have never amounted to anything on either side beyond a scare, and proving that once within the enemy's lines a good body of cavalry can travel either country with perfect freedom for a long time. . . .These raids make a big noise in the papers, and so glorify their commander; [Kilpatrick] is generally a man of that kind who court newspaper renown."[18] Kidd quite correctly observed, "There was . . . not much glory in the expedition for anyone, least of all for Kilpatrick himself."[19]

Heavily criticized for the failed raid, Kilpatrick was soon relieved of command of the 3d Division and sent west to take command of Maj. Gen. William T. Sherman's cavalry. Sherman later observed that Kilpatrick was "a hell of a damned fool, but just the kind of fool that I want to command my cavalry." Kidd now had command of the regiment because Colonel Gray was still incapacitated and Lt. Col. Henry Thompson, who was wounded at Hunterstown and had not yet recovered well enough to take the field, was detailed to command a camp for newly conscripted troopers. Kidd proudly pointed this fact out in a letter to his parents.

Hd Qrs 6th Mich Cavalry
March 20th 1864

Dear Father & Mother

I wrote you from Yorktown informing you of my safe arrival there. I also wrote when I arrived at Alexandria but was unable to send the letter. You have been anxious to hear from me, of my safety and health. When I started I did not expect to go through but my vigor kept me up and I am as good as new. That is more than I can say of my horses, however.

They are badly used up, worn out. The great raid on Richmond has ended and U.S. is satisfied Kilpatrick can't do everything. One thing at least he is unequal to the Captains of Richmond with Cavalry. I expected no more and am not disappointed. You have seen in the papers all we attempted to do and all we *failed* to accomplish. I can't tell you more. I don't want to go off on another such.

But I had a splendid ride by steamer & water from Yorktown to Suffolk, and back and from Yorktown to Alexandria touching at Fortress Monroe. This was something new and differed from other adventures in the experiences of last three weeks in having no slice of danger or fatigue. It is three weeks today since we left. Our cavalrymen, cavalry horses, etc. are about played out and for that matter so is somebody not mentioned whose name figured extensively in a certain raid not of long ago, but this I do not say. I only think, for by saying it I might compromise myself. Gen Custer you know distinguished himself as he always does. Lt Col Thompson[20] has been detailed at the Camp of Conscripts in Grand Rapids, so you can look to me as *"Maj Comdg Regt"* for some time to come. "Such is life." But every dog has his day. So shall I mine perhaps.

I shall now that I am back at Stevensburg try to be punctual in my correspondence again. How long we remain inactive, God only knows.

> Yours affectionately
> J H Kidd,
> Major

ON MARCH 3, Ulysses S. Grant received a promotion to lieutenant general and assumed command of all Union armies in the field. He decided to travel with the Army of the Potomac and soon moved his headquarters to Stevensburg. The new general in chief made a number of significant changes in the Army of the Potomac, one of which forever affected the Cavalry Corps.

In a meeting with President Lincoln, Grant expressed his dissatisfaction with the accomplishments of the Federal mounted arm, properly assessing that it might have done more under a more competent and more aggressive leader. Grant later recalled, "I said I wanted the very best man in the army for that command." Maj. Gen. Henry Halleck, who became the army's chief of staff upon Grant's promotion, was present at the meeting and inquired, "How would [Maj. Gen. Philip H.] Sheridan do?" Grant responded, "The very man I want." Lincoln told Grant he could have any man he wanted. Grant then acted quickly, telegraphing Sheridan, ordering him to report to the Army of the Potomac to assume command of the Cavalry Corps. Grant observed that Sheridan's appointment was not a negative reflection on Alfred Pleasonton, because Grant "did not know but that he had been as efficient as any other cavalry commander."[21] Kidd later described his new cavalry chief:

> He was well mounted and sat his horse like a real cavalryman. Though short in stature he did not appear so on horseback. His stirrups were high up, the shortness being of leg and not of trunk. He wore a peculiar style of hat not like that of any other officer. He was square of shoulder and there was plenty of room for the display of a major general's buttons on his broad chest. His face was strong, with a firm jaw, a keen eye, and extraordinary firmness in every lineament. In his manner there was an alertness, evinced rather in look than in movement. Nothing escaped his eye, which was brilliant and searching and at the same time emitted flashes of kindly good nature. When riding among or past his troopers, he had a way of casting quick, comprehensive glances to the right and left and in all directions. He overlooked nothing. One had a feeling that he was under close and critical observation, that Sheridan had his eye on him, was mentally taking his measure and would remember and recognize him the next time. No introduction was needed.[22]

Sheridan met with General Meade, still nominally the commander of the Army of the Potomac, and told him

> that, as the effectiveness of my command rested mainly on the strength of its horses, I thought the [extensive picket] duty it was then performing was both burdensome and wasteful. I also gave him my idea as to what the cavalry should do, the main purport of which was that it ought to be kept concentrated to fight the enemy's cavalry. Heretofore, the commander of the Cavalry Corps had been, virtually, but an adjunct at army headquarters—a sort of chief of cavalry—and my proposition seemed to stagger General Meade not a little. I knew that it would be difficult to overcome the recognized custom of using the cavalry for the protection of trains and the establishment of cordons around the infantry corps, and so far subordinating its operations to the movement of the main army that in name only was it a corps at all, but I still thought it my duty to try. . . . I told him that if he would

let me use the cavalry as I contemplated, he need have little solicitude in these respects, for, with a mass of ten thousand mounted men, it was my belief that I could make it so lively for the enemy's cavalry that, so far as attacks from it were concerned, the flanks and rear of the Army of the Potomac would require little or no defense, and claimed, further, that moving columns of infantry should take care of their own fronts. I also told him that it was my general object to defeat the enemy's cavalry in a general combat, if possible, and by such a result establish a feeling of confidence in my own troops that would enable us after a while to march where we pleased, for the purpose of breaking General Lee's communications and destroying the resources from which his army was supplied.[23]

Sheridan shook up the Cavalry Corps' command structure. Brig. Gen. Alfred Thomas Archimedes Torbert replaced Wesley Merritt, who had assumed command of the First Division upon John Buford's death in December 1863, and Brig. Gen. James H. Wilson replaced Kilpatrick. Merritt returned to command of the reserve brigade, attached to the First Division. Torbert was a West Pointer who had spent his career in the infantry, eventually commanding a brigade of New Jersey volunteers. One of Merritt's regular army officers keenly noted that Torbert was "a handsome dashing fellow, . . . a beautiful horseman, and as brave as a lion; but his abilities were hardly equal to such large commands."[24] Kidd was not impressed either, observing that Torbert was "an infantry officer whose qualifications as a commander of cavalry were not remarkable."[25] Kidd further observed that Torbert's "arrogant bearing made him exceedingly unpopular with Buford's and Kilpatrick's veteran troopers, who had been accustomed to serve under men who could do harder fighting with less airs."[26] Kidd's poor opinion of the new division commander would hurt his career later in 1864.

Sheridan's choice of Wilson was controversial. George Custer was senior to Wilson, whom Custer had known at West Point, and was entitled to take command of the Third Division. Sheridan observed, "At my request [Wilson] was selected to command the Third Division. General Grant thought highly of him, and expecting much from his active mental and physical ability, readily assented to assign him in place of General Kilpatrick."[27]

Custer did not share Grant's opinion, commenting that Wilson "has made himself ridiculous by the ignorance he displays in regard to cavalry."[28]

When informed of the change, Custer asked Grant and Sheridan, "Does that mean that my brigade is also to be advanced? Are they to be the First Brigade of the Cavalry?" After some thought, the two commanders told Custer that they had not considered that change. Custer reached into his pocket, pulled out a sheet of paper, and said, "If it means that I am to have my own brigade, the offer is very thankfully accepted; for they have earned for me all I enjoy of military celebrity; but if not, gentlemen, here is my commission." The two generals promptly replied, "Gen. Custer, your Michigan Brigade shall be promoted with you to the head of the cavalry line."[29] Apparently appeased, Custer wrote to his new bride, Libbie, "Everything is arranged satisfactorily now; I take my Brigade and join the 1st Division Cavalry Corps under Genl. Torbert, an old and dear friend of mine, and a very worthy gentleman. . . . Major-General Sheridan impresses me very favorably."[30]

Sheridan found that the "officers and men were in pretty good condition, so far as health and equipment were concerned, but their horses were thin and very much worn out by excessive, and it seemed to me, unnecessary picket duty." The men had a few weeks to nurse their mounts back to health, meaning that, when the spring campaigning season began, nearly ten thousand healthy horses were available to the Cavalry Corps.[31] As they rested, Kidd issued an order to all of his regiment's officers, which gives a good feel for his command style.

Special Order
No. 4

Hereafter Officers who are reported "for Duty" in the Morning Report will be required to perform such duties as they may be Detailed upon Officers who are not for Duty will so Report, otherwise the plea of sickness will not be considered.

By order of
James H. Kidd
Maj. Commanding Regt.[32]

A FEW DAYS later, Kidd decided to clamp down on regimental discipline.

Head Quarters 6th Mich. Cav
Stevensburg, Va April 3rd 1864

Regimental Order
No. 1

Hereafter the officer of the day will exercise a general supervision of all camp and police duties. He will see that all calls for duty are promptly attended. He will take charge of all the horses in the Regt at water call and formally conduct them to the place of watering. He will inspect the horses after recall from stable duty and the streets after fatigue and will cause all men violating existing orders to be arrested and punished. At retreat the Companies will move out on the Prolongation of their respective streets for Roll Call and inspection. The officers of the day posted in front of Regimental Head Quarters will there receive from the 1st sergeants reports of the men absent without permission from the several for duty during the day. On the morning when relieved he will furnish to the Adjutant a written report showing the condition and discipline of the portion of the command which was in camp the previous day showing which companies had their horses best groomed and what streets were best policed naming the Officers who did neglect to enforce the proper discipline and officers who allowed their men to shirk duty or violate orders. All orders which apply to the Companies, also apply to the Pioneer Corps and the extra and daily duty men.

The officer of the day will wear a sash.
By Order of
James H. Kidd
Maj Comdg Regt[33]

As THE ARMY prepared for its spring campaign, Kidd wrote home.

Hd Qrs 6th M Cavly
April 16, 1864

Dear Father

Yours of the 6th came night before last. It came slowly. I was glad to hear from you. Sorry the weather is interfering with your business. Saw a man a few days ago who knew you. He said you was getting *rich*. I hope so certainly. You deserve to and will if you plunge right in. We are having some big changes down here. Gen Grant is tearing down and build-

ing whether for good or bad remains to be seen. Pleasonton[34] has gone
west. Sheridan a western man takes his place. Gen Kilpatrick is also relieved
from the command of the 3rd Div. Who will supersede him is not yet
divulged.[35] Rumor says Gen Custer may leave us. "Bad luck" to those who
are instrumental in removing him. We swear by him. His name is our battle cry. He can get twice the fight out of this brigade that any other man
can possibly do.

T W Ferry[36] is here for what purpose I know not. We may be ordered
to move very soon. It is however raining which may interfere with active
operations for a while. When it does come it will come with a smash. This
campaign will squelch rebellion I opine. I wish we had no traitors nearer
home than the slave states. But we have and I fear they will split the north
on the war. If they do, then all patriotic men had better move to some distant land and set up a new government, and let this shattered old ship sail
to perdition, when [where] its inmates would certainly go. It has got to
be rather a disgrace than otherwise to be a soldier, particularly an *officer
at home*. I mean not here. If these northern croakers think it is such a fine
thing to be an officer, why don't they try it. They are politicians and politics run the thing. Without political friends you are nowhere. A scrip-
tural saying is "Those who sow shall in due time reap if they faint not."
This is true if you go to the political crib for your seed, not otherwise, I
fear. Perhaps you won't be able to see the point of all this strange talk.
Well if you can't you may perhaps after all be no worse off than I am myself.

Please give my love to all *our folks*, not omitting Grandfather, and my
regards to those who care for them if there are such. Hoping to hear from
you soon I am

Your affectionate son
J H Kidd, Major

As GRANT REORGANIZED the Army of the Potomac and prepared for the
spring campaign, the cavalry remained vigilant. On April 23, while ready-
ing the men for the coming campaign, Sheridan reviewed his new command. Custer crowed to Libbie, "We had a splendid review to-day.
General Sheridan reviewed the entire Division. My Brigade never looked
better. I was more than proud of it. We compared very favorably with the
other Brigades. . . . Genl. Torbert says that I have the finest and best brigade
of Cavalry in the entire army. I am laboring to make it still better." Kidd
led the 6th Michigan in the review, catching Sheridan's eye and prompting

a beaming Custer to write, "Tell Col. Gray that Genl. Sheridan said that his (Col. Gray's) regiment marched best of all in the command."[37]

A few days later, Kidd led the 6th Michigan on a rather futile reconnaissance in the vicinity of Madison Court House, Virginia.

> Hd Qrs 6th M Cavly
> 1st Brig 1st Div CC
> April 30, 1864

Dear Father & Mother

I recd your last last night. I am now in camp again. Day before yesterday I went out in the direction of Madison Court House, to support Col Devin[38] comdg the 2nd Brigade of this Division. I had under my command two regiments the 5th & 6th and a section of a battery. It was supposed that Longstreet was in that vicinity and I was sent to prevent a flank or rear attack on the 2nd Brigade. The reconnaissance disclosed no enemy in that direction except a few guerrillas whom we captured. I confidently expected to meet with heavy resistance. When our brigade went to Madison Court House last year they got pretty badly flogged by the enemy's cavalry and infantry.

We returned to camp, where we now are awaiting events. An immense army is assembling here which cannot remain lying idle. I expect a tremendous struggle the coming campaign with what result I cannot predict If Grant is successful look for a speedy termination of the war. If not it's indefinite prolongation, so I view it.

I like Grant's style and I am glad he has *actual* authority.

I hear Sarah is to be married. I am glad of it. She is old enough and Spence is good enough.

I don't hear from Uncle Rich nor any of my friends. I suppose I do not write sufficiently often. I hope they will not *entirely* forget me.

You need not expect me at home this summer. I probably shall command the regiment during the campaign, and it would be utterly impossible to get away under any circumstances unless wounded. Give my love to all and believe me.

> Your affectionate son
> J H Kidd

ON MAY 3, Grant attacked Lee's Army of Northern Virginia in an area known as the Wilderness, near the old Chancellorsville battlefield. In a harsh two-day battle, Lee defeated Grant's huge army, inflicting heavy casualties, with the Cavalry Corps playing a significant role in the severe fighting. The Michigan Brigade remained active, engaging in scouting and fighting.[39]

Grant broke off the engagement with Lee, but instead of retreating moved ten miles southeast of The Wilderness, and re-engaged at a place called Spotsylvania Court House. There, the two armies remained locked in combat for nine brutal and bloody days. "I propose to fight it out on this line if it takes all summer," declared Grant.[40] As the two armies bloodied each other in the trenches at Spotsylvania Court House, Sheridan and George G. Meade, still nominal commander of the Army of the Potomac, disagreed over the role of the cavalry in the campaign. The two generals, both of whom possessed fiery tempers, had quite a row over the role of Sheridan's cavalry. Meanwhile, Sheridan loudly proclaimed that he would whip J. E. B. Stuart's Confederates, if only Meade gave him the chance. When Grant heard this, he said, "Did Sheridan say that? Well, he generally knows what he is talking about. Let him start right out and do it."[41] Kidd observed that this excursion was "a second edition, only on a much larger scale, and under a very different commander, of the Kilpatrick raid."[42]

Sheridan led the First and Second Cavalry Divisions, commanded by Brig. Gens. Wesley Merritt and David M. Gregg, respectively, on a raid around Lee's right flank and toward Richmond. After a hard fight near Goodall's Tavern, Sheridan encountered Stuart near Yellow Tavern, which prompted Sheridan to comment, "Our move would be a challenge to Stuart for a cavalry duel, behind Lee's lines, in his own country."[43] Kidd noted, "General Custer, who was to lead, ordered that the Sixth Michigan move out first and thus it fell to my lot to be in the van at the outset of that historic expedition."[44] The two forces made contact on May 11. In his diary Lt. George W. Hill of the 7th Michigan recorded, "This is a day to be remembered by many."[45]

In a whirling melee, Sheridan's horsemen thrashed the Confederate cavalry, with one of Custer's Wolverines, Pvt. John A. Huff of the 5th Michigan, mortally wounding Stuart on the first day of the battle. Trooper Robert Hudgins of the 3d Virginia Cavalry saw the action: "As the man fired, I saw Stuart sway in his saddle. I suppose I was approximately one hundred feet from him and I could easily tell he had been shot because his head drooped and his famous plumed hat fell to the ground. . . . Later I heard that he was badly wounded and would probably not live."[46] Writing

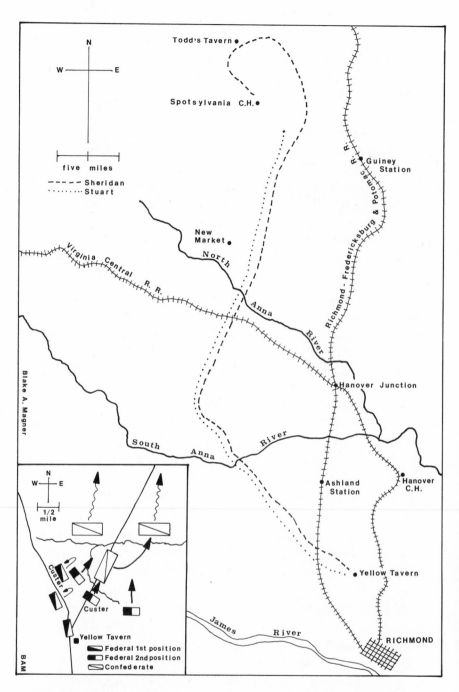

Sheridan's Raid on Richmond and the Battle of Yellow Tavern (Yellow Tavern map based on Gordon C. Rhea, The Battles of Spotsylvania Court House and the Road to Yellow Tavern, May 7–12, 1864 *[Baton Rouge: Louisiana State University Press: 1996], 202).*

about Yellow Tavern, Custer noted, "The 6th Michigan, under Major Kidd, also crossed [a] bridge [over the Chickahominy River. Along with the 5th Michigan] these two regiments advanced far enough to protect the pioneers while building [a temporary] bridge [over the river]. This being done, the 7th Michigan, two regiments from Colonel Devin's brigade, and two regiments from General Merritt's brigade, crossed the bridge to support the 5th and 6th Michigan."[47] During the fight, Custer personally led the Wolverines in a mounted charge against Confederate horse artillery. Sheridan reported, "Custer's charge . . . was brilliantly executed; first at a walk, then at a trot, then dashing the enemy's line and battery, capturing the guns and gunners and breaking the line."[48] Sheridan congratulated Custer, saying, "The Michigan Brigade is at the top of the ladder."[49] Kidd proudly noted, "One thing is certain. Stuart's death befell in front of Custer's Michigan brigade and it was a Michigan man who fired the fatal shot."[50]

The tide had turned. No longer was the Federal mounted arm inferior to that of the Confederacy. One of Meade's staff officers commented, "It is curious that the southern cavalry cannot now cope with ours. We have beaten them every time this campaign; whereas their infantry are a full match for us."[51] Capt. Moses Harris, a regular army cavalryman, noticed, "And now, at last, under a leader worthy to command it, the Cavalry Corps of the Army of the Potomac is given an opportunity to show its value as an independent fighting force."[52] This fact was not lost on Sheridan. Later that year, he proudly observed: "It will be seen . . . that the idea advanced by me at the commencement of the campaign, viz, 'that our cavalry ought to fight the enemy's cavalry and our infantry the enemy's infantry' was carried into effect immediately after the battle of the Wilderness. The result was constant success and the almost total annihilation of the rebel cavalry. We marched when and where we pleased; were always the attacking party, and always successful."[53]

Not getting much of a respite, the Cavalry Corps returned to the Army of the Potomac, advancing toward the important crossroads of Cold Harbor, near the old Gaine's Mill battlefield of 1862. As the two armies turned the landscape into an unbroken line of earthworks and engaged in trench warfare resembling that seen fifty years later in World War I, the Cavalry Corps remained active. On May 26, Custer's men fought the Confederates at Hanovertown, Virginia, and on the 28th, a major battle occurred at a place called Haw's Shop.

Seeing Gregg's men fighting against three brigades of Confederate cavalry, Sheridan called for Custer. When the young general arrived, Sheridan

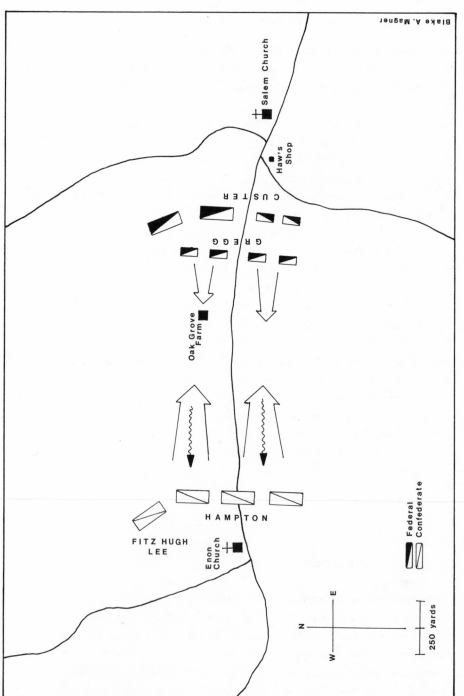

Blake A. Magner

Salem Church

Haw's Shop

CUSTER

GREGG

Oak Grove
Farm

HAMPTON

FITZ HUGH
LEE

Enon Church

N

W — E

S

250 yards

Federal
Confederate

The Battle of Haw's Shop.

pointed at Gregg's predicament and said, "Custer, I want you to go in there and give those fellows hell!" Custer obeyed, leading the Wolverines in "one of the most gallant charges of the war."[54] Kidd later described the effect of this charge:

> Custer formed the brigade, dismounted in double ranks and, riding ahead of the line, accompanied by a single aide, waved his hat over his head and called for three cheers. The cheers were given and he led his men in a charge into the woods where Butler's South Carolinians were just coming into action on the other side. Then it was face to face, and eye to eye. The effect of Custer's splendid courage was to inspire his Wolverines to more than their wonted bravery. In a few minutes the men from the Palmetto state were in headlong flight, leaving their dead and wounded. About one hundred officers and men were killed and wounded in the Michigan brigade and it all befell within a very few minutes after the charge into the woods.[55]

Praising the efforts of the Michigan Brigade, Torbert, back in command of the division, noted, "Too much praise cannot be awarded General Custer and his brigade for the manner in which they fought on that day."[56]

On May 30, the cavalry took the strategic crossroads of Cold Harbor, holding the area until the infantry arrived and prompting Custer to write, "The Mich. brigade turned the tide (as usual)."[57] On June 2, the Wolverines went into camp near Bottom's Bridge over the Chickahominy River, giving the men a well-earned break from the constant campaigning. Kidd finally found time to recount the exploits of the Army of the Potomac's cavalry.

Head Quarters, 6th Mich
Cavalry
June 3rd 1864

Dear Father & Mother

Since I last wrote we have had some hard times. In the fight at Hawe's Shop on the 28th past I lost 12 men killed and 21 wounded. The day before I lost 3 killed and one wounded. These were some of our best men. Seth Carey[58] whose wife you will recollect, used to inquire so anxiously respecting her husband was killed instantly. Tell her that he died like a soldier, fighting bravely and not before he had killed his man. He was buried beside a brick church in the field and his resting place marked by a board inscribed with his name. He was one of our bravest *best* men.

Miles Hutchinson[59] was wounded *not* dangerously. He will recover. I saw him when he was shot. He fell at my feet. This fight was terrific. Gen Gregg's men[60] had been fighting all day, and could but just hold their own with terrible loss. The rebels were receiving reinforcements, and would probably drive them from the woods when they moved full back across the open country for nearly a mile. Almost every man must inevitably have been shot. The enemy were doubling their execution. Cannon were raining grape and canister into our ranks and fresh troops pushing forward with a shock. At this critical juncture, our brigade came up. The men all dismounted and advancing up the road in column of fours formed in line just back of the woods. The 5th Mich took the left of the road. The 6th Mich the right our flank resting on the road. The 1st was on our right. The 7th on the left of the 5th. Then we advanced, Gen Custer riding ahead of the line, took off his hat and called for three cheers. The cheers were given and in we went. In two minutes we were within two rods of the enemy. A new brigade of S.C. Cavalry[61] armed with Enfield rifles, Infantry guns. They fought desperately but then had to give way. Many of them refused to surrender and were shot down. The 5th Mich and the 6th had each about 150 men in the fight. They lost 50 men. We lost 34. The ground was covered with rebel dead and wounded. One of the regiments alone lost 160 men. We captured a large number of prisoners.

After our line had advanced some distance, I found that some men were firing on us from the rear. Several bullets whistled so close as to convince me that they were designed for my especial benefit. I sent back an officer and some men who found that a party of rebels had been left behind in the eagerness of the pursuit and these men paying their compliments to us in regular Free Pass style. They were captured. For all that this Brigade has accomplished all praise is due to Gen Custer. So brave a man I never saw and as competent as brave. Under him a man is ashamed to be cowardly. Under him our men can achieve wonders.

The trees small saplings where we fought were riddled.

The next day Rebel infantry was whipped by our cavalry our brigade participating. The 30th we drove a force of rebel infantry out of Cold Harbor and receiving orders from Gen Meade to hold the position at any cost, until our infantry came up, we spent the night building breastworks behind which we laid all night, awaiting an attack. Before daylight the sound of bugles in our front announced that the rebel Cavalry was moving. To have them attack us was what we wished for. They however ignored us entirely

and went we know not where. In the middle of the forenoon, the crack-
ing of muskets, from a line of Infantry, told us that we were not to be "*left
alone.*" The front when the 5th 6th 7th & 1st Mich was posted they did
not attack, but by a rapid flank movement attempted to drive us from our
breastworks. On the right they encountered the regular brigade, who, with
the aid of 10 cannon and two squadrons of the 1st Michigan Cavalry, drove
them back, although they charged with bayonets fixed. Shortly afterwards
three army corps of Infantry came up and there the same night a severe
fight took place. From there we came here when I suppose we are watching the left flank again.

Gen Grant has I think demonstrated the practicality of the "Rapidan"
route to Richmond as he is now in nearly the same ground reached by
McClellan via the Peninsula. Unbounded confidence we have in our great
leader and if we *are to conquer,* it must be speedily.

I sent to Mr Powell[62] a list of our killed and wounded for publication.
If he does not receive it, I will send it again. Company E (my old company), has lost nine of its *best* men. Brave they were without exception and
to me like brothers.

Col Gray has resigned;[63] Angelo is sick and has been a good deal. I
think he ought to resign. His health is not good enough to endure. We
all know his worth and his bravery, and to resign would not implicate him
in anything discreditable.[64] If I am fortunate enough to survive this Campaign (and if I do that, I believe I shall see the end of the war) I shall be
as glad of peace as any one can be. If you think any portion of this letter
would be of interest to the friends of those in the regiment, you are at liberty to have such portions published in the Gazette. I write in great haste.
It is not often that I can get at our wagons where my writing materials
are. Love to all.

Yr affectionate son
J H Kidd

DURING THIS BREAK, the regiment began to receive new weapons.
Throughout their time in the field, the men of the 6th Michigan had carried Spencer repeating rifles. In early June, the rifles were traded for
shorter-barreled Spencer carbines. The new weapons were also seven-shot
repeaters, but they had shorter barrels, meaning that they had a much
shorter range. The new guns were also easier to use on horseback. The
firepower of the carbines made a difference in the coming months.[65]

As the cavalry continued its advance, it passed the Cold Harbor battlefield. Lt. Wallace of the 5th Michigan saw this vivid picture, which stuck with him for the rest of his life: "Our division passed over the ground on our way to another expedition, and we found the dead still lying scattered about. Some had been drawn up side by side but were still uncovered. The stench was terrible. Hogs had torn many of the bodies, and the ravens were having a feast. Here was the very skeleton of war laid bare, stripped of all of its pomp and glitter, and a gruesome sight it was. In it was none of the glory of war."[66]

Two days later, Kidd's father wrote, "I have noted by the papers *all* the movements of your army . . . and have looked anxiously for your department and hope you . . . may . . . escape unharmed." His father was aware that both Gray and Thompson were unfit for duty, and noted, "I think Thompson will not be Col. of your Regiment unless you are killed." Kidd's father continued: "Sarah is to be married next month and we would all be glad to have you at home if you could possibly come."[67]

That same day, Congressman Kellogg also wrote to Kidd, "Lt. Col. Thompson got here yesterday resigned & I got his resignation accepted today. I hope you will be made Colonel now as I know no one else who deserves it more." Kellogg offered to intervene with Gov. Blair and asked Kidd to remember his two nephews, officers in the regiment, when it came time for a round of promotions. In a postscript, Kellogg commented, "If Gen'l Custer should write the Governor soon in your favor it would help." A second postscript stated, "Major—you are Col Kid. The Gov said tonight you should have a commission soon as possible. God bless you Colonel."[68] Kidd owed much to Kellogg—for giving him his first commission and for pushing his promotion to colonel.

When Gray finally resigned, the officers of the 6th Michigan prepared and circulated a petition to the governor of Michigan, asking that Kidd be promoted to colonel. George Custer, who forwarded it to Gov. Blair, endorsed this petition.

> Headquarters 1st Brig.
> 1st Div. CC
> June 3, 1864

To His Excellency
Gov. Blair

I most cheerfully and earnestly recommend that the foregoing petition may be granted. Major Kidd has commanded his regiment for several months. He has distinguished himself in nearly all of the late severe engagements of this corps. Michigan cannot boast of a more gallant and efficient officer than Major Kidd and I am confident that his appointment as Colonel of the 6th would not only produce entire satisfaction in his regiment but would seem to increase the already high but well earned fame of the Michigan Cavalry Brigade.

Very respectfully &c.

G A Custer

Brig. Genl Comdg

THE PETITION READ:

Headquarters 6th Michigan Cav.

1st Brig. 1st Division Cav. Corps

Bottoms Bridge Virginia

June 3rd 1864

His Excellency

Austin Blair

Governor of the State of Michigan

We the undersigned officers of the 6th Regt Mich. Cav.[69] do respectfully petition Your Excellency that Major James H. Kidd be appointed to the Colonelcy made vacant by the resignation of Col. George Gray. Major Kidd has led the Regiment through all the engagements of this campaign and fully demonstrated his fitness to command. He has the confidence of the officers and men of this command. We would earnestly recommend that he be promoted to the position the duties of which he has so long and so ably performed.

Charles W. Deane, Major 6th Mich. Cav.

H. N. Throop, Captain Co. K, 6th Mich. Cav.

Manning D. Birge Captain Comdg Co. A 6th Mich. Cav.

Harvey H. Vinton Captain Comdg Co. M 6th Mich. Cav.

Don G. Lovell Captain Comdg Co. F

Wm. Hyzer Captain Comdg. Co D 6th Mich. Cav.

William Hull Lieut Comdg. Co. G 6th Mich. Cav.

J. L. Shelton Lt. R.C.S. 6th Mich. Cav.

Levant W. Barnhart 1st Lt. A. Adjt. 6th Mich. Cav.

C. H. Patten 1st Lt. R.Q.M. 6th Mich. Cav.

D. G. Weare, Surgeon 6th Mich. Cav.

Elias P. Stone 2nd Lt. Comdg. Co. I 6th Mich Cav.
Osmer F. Cole Lt. Comdg. Co. L
Jacob O. Probasco 2nd Lt. Comdg. Co. E 6th Mich. Cav.
Wm. Creery Lieut. Comdg. Co. C 6th Mich. Cav.
Geo. W. Simonds 2nd Lieut. Co. L 6th Mich. Cav.
L. G. Kanouse 2nd Lieut Co. D 6th Mich. Cav.

COL. GRAY, WHO remained in Washington after his resignation, whole-heartedly endorsed Kidd's promotion and intervened with the governor to bring it about.

Washington, June 5 1864

My dear Major

Gov. Blair is here being a delegate to the Baltimore Convention. I have had an interview with him to-day, and he says he will forward you your commission as Colonel of the regiment immediately. I suppose he will do so when he returns to Detroit after the Convention. I shall remind him of it and shall see that it is not delayed. I heartily congratulate you on your safety so far, and your continued success and earnestly hope to hear the like of you and the regiment until this contest is over. I wrote you a very hastily written letter sending it by Capt. Judson,[70] and suppose you have rec'd on this. Please let me hear from you when you can find time to write. I will always want to hear of you and our noble 6th. I shall never cease to entertain the most lively interest in your progress for the affection I entertain for the gallant regiment, officers and men is part of my existence.

Wishing you & them all success and honor in your career, fervently desiring your safety in the hour of battle, and your speedy return to your home and friends.

I am ever
Most truly yours
Geo. Gray

WHILE THE WHEELS of bureaucracy ground on, the Cavalry Corps took to the field again. To cover a move across the James River, toward Petersburg, Grant sent Sheridan's cavalry on a raid toward Gordonsville. The raid had two stated objectives: the destruction of the Virginia Central Railroad, which ended in Gordonsville, and the linkage of Sheridan's cavalry with the army of Maj. Gen. David Hunter, advancing up the Shenandoah

Valley toward Lynchburg. Taking the First and Second Cavalry Divisions, Sheridan departed on June 7. He planned to march along the course of the North Anna River to a spot near Trevilian Station, cross the Virginia Central line there, capture the train station, and destroy the railroad from Louisa Court House to Gordonsville, and then link with Hunter's army at Charlottesville.[71]

The Rebel cavalry, commanded at that time by Maj. Gens. Wade Hampton and Fitzhugh Lee, caught up to Sheridan's column at Trevilian Station. A two-day fight took place there; the Battle of Trevilian Station was the largest all-cavalry battle of the Civil War. On the first day, Custer found a hole in the Rebel line and captured a large wagon train. The Confederates reacted quickly, surrounding Custer and forcing him to fight his way out. Only Custer's quick thinking and hard fighting by the men of the 6th saved the Michigan Brigade from being destroyed. Kidd himself was briefly captured on June 11, but escaped when a charge by the 6th freed him.[72]

On the second day, the Wolverines launched numerous dismounted attacks against a strong Confederate position anchored along the railroad bed. Kidd later wrote, "The Michigan brigade was on the left of the line. It was the first brigade engaged. It began the fight and stayed in it till the end. Harder fighting has rarely been done than that which fell to the Michigan men in that battle."[73] Casualty statistics supported this conclusion; from May 6 to June 12, the Wolverines lost 148 officers and men killed.[74]

The Union horsemen slowly fell back to the James River line after their defeat at Trevilian Station, the raid's two primary objectives unfulfilled. Kidd described the action.

> Hd Qrs 6th Mich Cavly
> 1st Brig 1st Div Cav Corps
> White House Landing
> Va. June 21, 1864

Dear Father & Mother

On the 7th instant we left Newcastle and the army and started on a raid, the object and destination of which was a profound secret to all except those entrusted with the command. For 14 days since that time we have been constantly in the saddle, often marching night and day. What the object sought to be accomplished may have been I am of course ignorant. It may have been to form a junction with Hunter, supposed

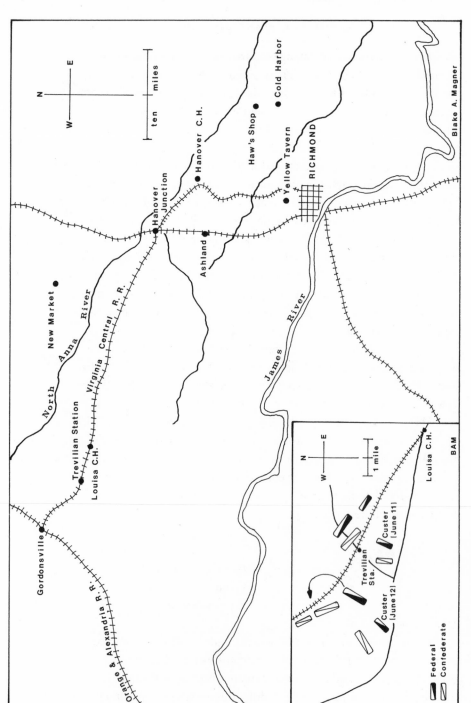

Sheridan's Trevilian Station Raid.

to be at Staunton or that vicinity or it may have been to sever the R.R.[75] communication north of Richmond or possibly to cross the James west of Richmond and *"strike"* for Lynchburg. If the former the route attempted via Gordonsville was the wrong one and the expedition failed, for we did not reach Gordonsville and were certainly repulsed, not that we could not match the enemy, fight him and whip him on an even game but that we were unable to force a passage through his breast-works and strongly entrenched on a commanding position especially since one third of our force had been left with the Army of Potomac and he had his entire force.

At Trevilian Station on the 11th the Mich. Brigade through no fault of Gen Custer, but through the fault of the officers who ordered us there, became wedged in between Wade Hampton's & Fitz Lee's Divisions,[76] and fought the entire force single-handed for three hours. In a charge which I made mounted with one squadron, I was captured and was a prisoner about a quarter of an hour. They had me nearly to their reserve, when the rest of the Regt charged and I made my escape to be engaged in a severe fight that day and the next. In the two days I had killed 7 wounded 23 missing 75 total 105. In the first day's fight we captured a great many prisoners and horses but had not men enough to hold them, our brigade having such superior numbers opposed to us. We however kept about as many as we lost. I have been told by several correspondents that I am promoted to Colonel. It is a position I have not sought and my friends can only blame themselves if I do not prove myself so good a man for the place as they expected.

A petition went to Gov Blair I am told which I never saw, asking that I be appointed. This signed by all our officers. Also Gen Custer wrote a very complimentary letter of which I am prouder than of the commission if I get it. I have tried to perform my duty and shall do so. Nothing however do I wish for so fervently as that peace may speedily come and the Union restored. Gen Grant's strategy strikes me as being immensely superior to anything before evinced by Potomac commanders. I think he has on several instances outwitted Lee, and has shown himself entirely his equal from the beginning. But the real campaign is yet to come. Richmond has not fallen. Grant is across the James and we are at White House and a Rebel force in front of us disputing our further progress. What route we shall take hence I cannot conjecture. One thing is certain we are wanted with the army. I recd yours dated June 5th. Tell Kate I recd her letter. I rarely have opportunity to write. I ride all [day] when not fighting and lie down at night completely exhausted to sleep. One thing about Gen Sheridan. He takes things very coolly, never gets excited and gives us all the rest possible. But it is getting dark. I must close. Love to all. Remember me to all my friends, and ask them to write. Is Uncle Rich well & how is his family. Tell my new Brother-in-law that is to be that I shall be right glad to establish intimacy and shall write to him soon if possible.

Yours affectionately
J H Kidd

As the Trevilian Raid came to an end, Kidd was commissioned colonel of the regiment, with an effective date of May 19, 1864.[77] Whereas the letter transmitting the commission was dated June 23, Kidd did not receive it until July 9. Here is the laconic description given in his memoirs: "[W]hile at Lighthouse Point I received my commission as colonel and, July 9, was mustered out of the United States service as major—with which rank I had been commanding the regiment—and was mustered in in the new grade. The promotion, which was unsought, was due to a request made to the governor, signed by all the officers of the regiment serving in the field, and recommended by General Custer."[78]

The Cavalry Corps settled into the siege lines near Petersburg, and things fell quiet for almost a month. The men needed the rest; Sheridan keenly noted that his horsemen "had marched and fought for fifty-six consecutive days."[79] Kidd observed, "From July 2, when we returned to Lighthouse Point on the James River, to July 26 was quiet and uneventful. Many hundred convalescent wounded and sick men returned from hospital to duty; many also who had been dismounted by the exigencies of the campaign returned from dismounted camps."[80] On July 8, a war correspondent reported, "We have just completed one of the heaviest cavalry expeditions which are on record. For the first time since we crossed the river have we had our tents pitched, and a dirtier lot of fellows you never saw. The dust on the road any where is from six to ten inches deep, and I have many times seen it so thick upon the faces of the men that it was impossible to tell the white from the black."[81]

During this respite, the 1st Michigan Cavalry also got a new commander; Col. Charles Town was dying of tuberculosis and could no longer stand the rigors of the field. Lt. Col. Peter Stagg, his second in command, assumed leadership of the regiment. Like Kidd, Stagg was also promoted, although his commission was dated August 17, 1864.[82] One of his troopers noted, "Lieut. Col. Stagg . . . is much liked by the command, and is in high favor at headquarters."[83] This may have been true with the men of the 1st Michigan Cavalry, but Kidd and Stagg eventually came into conflict over issues of seniority. For now, though, Kidd found time to write to his father several times before the 1st and 2d Divisions were dispatched to the Shenandoah Valley in early August. Meanwhile, new recruits arrived, convalescents returned, and the regiment received new horses and equipment.

On June 14, Kidd's father wrote, asking Kidd whether he could intervene to arrange a promotion to major for the son of a friend, Capt. Donald G. Lovell. He also reported, "Everybody here says Kidd must be Col. and Col. Kellogg writes home to his friends he is brave and always stays at the head of his Regt. & we want him appointed before he is killed."[84] Kidd responded a few weeks later.

HdQrs 6th Mich Cavly
July 12, 1864

Dear Father

Your letter with reference to promoting Don Lovell[85] was recd. I had been written to by Mr. Lowell, and Uncle Rich with regard to his appointment, but I must tell you what I told them. It can't be done. I had made the appointments before I recd their letter and moreover Don is not entitled to a majority in the regt and I am surprised if he had anything to do with this application. I should not like to think that Don were working to supplant his senior officers.

I do not hear from you often, nor do I often hear from Ionia. I should like an occasional Gazette.

You have known by the papers what we did. The account of the Trevilian fight in the Detroit Tribune tells it about as it was. That detracts from nobody. We are now near City Point VA recruiting and are in as good condition as at any time since the campaign began. The weather is appropriately hot and dusty. No rain yet of consequence. The raid into Pennsylvania and Maryland[86] we fear may make us trouble but as yet we know nothing definite here about it. What I hope is that they may be driven out before they get horses enough to mount their cavalry and infantry.

They fear Sheridan and will make greater efforts to crush than for any other single object; Lee I imagine will hardly but general Grant very much.

I heard yesterday through Capt Vaspur or Vapur[87] (some such name), a man from Saranac that a cousin of mine, William Kidd, was in the army. I did not see the Captain, but he sent me word that my cousin had been sent off from City Point sick. This must be Uncle Thomas' son—but if I ever knew he was in the army I had forgotten it. I will investigate the matter when I can go down to the Point.

Gen Custer is sick and has got a 20 days' leave. I could not imagine a greater disaster from brigade if he does not return before we take the field again.

I am mustered in as colonel. Hoping to hear from you and all of you soon. With love to all, I am

Yours affectionately
J. H. Kidd

On July 14, Kidd's Uncle Rich wrote, stating, "I must not tell you how anxious we are (constantly) about you and . . . thank God most fervently that he has kept you thus far in safety. . . . Yr. mother . . . prays every day that God will make you a *brave valiant* good man & deliver you safely to us." Rich reported that the family business was prospering and that everyone hoped that the war would end soon.[88]

Hd Qrs 6th Mich Cavalry
July 20, 1864

Dear Father

I have today sent to you by Express $450.00. Please acknowledge the receipt of it at once or inform me if you do not receive it. I recd your letter by Charley Connell[89] a day or two ago, also your last, one from Sarah and one from Osgower. Uncle Rich's letter I recd last night. I was very glad indeed to hear from you all.

We are still at City Point (never these). How long we shall remain I cannot tell, probably not much longer. I see by the papers that the Northern people expect Sheridan's Cavalry to intercept and gobble the force which frightened them all out of their senses.[90] What they were afraid to go out and march they expect us jaded and worn by hard marching and fighting to annihilate. The apathy and cowardliness of the people across the Potomac is disgusting and disgraceful. Why in God's name didn't they turn out and repel the invasion instead of taking to their legs. Hiding their cowardly heads behind the fortifications & calling on Grant or Sheridan, while a few guerrillas were plundering their country and a force not so large as the no. of clerks employed in the departments or the number of well men kept in hospitals & like places to black boots for Surgeons etc were threatening the Capitol. Why didn't every man shoulder his musket & fight.[91] No cover from them for us. So long as the Northern people at home show the spirit of cowardliness & apathy which characterizes the citizens of Maryland of Pennsylvania and of *Washington*, during the last *"invasion,"* so long we may go on fighting for no purpose.

Yrs affectionately
J H Kidd

ON JULY 26, the Wolverines participated in the Second Army Corps' movement to the north bank of the James River. Kidd commented, "The object of the movement was to draw the enemy's attention away from the lines around Petersburg preparatory for the explosion of the mine which was to take place on the 30th."[92] Although the deception succeeded, what became known as the Battle of the Crater was an unmitigated disaster for the Army of the Potomac. When the mine exploded, Sheridan's horsemen were at City Point, waiting for transports to take them to Washington for a move into the Shenandoah Valley. The failed attack at the Crater meant that the two armies settled into siege warfare along the Petersburg lines. Grant clamped a death grip on the Confederate army, forcing Robert E. Lee to acknowledge, "We must destroy this army of Grant's before he gets to the James River. If he gets there, it will become a siege, and then it will be a mere question of time."[93]

The Cavalry Corps had fought and marched hard, enduring constant campaigning for nearly four months. His spring adventure ending, Sheridan proudly noted, "In all the operations the percentage of cavalry casualties was as great as that of the infantry, and the question which had existed 'Who ever saw a dead cavalryman?' was set to rest."[94]

On July 24, Kidd forwarded a sketch of his picket lines to Col. Russell Alger of the 5th Michigan, temporarily commanding the Michigan Brigade while Custer was on leave. This was the last letter before the Cavalry Corps went west into the Shenandoah Valley with Sheridan.

Hd Qrs 6th Mich Cavalry
July 24, 1864

Col.

I have the honor to forward in obedience to orders the enclosed sketch of our picket lines.[95] It is the best we can do, having not communications with which to work.

Very respectfully
Yr obdt servant
J H Kidd
Col Comdg.

Perhaps you have heard that Rebel papers (Petersburg 25) state that *Sherman* has been badly defeated.[96]

Yours truly,
J. H. K.
Col. R. A. Alger
Comdg. Brig.

KIDD WENT INTO the Shenandoah campaign as a twenty-four-year-old, battle-tested colonel. Now accustomed to command, he faced new challenges and disappointments in the Valley.

5

Sheridan's Shenandoah Valley Campaign

"A speedy & honorable peace" is what we all want.

DESPERATE TO BREAK Grant's hammerlock at Petersburg, Robert E. Lee gambled. Remembering that Stonewall Jackson's Army of the Valley had drawn forces away from Richmond in the summer of 1862, Lee decided to try the same ploy again. He sent Lt. Gen. Jubal A. Early's Second Army Corps away from the lines at Petersburg, putting his force on trains of the Virginia Central Railroad and transporting them to Lynchburg, where they arrived just in time to repulse the advance of Maj. Gen. David Hunter's army, which was moving up the Shenandoah Valley.[1] Early then joined forces with the small army of Maj. Gen. John C. Breckinridge at Lynchburg. This combined force advanced down the valley toward the Potomac River.

Early crossed the Potomac, defeated a scratch force of Union troops under Maj. Gen. Lew Wallace at Monocacy Junction, Maryland, and then marched on Washington, D.C. Grant dispatched the Sixth Army Corps from Petersburg, which arrived just in time to repulse Early. Early then retreated, sending a cavalry force under command of Brig. Gen. John McCausland into Pennsylvania. McCausland's troopers burned the town of Chambersburg and then rejoined Early in the Shenandoah Valley, where Early defeated a force under Brig. Gen. George Crook at Kernstown, just south of Winchester. With a force of less than twenty thousand men, Early waited for the Yankee army to come after him.

Enraged, Grant sent Sheridan to Washington, where he took command of the Sixth and Nineteenth Army Corps, Crook's Army of West Virginia, and the available cavalry forces. Grant's orders were specific: "I want Sheridan put in command of all the troops in the field, with instructions to put himself south of the enemy and follow him to the death. Wherever the enemy goes let our troops go also."[2] After consulting with Grant at Monocacy on August 6, Sheridan moved toward Winchester. Grant's orders were explicit:

> In pushing up the Shenandoah Valley, as it is expected you will have to go, first or last, it is desirable that nothing should be left to invite the enemy to return. Take all provisions, forage, and stock wanted for the use of your command; such as cannot be consumed, destroy. It is not desirable that the buildings should be destroyed; they should rather be protected; but the people should be informed that so long as an army can subsist among them recurrences of these raids must be expected, and we are determined to stop them at all hazards. Bear in mind the object is to drive the enemy south, and to do this you want to keep him always in sight. Be guided in your course by the course he takes.[3]

Sheridan obeyed his orders. His consolidated force of almost 45,000 men was dubbed the Army of the Shenandoah and was responsible for the defense of the Middle Military Division, consisting of Maryland and the Shenandoah Valley region. Grant also gave Sheridan authority to place the officer whom he wanted in command of the cavalry. Brig. Gen. William Woods Averell, senior division commander, was entitled to the command, but Sheridan exercised the discretion granted him by Grant and appointed Torbert instead. Merritt took command of the First Division, Averell commanded the Second, and Wilson the Third.

The two armies jousted for a couple of weeks as Sheridan consolidated his new command. On August 11, Custer's brigade crossed the Opequon Creek and moved toward Winchester, where it soon encountered Confederate infantry. Kidd noted, "A sharp fight followed which showed that Early was retreating up the valley. Ransom's regular battery, attached to the brigade, was charged by Confederate infantry, which was met and repulsed by a countercharge of one battalion of the Sixth Michigan Cavalry, led by Captain James Mathers, who was killed."[4] On August 16, the Wolverines marched on Front Royal. Finding no enemy, they dismounted and lit fires, preparing dinner. Maj. J. H. Vinton of the 6th Michigan, who commanded the brigade picket line, soon came under fire from Fitzhugh

Lee's cavalry. Custer quickly mounted his command and led a bold counterattack across a ford over the Shenandoah River, catching the Confederates unaware and capturing many of them, which turned a defeat into
a victory.[5]

Another skirmish took place on August 25, near Shepherdstown. Again
caught by surprise, Custer turned the tables on the Rebels, sending Kidd's
6th forward in a mounted saber charge. Kidd acerbically noted, "That [the
Michigan Brigade] escaped no thanks were due to General Torbert."[6]
George Custer temporarily left the army for a few days in early September, leaving Kidd, the senior regimental colonel, in command of the Michigan Brigade. The new brigade commander found time to write home.

> Hd Qrs 1st Brig. 1st Div. Cav.
> Middle Military Division
> Near Berryville VA
> Sept 9, 1864

Dear Father & Mother

I have heard through other sources than your own letters that you had
not heard from me for a month and that you were anxious to know of me.
Although I have not written so often as "was my want," I think some of
my letters must have failed to reach you for I am sure I have written within
that time.

We have been constantly on the move since coming up here, not so
much fighting as in the Army of the Potomac but more marching. Back-
wards and forwards and forward and backward again, has been the pro-
gramme. Our wagons with desks trunks paper pens ink etc, we have scarcely
ever seen. Not foreseeing this, I failed to provide myself with conveniences
and consequently could not write; when I last wrote you I think I stated
that I had so much official correspondence that I could spare but a moment
for you. That same night we packed up, and have been moving around
ever since. We are now in camp. Gen'l Custer is absent and I am temporarily comdg Brig. You undoubtedly are surprised that Sheridan doesn't
fight Early, but I suppose his orders are merely to engage his attention
and keep him in the Valley as long as possible. If this can best be accomplished without fighting I think all parties ought to be satisfied. We certainly shall be. The Cavalry however are not likely to have very easy work
under any circumstances: constant reconaissances are necessary to ascertain the movements of the enemy, and in doing this encounter Infantry

oftener than Cavalry. In fact in nearly every fight we have had in the valley we have been pitted against Infantry and against several times our number. The Mich. Brig. has lost no honor but that kind of fighting is about *"played"* even with them.

Sherman's and Farragut's[7] victories have put heart into the army. The unexpected turn "volunteering" has taken, also is cheering.

Politics we care little about but think Lincoln ought to be reelected because we know he is all right. Somebody else *may not be* "A speedy & honorable peace" is what we all want. Hoping for this with love to all, I remain

Yr affectionate son

J H Kidd

ON SEPTEMBER 19, Sheridan attacked Early at Winchester. Cavalry Corps chief Torbert's instructions to his subordinates were clear and simple: "The move means fight."[8] These instructions proved prophetic. The gigantic Federal mounted force vastly outnumbered Early's horsemen, and this numeric disparity tipped the balance in the fight at Winchester.

Torbert's horse soldiers kicked off the attack, splashing across Opequon Creek at sunrise, as his infantry moved on Early's troops. Custer gave Kidd orders "to engage the attention of the enemy as closely as possible."[9] Kidd commented, "At three o'clock I mounted my favorite saddle horse 'Billy' and by order of General Custer, led my regiment in advance of the division, toward Locke's Ford on the Opequon Creek. Nothing was said, but every one knew that the army was in motion and that great things were in store for us."[10] Led by the Michigan Brigade, the Union cavalry drove off the Confederate pickets and moved toward Winchester. Kidd himself did not fare so well. He wrote: "The charge prostrated me. I succeeded in getting across the field, cheered on by the gallant Custer, who rode half way, but then fell down and for a minute or two could not stand on my feet. I suppose my pale face and weak condition made a very fair presentment of a colonel demoralized by fright. It was a case of complete physical exhaustion. While it is probably for the most part moral rather than physical courage that spurs men into battle, it is equally true that good health and a sound body are a good background for the display of moral courage."[11]

Kidd soon rallied and rejoined his troops while Sheridan's infantry engaged Early's infantry, thus beginning a long and very bloody day of fighting. As the infantry fight raged, the cavalry waited for the outcome.

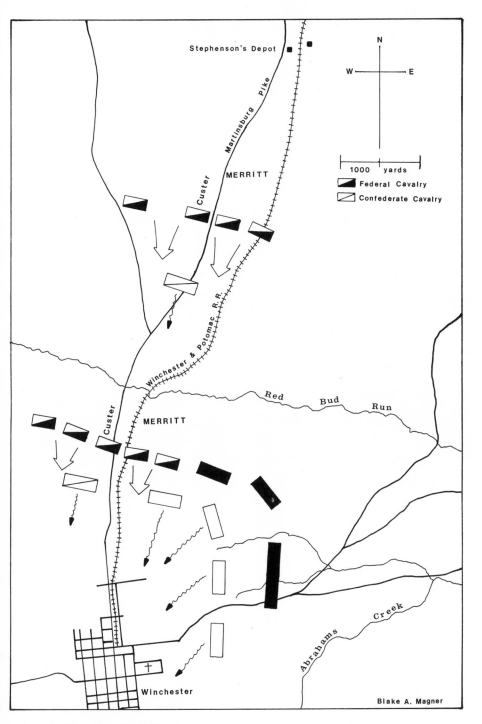

The Third Battle of Winchester.

Kidd remembered: "During the long hours of morning the dismounted troopers reclined on the ground in front of their horses, gaily chatting and smoking, or cooking coffee, giving little heed to the ever-increasing roar or artillery and rattle of musketry, which, though it could not intimidate, too plainly indicated the desperate nature of the conflict. The sun had reached the meridian, and still the din of battle did not recede."[12]

When the infantry failed to prevail at around 3:00 P.M., the Union cavalry engaged a substantial force of Confederate horse soldiers north of the town, near Stephenson's Depot. Custer painted a vivid picture of the massed attack launched by the Yankee troopers: "The bands playing national airs, presented in the sunlight one moving mass of glittering sabers. This, combined with the various and bright-colored banners and battle-flags, intermingled here and there with the plain blue uniforms of the troops, furnished one of the most inspiring as well as imposing scenes of martial grandeur ever witnessed on a battle-field. No encouragement was needed to inspirit either man or horse."[13] Kidd described the spectacle:

> The Michigan brigade was on the left of the turnpike; to its left, the brigades of Devin and Lowell;[14] on the right, Averell's division of two brigades—five brigades in all—each brigade in line of squadron columns, double ranks. This made a front of more than half a mile, three lines deep, of mounted men. That is to say, it was more than half a mile from Averell's right to Merritt's left. At almost the same moment of time, the entire line emerged from the woods into the sunlight. A more enlivening and imposing spectacle never was seen. Guidons fluttered and sabers glistened. Officers vied with their men in gallantry and in zeal. Even the horses seemed to catch the inspiration of the scene and emulated the martial ardor of their riders.[15]

The vast mounted blue juggernaut quickly swept away the opposition. The road to Winchester was free and, as Wesley Merritt later observed, "The field was open for cavalry operations such as the war had not seen."[16]

The infantry having pinned down the Confederate forces and the Confederate cavalry having been dispersed, Torbert ordered a massed mounted charge along a five-brigade front.[17] The Yankee troopers started forward, first at a walk, then at a trot, and finally at a gallop. One Ohio foot soldier recalled that it was "the most gallant and exciting cavalry charge I ever saw." One member of the 5th Michigan proudly remembered, "Ten thousand troopers went forward on a charge with sabres gleaming in the sun and with a cheer that would enthuse a dead man. The scene was grand beyond description."[18]

Dropping like a bombshell, the massed cavalry charge shattered Early's lines and drove them from the field in a wild rout. Kidd recalled, "I marvel exceedingly that then and there no effort was made to resist the charge by forming the hollow square, with its wall of bayonets; nor do I remember that it was resorted to under similar circumstances, during the war, although every regiment in either army was drilled in the evolution."[19] With the Wolverines in the van, the overwhelming blue wave tipped the scales of the battle. Kidd received his second combat wound: "As my horse swerved to the right, a bullet struck my right thigh and, peeling the skin off that, cut a deep gash through the saddle to the opening in the center. The saddle caused it to deflect upwards, or it would have gone through the right leg. . . . I . . . found that it was one of those narrow escapes which a pious man might set down to the credit of providence or a miracle. The wound was not serious."[20] Kidd's beloved warhorse, Billy, was also slightly wounded in the charge, but, like his master, Billy survived.

Only a stubborn stand by Confederate cavalry south of Winchester saved Early's army from total destruction. It was a great victory for Sheridan, brought about by good coordination between the infantry and the cavalry. Early later wrote, "The enemy's very great superiority in cavalry and the comparative inefficiency of ours turned the scale against us."[21] Analyzing the victory, Kidd accurately observed that Sheridan "was the only general of that war who knew how to make cavalry and infantry supplement each other in a battle."[22] Custer praised Kidd's valor in leading his men from the front in the grand charge.[23]

Early fell back to a position near Fisher's Hill, between Winchester and Strasburg, where his battered army licked its wounds and waited for Sheridan's inevitable pursuit. On September 21, the cavalry leading the way again, the Army of the Valley made its move on Fisher's Hill. In a vicious frontal and flanking attack, Sheridan swept Early's little army off Fisher's Hill. On the 22d, the Wolverines led an expedition up the Valley toward Luray. In a running fight, they encountered Thomas T. Munford's Rebel cavalry strongly positioned on high ground. Calling off the attack and unsure of the results of the fight at Fisher's Hill, Torbert balked. He justified his timidity in his report to Sheridan: "Not knowing that the army had made an attack at Fisher's Hill, and thinking that the sacrifice would be too great to attack without that knowledge, I concluded to withdraw to a point opposite McCoy's Ferry."[24]

On September 26, Sheridan relieved Averell and placed Custer in command of the Third Division. This move was very unpopular with the men of the Michigan Brigade; over four hundred of them signed petitions asking that the Wolverines be transferred to the Third Division—a request that Sheridan denied.[25] As its senior colonel, Kidd formally assumed command of the Michigan Brigade. Sheridan pulled back toward Winchester and consolidated his force and his gains. Kidd was not entirely thrilled about the change, commenting, "The Michigan Brigade without Custer . . . was like the play of Hamlet with the melancholy Dane left out."[26] Kidd himself considered the promotion "an unsought and unwelcome responsibility."[27] The army went into camp along the banks of Cedar Creek, south of Winchester.

While the Wolverines camped there, Kidd, always politically astute, got a new lieutenant. Thomas Custer, younger brother of the general, was commissioned into the 6th Michigan Cavalry at Kidd's behest. The choice was a good one; Tom Custer was later awarded two different Medals of Honor in the spring of 1865, making him one of only two Union soldiers to be awarded two such medals during the war.[28]

In the interim, Early received reinforcements, including a division of infantry and the cavalry brigade of Brig. Gen. Thomas L. Rosser, Custer's West Point classmate and close friend. Rosser, who commanded a veteran brigade of cavalry drawn from the Shenandoah Valley, was dubbed "Savior of the Valley" by the locals, a moniker that haunted him during the coming weeks. Rosser's men knew what to expect. Gunner George M. Neese of Chew's battery of horse artillery noted in his diary on October 4, "General Sheridan is in command of the Yankee army in the Valley of the Shenandoah, and if he has the men that he had at Trevilian Station, there will be some tough work on the boards yet this fall, for his cavalry is made out of first-class fighting stuff."[29]

On October 3, Merritt ordered Kidd to take the Michigan Brigade to Cross Keys and to "picket your front at Cross Keys and connect by patrol with regiment at Port Republic. Watch the country toward Brown's Gap and Piedmont. By all means make frequent reports to these headquarters."[30]

In the first weeks of October, Sheridan ordered the destruction of the Shenandoah Valley, thus taking the war to the civilian population. Known as "The Burning," the devastation of civilian farms and farm stocks enraged

the locals and incurred the wrath of John Singleton Mosby, whose guerrillas fell upon the Yankees. An ugly episode of mutual hangings took place,
with several of the Wolverines hanged in retaliation for the hanging of
several of Mosby's men upon Torbert's orders.[31]

Kidd did not relish the task of destroying the beautiful valley and later
commented, "What I saw there is burned into my memory."[32] A year after
the war, he wrote, "The Valley of the Shenandoah . . . before the rebellion was the 'Eden of America,' but at the war's termination, was a desolate mass, with scarcely a barn, storehouse, mill, or fence, to relieve the
monotony of the scene."[33] As the inferno spread northward, Kidd drew
the unwelcome duty of providing the picket support for Merritt's division
and, later, for Sheridan's infantry. In both instances, Kidd's flanks were
constantly annoyed by the probing attacks of Rosser's troopers.[34]

Sheridan later reported that more than two thousand barns filled with
grain and implements and more than seventy mills laden with wheat and
flour had been destroyed. In addition, more than seven thousand head of
livestock were either confiscated or killed. He proudly noted, "This
destruction embraces the Luray Valley and Little Fort Valley as well as
the main valley. . . . [W]hen this is completed, the Valley from Winchester up to Staunton, ninety-two miles, will have little in it for man or beast."[35]

In response, Early ordered his cavalry "to pursue the enemy, to harass
him and to ascertain his purposes."[36] In obedience to Early's orders, Rosser
moved to intercept the cavalry forces that were destroying the valley. On
October 8, when Custer and Merritt turned to meet Rosser, the forces
collided at Tom's Brook, south of Strasburg. "Mad clear through" with
Rosser's harassment, Sheridan ordered Torbert to "start out at daylight
and whip the rebel cavalry or get whipped," in short, to "finish this 'Savior of the Valley.'"[37]

On the morning of October 9, a massed attack by the Federal cavalry
at Tom's Brook near Woodstock caught the Confederates in both the front
and the flank. Kidd's Wolverines attacked Rosser's center, while the rest
of the Yankee cavalry forced the advance. The Rebel horsemen were driven
off in a wild rout, with their Yankee foes following for twenty miles before
finally giving up the pursuit.[38]

Custer captured Rosser's personal baggage and gleefully wore his old
friend's dress uniform coat, even sending Rosser a taunting note asking
"if he would have his tailor make the coattails of his next uniform somewhat shorter so it would fit better when he captured it."[39] Sheridan lost

only nine killed and forty-eight wounded achieving a victory "beyond my power to describe."[40] He noted in his memoirs: "After this catastrophe, Early reported to General [Robert E.] Lee that his cavalry was so badly demoralized that it should be dismounted; and the citizens of the valley, intensely disgusted with the boasting and swaggering that had character-ized the arrival of the 'Laurel Brigade' in that section, baptized the action (known to us as Tom's Brook) the 'Woodstock Races,' and never tired of poking fun at General Rosser about his precipitate and inglorious flight."[41]

In fact, Early complained, "God knows I have done all in my power to avert the disasters which have befallen this command; but the fact is that the enemy's cavalry is so much superior to ours, both in numbers and equipment, and the country is so favorable to the operations of cavalry, that it is impossible for ours to compete with his." Early concluded, "It would be better if they could all be put into the infantry; but if that were tried I am afraid they would all run off."[42]

After the great victory at Tom's Brook, the Army of the Valley returned to its camps near Cedar Creek, blissfully unaware that Early was about to unleash a massed attack on its camps. Finding an interlude in his duties, Kidd wrote a hasty letter home on October 15.

> Hd Qrs 1st Brig. 1st Cav. Div.
> Near "Cedar Creek" Va
> October 15 1864

Dear Father & Mother

I wrote you after our last fight informing you that I am well. Your last letter is recd. The scratch I recd at Winchester was not serious and has now healed entirely. We are about to start on some sort of an expedition I know not what or where. You will hear I presume before I am able to write again through the papers.

I suppose every exertion will be made to make the most of the remain-ing time between this and winter. If rebellion can be crushed it will be done but if we have to go into winter quarters another season will cer-tainly finish it.

Things look very much brighter than last year at this time. Hoping to hear from you often, and of your well-being and prosperity. With love to all, I am

> Yr affectionate son
> J. H. Kidd Col.

ON THE MORNING of October 19, while Sheridan was in transit to Winchester from strategy meetings in Washington, Early launched a massive surprise attack upon the Army of the Valley. He met with quick success, driving the Union solders for several miles before they rallied and stiffened their resistance. Early made a fatal error, pausing in the middle of the afternoon to consolidate his lines and failing to exploit his breakthrough. This pause allowed sufficient time for the Federals to rally and re-form their lines. In the meantime, hearing that his army was being routed, Sheridan galloped nearly twenty miles to the battlefield, arriving in time to rally his troops.[43]

Rosser was ordered to "occupy the enemy's cavalry" while the infantry attack stepped off, and his skirmishers pinned down the Wolverines along the banks of Cedar Creek.[44] Kidd had spent an uneasy night, worrying about his dispositions. Alerted by the picket firing, he ordered his men to deploy but cautioned them not to use the bugles, to avoid attracting the attention of the nearby Confederates. Torbert quickly awoke and immediately deployed his cavalry.[45]

The Yankee troopers marched across the farm fields, coming under artillery fire the whole way. The Wolverines moved east along the Old Forge Road and then took up positions to the east of the Valley Road, staying mounted, ready to go into combat at a moment's notice. There they had a vista of the fight unfolding in front of them. Kidd recalled:

> The full scope of the calamity which had befallen our arms burst suddenly into view. The whole battle field was in sight. The valley and intervening slopes, the fields and woods, were alive with infantry, moving singly and in squads. Some entire regiments were hurrying to the rear, while the Confederate artillery was raining shot and shell and spherical case among them to accelerate their speed. Some of the enemy's batteries were the very ones just captured from us. It did not look like a frightened or panic stricken army, but like a disorganized mass that had simply lost the power of cohesion. A line of cavalry skirmishers formed across the country was making ineffectual efforts to stop the stream of fugitives who had stolidly and stubbornly, set their faces to the rear. Dazed by the surprise in their camps, they acted like men who had forfeited their self-respect. They were chagrined, mortified, mad at their officers and themselves—demoralized; but, after all, more to be pitied than blamed.[46]

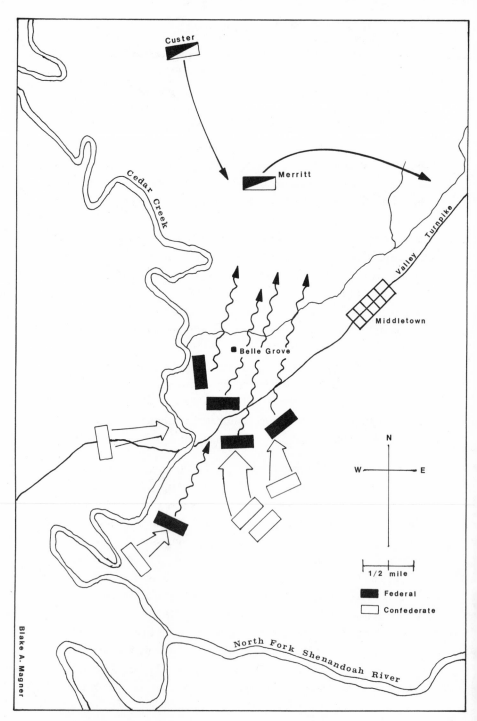

The Battle of Cedar Creek.

Once the infantry rallied and began to turn the tide during the afternoon phase of the fighting, Sheridan arrived on the field. Around 4:00 P.M., as he prepared to commence an all-out infantry counterattack, Sheridan ordered Merritt to charge a Rebel battery. Merritt sent three brigades, including Kidd's, forward across the farm fields, which chased away the battery and cleared the way for the infantry attack. Kidd commented, "Heavens, what a din! All along the Confederate line the cannon volleyed and thundered. . . . [T]he Union artillery replied, the roll of musketry became incessant."[47]

Merritt later wrote, "The [Michigan Brigade], in column of regiments in line, moved forward like an immense wave, slowly at first, but gathering strength and speed as it progressed, overwhelmed a battery and its supports amidst a desolating shower of canister and a deadly fire of musketry at short range." He crowed, "Never has the mettle of the division been put to a severer test than at this time, and never did it stand the test better."[48] Thomas L. Rosser recorded, "The enemy came down upon us all along the line and General Early and his little army were brushed out of the way and scattered like forest leaves before a mighty cyclone." Rosser continued, "It was the cavalry that destroyed" Early's army.[49]

Sheridan's counterattack caught the Confederates by surprise and chased them from the field with heavy losses, including one of Early's division commanders, Maj. Gen. Stephen Dodson Ramseur, who fell mortally wounded. The 6th Michigan pursued the routed Confederates as far north as Buckton on the North Branch of the Shenandoah River before finally giving up the chase. What began as a potential disaster for Sheridan turned into a great victory, with Early's army once again scattered and demoralized, never to be a factor again. Kidd correctly observed of Early, "His prestige was gone, his army destroyed and, from that moment, for the Confederacy to continue this hopeless struggle was criminal folly."[50] Two days after the great battle at Cedar Creek, Kidd wrote home to his father.

> Hd Qrs 1st Brig 1st Cav Div
> Oct. 21, 1864

Dear Father

Yours of Oct 8th and one of a previous date are both received. I am very glad indeed to hear that you are doing well and that the prospect of relieving yourself of debt is good.

I have prayed for that result of your efforts for years and nothing will please me so much as to hear that you are unencumbered. Once free, give yourself rest. Do not attempt to get *rich*. Try to make yourself and family happy and let *wealth* alone the rest of your life. You have children enough to do the hard work, and who will be only too glad if necessary to support you and see you and our Mother *enjoy* a tranquil old age. We are getting old enough to do something and I can be expected to do something.

If you can close out your indebtedness this year be content with what you have got, doing only a *moderate* business. Above all stay at home and learn to prize those blessings which it affords. I do not understand what you say about selling the old homestead in one letter and I, making the old house answer for another year in the other—Have you sold it?

I cannot believe it. If so, annul the bargain or buy it back the first opportunity.

Am I to come home to find somebody besides my own parents living in *the* house where I passed my childhood? I hope not: you speak of building a new house. Know that that old "homestead" would (if occupied by Father, Mother, brothers and sisters), [possess] more attractions for me than the most costly edifices. I would like, if you could afford it, to see some money "layed out" in beautifying the grounds, and the *"old house at home"* might be enlarged and repainted, if necessary and *it could be afforded* not otherwise. No one can appreciate like a soldier the comforts of the humblest home. *It is home.* That's enough. I have slept without a roof to shelter me too often to scribble about taking up my abode when every shingles is not entire and the ceilings of a certain height. *Keep the old homestead* and be satisfied. Lay out a spare dollar occasionally in buying a choice *tree*, or in building a new fence, or in planting a strawberry bed, something good, substantial, and real. Show is nothing. *Home happiness* is what every man ought to have what *few find*. If I can be there with you all I shall be content. Am I old enough to venture these suggestions? If not, overlook them, but for God's sake if you can avoid it do not part with that old homestead. The money required to build a fine *new house*, which you can do without, will make a paradise of it. The little money I shall be able to send home you will use as your judgment shall dictate. Use it to pay your debts if needed. If not, fix up [the] house, make it a pleasant place to stay. Make it inviting so that all your children *and* their friends will like to come there. The *"gim crackey"* of life I have learned to care very little about. You and all of us are always cared too little for home. Uncle Rich values it more highly.

You want to know something about me (us) and I am impatient at all this talk about what you will consider of little moment. (You will not always think so)

I wrote you once since the cavalry when we chased the "Saviour of the Valley" on the keen run for over twenty miles.

We then came to Cedar Creek and went into camp, waiting for supplies from Winchester making our rolls, reports etc. writing letters and making ourselves as comfortable as possible after what we are entitled to consider a very honorable campaign. Early however seems to have been determined not to be "squelched." He soon appeared in our front at his old stronghold Fisher's Hill, which by the way is an impregnable position to direct assault. He began to worry our pickets, making night reconnaissances and attempts at surprise in which he was severely foiled. Gen. Sheridan for some reason went to Washington and the army was commanded by *Major Gen Wright*.[51] On the night of the 18th inst. Early broke camp and marched to attack us. His attempt to surprise us was I regret to say successful. The 8th Corps was surprised at about 4 o'clock in the morning *in bed*. Everybody was alarmed and got ready for action. A little after daylight their attack commenced along our entire line and a scene ensued which made us all ashamed of the name of soldier. The 8th Corps, and some portion of the 19th ran without firing a shot, whole regiments led by their officers *ran* to the rear. Gen Wright *it is said was drunk*.[52] As soon as possible the Cavalry was formed in rear of these poltroons to *force* them into action, and partially succeeded. Many however threw away their arms and did not stop their disgraceful stampede until they were many miles distant from the sound of battle.

About twenty cannon and 1800 prisoners were taken by the rebels. The fighting then became terrific. The Cavalry I am proud to say it behaved with more than usual gallantry, and the 6th Corps of Infantry. The rebels turned our own captured guns upon us and since I have been a soldier I have never been exposed to such murderous discharges, but nothing could demoralize the men who constitute the superb cavalry force of the Middle Military Division. This I say with pride and *truthfully*. The Cavalry gained the day at *"Winchester"* the 19th September, and the Cavalry saved the day at Cedar Creek the 19th October. But Early's triumph was short-lived. Sheridan on his way back met the flying cowards at Winchester putting a line across the road. He stopped them, and turned their faces the other way, then putting spurs to his horse. He flew to the scene of action, staff escort and everything was outstripped, with his horse's "bridle (literally) far outstreaming, his flanks all blood and foam" he came, just at the time when we were about to give up in despair, ready to fight, needing only a leader to wipe out the disgrace of the forenoon. You should have heard the cheer that went up when it was known that "our glorious leader was again with us." The 6th and 19th Corps and the Cavalry were formed in a new line and a *charge* ordered. Sheridan himself led the 19th Corps. The 6th and the Cavalry (1st and 3rd Divisions) needed no leaders. *Every man was a general.* Then was seen one of the severest fights known I verily believe. Lines of Infantry we charged, and batterys vomited storms of iron into our ranks but Sheridan was there and we knew it. Soon the victorious legions of the morning were routed in turn and such a rout was never known. 47 pieces of artillery with wagons ambulances small arms and prisoners attest the completeness of our victory. Two hours more of daylight and we should have captured the whole army.

They scattered completely, broken in all directions, to the ravines and mountains. It was nearly dark when the charge was made, and of course they succeeded in making their escape. Nothing but gross carelessness gave them temporary success and somebody ought to be dismissed if regulations allowed it. I should say *hurry.* General Sheridan's absence came near producing fatal results. If we had three Army Corps like the 6th and the Cavalry, we could defy anything under any circumstances. The Rebel Cavalry is of little account. Fighting them is only a *"side-show."*

Early will collect his scattered forces and may advance down the valley again, but he will get whipped every time he comes, rest assured of that.

I am still comdg Brigade, but do not think myself competent for the command. Hoping to hear from you often with love to all I am.

Yr affectionate son

J H Kidd

SHERIDAN ORDERED a brief pursuit of Early but called it off within a few days. Instead, the Army of the Shenandoah went back into camp near Cedar Creek. Rosser wryly commented, "There was no effort made by Sheridan to pursue us and really he did not appear to realize the completeness of his victory. If he had pursued vigorously on the morning of the 20th, he could have galloped over every obstruction we could have thrown in his path and could have captured Early and his army."[53] The capture of Early and his plucky little army would have denied Robert E. Lee the return of its elements to the siege lines at Petersburg and might have shortened the war by a few weeks. Thus, Sheridan squandered a great opportunity by not pursuing the ragged and beaten Army of the Valley with more vigor.

Despite his failure to follow up on his great victory of October 19, Sheridan correctly observed that Cedar Creek "practically ended the campaign in the Shenandoah Valley. When it opened we found our enemy boastful and confident, unwilling to acknowledge that the soldiers of the Union were their equal in courage and manliness; when it closed with Cedar Creek this impression had been removed from his mind, and gave place to good sense and a strong desire to quit fighting."[54] Its assigned task evidently completed successfully, Sheridan's grand army started disbanding as its elements returned to their original commands. The 6th Corps returned to the Army of the Potomac, but the cavalry remained, with some hard work remaining unfinished.

From October 20 to 24, the Michigan Brigade did little other than reconnoiter the area. On the 25th, Kidd took his brigade through the Little Fort Valley toward Milford. As he later reported, the excursion was not successful: "After having lost about two hours by a misunderstanding in regard to the roads I found the passage through the mountains so obstructed that, in my own opinion and that of every officer whom I consulted, it was impossible to accomplish anything that day. This fact I reported to [Merritt] and also to [Torbert], and received orders to return to camp."[55]

The next day, Torbert relieved Kidd of command of the Michigan Brigade and replaced him with Col. Peter Stagg of the 1st Michigan.[56] Having drawn the ire of Torbert, the corps commander, for his alleged lack of aggressiveness at Cedar Creek, Kidd returned to command the 6th Michigan Cavalry under a stigma. Custer, ever loyal to his subordinate, found time to pen a few words of support.

> Headquarters Third Division
> Cavalry M.M.D
> October 27th 1864

My dear Col:

I am deeply pained at the intelligence of the charge which has been made in your command and without questioning or criticizing the action of my superiors I cannot but feel that there has been a misunderstanding upon the part of those who have ordered the charge. Prior to the reception of your note, I had been briefly informed of the supposed cause of your removal by a staff officer of Genl Torbert's, and it in no way reflected upon your capacity or courage as a commander & whose opportunities of fighting in regard to this question are far superior to those of any other officer. I am confident that your management of the Brigade since I left it has been highly creditable to you and satisfactory to the Brigade. My advice to you now, is to continue in the future, as you have in the past, to discharge your duties as an officer and a soldier. Your career while under my command was not only unreproachable but in every respect highly commendable and satisfactory. I trust that the command of the Brigade will be so arranged as to give satisfaction to all concerned.

With hearty best wishes for your success and happiness I am Col

Your sincere friend

G A Custer

ON NOVEMBER 5, Kidd's Uncle Rich wrote, "Your description of the Rebel repulses & flight is quite animating & cheering. I wish we could hear of their flying from all of this strong holds and although I have an abiding faith that we shall conquer them in the end but moves slow & I get discouraged sometimes." He continued, "We have *full* confidence that Lincoln will be reelected over all Copperhead opposition and fraud. . . . I am proud, that's the word, of your promotion & . . . believe you deserve them all."[57]

Two days later, James M. Kidd wrote to his son. This long letter described the state of the elder Kidd's business and reported on political campaign activities in Ionia. Referring to young James's letter of October 21, Kidd stated, "Your advice in your letter is very good. . . . [T]he small farm of your Parents and home is and will always be a source of gratification to me." The father's letter set forth a strategy for improving his financial condition consistent with his son's suggestions, and the elder Kidd sounded an optimistic note for the future of his business. The long letter concluded by encouraging James to obtain a furlough and return home once the army went into winter camp: "Once the elections are over, I think the army will go into winter quarters then we shall *all* be glad to see you home. Get as long a furlough as you can. Try and get one for the winter others have done so and you better try and do so too. You have worked hard and should have a winter's rest."[58]

A week later, Kidd's sister Catherine, known as Kate or Katy, wrote, "The wind blows hard howls terribly tonight and I can't help but think of the poor soldiers lying on the ground such a night as this—but 'there is a good time coming.' Wait a *little longer* and we will have our soldiers all home again." She ended, "Accept my love, write when you can and never for a moment think that you are forgotten by your ever loving sister Katy."[59]

On November 10, the Michigan Brigade broke camp at Cedar Creek and moved into Winchester for its winter encampment. The Wolverines spent much of the winter picketing and confiscating resources of value to the enemy. It was, once again, an unpleasant duty that Kidd definitely did not enjoy.[60] As fall broke, Kidd issued orders that plainly demonstrated the tedium of the regiment's daily routine after the campaign season had ended.

Headquarters 6th Mich Cav
Oct 29th 1864

Special Order
No. 14

Until further orders the following bugle calls will be sounded at these Headquarters and the following order is published respecting their observance.

Reveille	6	o'clock	A.M.
Stable Call	6:30	"	"
Recall	7	"	"
Water Call	9	"	"
Fatigue	10	"	"
Orders	11	"	"
Water Call	3	"	P.M.
Guard Mounting	3:30	"	"
Dress Parade 1st Call	4	"	"
" " 2nd Call	4:20	"	"
Stable Call	5	"	"
Recall	5:30	"	"
Retreat	Sunset		
Fallow	8	"	"
Taps	8:30	"	"

All stable calls must be attended by an Officer of each Company and water call by the Officer of the Day. Men will be required to continue the grooming of horses until Recall sounds.

The officer of the guard who will also officiate as camp officer of the day, and will be held personally responsible for the enforcement of this Order and the general police of the camp.

The old guard relieved the preceding day will be required under charge of the Sergeant of that Guard to police the camp outside the company quarters, at Fatigue companies will police their own ground. The Assistant Surgeon in charge will see that quarters are kept clean and all offal and filth promptly removed and the sinks daily kept in repair. These regulations are believed to be necessary to maintain the morale and discipline of the command aside from consideration of health, convenience, and comfort.

All officers are urged to assist in the prompt execution of all orders respecting the government of camps.

By order of
Jas. H. Kidd
Col. Comdg Regt.[61]

CHAFING AT THIS boring routine, Sgt. Hiram Rix Jr. of the 6th Michigan complained that the regiment's mounts were "fed better than we are . . . we get enough of bread and meat, coffee and sugar." This decent fare helped him and the other men of the 6th make it through "the usual routine of duties," which included getting "up at daylight, [going] to roll call, then tak[ing] care of our horses, get[ting] breakfast, [and joining] the detail for guard duty, also the pickets."[62]

Hd Qrs 6th Mich Cavalry
Dec 5th 1864

Dear Father

Your long letter dated just one month ago was received some time ago. I plead guilty for not writing home sooner and oftener: Osmond's wife[63] wrote that you were all anxious about me not having heard from me in more than a month. You need never be anxious. If I am not well you shall know it: I am very well now. Have been on a great *marauding* expedition into Mosby's territory on the east side of the Blue Ridge. We destroyed millions of dollars worth of property drove off all the stock amounting to more than two thousand head of cattle, ditto sheep, and one thousand head each of horses and hogs.

How the people of Virginia will live this winter I cannot imagine. Nothing is left where we have been but corn and not much of that. Barns and mills all are destroyed. Hay and grain has been given to the flames. As relentless war this we are now waging but it may be the best speediest way.

Winter seems to bring no respite. The war goes on in spite of weather and the elements. All eyes are now turned to Sherman as the bright particular star who is to guide us to a haven of peace, and Sherman is just the man to succeed in the bold, audacious movement he has commenced. His strategy is unexampled in these times and his genius is undoubted. This whether he succeeds in his present expedition or not (I do not believe he can fail).

I hope before spring the war will end. I shudder to think of another campaign like this, but if it must be let the nation do its best. Now that Abraham Lincoln is elected there can be but one heart and one voice: (however honestly a portion of the north may have opposed his re-election) that for united support of his administration and of the war. I believe the loyal people of all parties will now give cordial and undivided encouragement for the prosecution of the war if necessary.

As you will probably hear or have heard that I was for a few days *under arrest*. I might as well explain so that you may have no trouble about it. The Colonel at present by General Torbert's order commanding the brigade having taken command after the fighting was over, imagining that I stood in his way, for promotion to Brig General which he is exceedingly ambitious to be, placed me in arrest on a very trivial charge, at the best, or at least supported by a very trivial specification. The charge was "disobedience of orders". As soon as he sent the charges to me I forwarded them to Genl Devin comdg the Division, who ordered him to release me to take command of my regiment as we were

[The balance of the letter is missing.]

THE EPISODE BETWEEN Stagg and Kidd spoiled their relationship forever. As Kidd pointed out, Stagg was an ambitious officer, eager for promotion to general. As Custer's handpicked successor, Kidd stood in Stagg's way, even though Kidd had been serving on court-martial duty in Winchester since mid-December. Although the charges seem to have been based on trivial violations, the situation caused the feud between the two men to fester. According to Edward Longacre, "When Kidd went over Stagg's head by bringing his arrest to the attention of General Devin, commanding the division, he was immediately released, to the irate displeasure of his jailor. From that time on, the two men had been unable to serve together without rancor."[64] This incident prevented Kidd from participating in the war's decisive campaign, much to his chagrin.

Uncle Rich's wife wrote to Kidd the same day. Chiding him for his lack of piety, she wrote, "James it would make me very happy to know that you acknowledge His care, His protection. He has sent His angel to encamp around you or your record would be oh how sad to us at least." She continued, "I love to hear of your success of your promotion as I would if you were my own son."[65]

Two days later, Kidd's father wrote to James: "Glad to hear from you that you are well and have your . . . complaint settled. Hope that what is already done is to be the end of it. Osmond's wife told me of it but I think the matter is not known in town beyond her and Angelo and our Family except your mother knows nothing of it." Kidd's father reported on the health of the family and closed by encouraging his son: "I must close by adding you must make us a visit if possible and soon if convenient."[66]

The commanders of Michigan regiments were required to file an annual report with the state adjutant general, recapping the year's exploits. On December 17, Kidd filed an excellent summary, which does not appear in the official records, but has been printed in this volume as Appendix B.

Alfred Torbert took Stagg's side in the dispute. Kidd had long disliked Torbert and apparently did not have much respect for the cavalry commander. As Kidd made little effort to disguise his contempt for the former infantryman, it is no surprise that Torbert blocked Kidd's every effort to return to active duty with his regiment. Kidd's dispute with Torbert exiled him to presiding over a protracted series of courts-martial and prevented him from commanding his Wolverines in the war's final days. Instead, he spent his days tending to routine matters.

> Head Quarters 6th Mich Cav
> Dec. 6th 1864

Special Order
No. 42

Company commanders of this Regiment are required to make requisitions for a full compliment of Forage caps, cross sabers, numbers and letters of their Companies.

Special Order No. 40 from these Hd.Qtrs. dated Nov. 24, 1864 is so far modified as to read that all non commissioned [officers] will provide themselves with chevrons and stripes to be always worn while on duty. Such non commissioned officers as shall not have complied with this order before the 9th inst. will be recommended by their Company commanders for reduction.

> By order of
> James H. Kidd
> Col Comdg Regt.[67]

To HIS GREAT DISMAY, Kidd missed the greatest days of the Army of the Potomac's Cavalry Corps.

6

Missing the End of the War

General Sheridan is accomplishing much & I should like to share the honor.

KIDD SPENT THE WINTER of 1864–65 in Winchester, presiding over a court-martial board. He now proudly wore a gold "Custer badge," presented to him by the officers of the 6th Michigan Cavalry and issued at the behest of the Boy General himself. The badges, made by the Tiffany Company of New York, consisted of a gold Maltese cross with Custer's name inscribed on it and topped off by a single gold brigadier's star. Only upon Custer's specific request would a man receive the badge, and it was quite a symbol of pride and honor for those lucky enough to wear one. When Kidd received his, he said, "The gold in this badge is not more precious, it is not rarer, than the frankness, the generosity, the want of distrust which has always characterized your intercourse with me. . . . The associations—the Michigan Brigade of Cavalry, its leader, Custer, his deeds and theirs, are enough to make your gift one of inestimable value always."[1]

Despite Kidd's obvious pride at the esteem in which Custer held him, Kidd was very unhappy and made no secret of it, making multiple requests to be relieved of his unhappy duty and sent back to his regiment. These requests were all rejected.

As Kidd brooded over the rejections, George and Libbie Custer hosted a "Michigan Brigade Ball" at a local school, York Academy. "The occasion paired local ladies of unionist persuasion and Custer's subordinates. As snow drifted down outside, the officers and their partners waltzed the night away to the accompaniment of the Michigan Brigade band."[2] It is not known whether the pouting Bob Kidd attended the event. His father did not help things, writing, "I have been expecting daily to see you at home to make us a visit. Other officers came home. I did not see why you would not come and at least spend a few days."[3]

In the meantime, Sheridan prepared for the destruction of Early's remaining forces, which were camped near Waynesborough at the head of the Shenandoah Valley. Torbert was away from the army on a leave of absence, and Merritt assumed command of the Army of the Shenandoah's Cavalry Corps. Kidd would not miss Torbert, whom he did not care for, but he respected Merritt a great deal. Not long after the end of the war, he praised Merritt profusely: "During the many hotly contested cavalry engagements, from Upperville and Aldie to Five Forks, he was not accustomed to view the progress of the battle from a distance, but plunged into the fray, encouraging his men by actual presence, and would not hesitate to place himself at the head of a single squadron for a charge, even when commanding a division. By his coolness and intrepidity in action, he won for himself an enviable reputation, and enjoyed a high degree the confidence of Gen. Sheridan."[4]

Merritt also held a high opinion of Kidd, and asked Sheridan to reconsider the decision to keep Kidd on the court-martial panel.

> Head Qrs Cavalry
> Mid Mil Divn
> Feby 26th 1865

Brig. Gen. Forsyth[5]
Chief of Staff
Hd Qrs Army
General

In a conversation had with you I understood you to intimate that Col. Kidd did not wish to accompany the expedition tomorrow. The Colonel does want to go and has applied to me personally to go.

I can truly say that I should like very much to have Col. Kidd along in command of his regiment which is one of the largest in the First Division. If it can be arranged without detriment to the service, give Col. Kidd the permission he asks for and you will much oblige.

Yrs truly
W. Merritt
Bvt. Maj. Genl.
Comdg

THIS REQUEST WAS also rejected. The next day, Sheridan formally relieved Torbert and replaced him with Merritt. A newly promoted Brig. Gen. Thomas C. Devin took command of the First Cavalry Division and the Michigan Brigade.

On March 1, Custer led the First Division in an attack on Early's small force at Waynesborough. Sweeping down on the ragged Confederate veterans, Custer's juggernaut shattered Early's small force, dispersing it and effectively ending Rebel resistance in the Shenandoah Valley. The glory for the victory went to Custer's Third Division. A Michigan sergeant complained loudly to one of Custer's staff officers, "Why since Custer left the 1st Division it has done nothing. . . . Now all you hear about is the 3rd Division. The 3rd Division captured so many battleflags, nothing but the 3rd Division, while the 1st Division is scarcely heard of. The fact is you have Custer now."[6]

After shattering the Rebels, the horsemen moved off toward Charlottesville, navigating "the rain-soaked roads of red Virginia clay, churned into thin mortar by the hoofs of many thousands of horses."[7] Kidd's good friend from the 6th Michigan, Capt. Benjamin F. Rockafellow, commented, "No human language . . . can describe the rain, the mud and the raging, foaming rivers that we have waded through."[8] Capt. Harlan Lloyd Page, an officer in a Third Division regiment, wrote:

> Our course was marked with the destruction of railroads and of the locks of the James River Canal, and of such supplies as were most needed by Lee's army. It was a most difficult and toilsome march for men and horses; the rain still fell in torrents every day; the weather was bitterly cold for marching; the roads were as bad as possible. We were in a section not hitherto traversed by our armies. Topographical maps were unknown, and it was difficult to find the way to many points which General Sheridan desired to reach. We had one rendezvous at Columbia, and we examined the James River at many points, hoping to find a possible fording place, but were unable to cross the river without pontoons. . . .
>
> The horses were badly worn out, and the men were very tired, but all hearts were jubilant, and soldiers were never known in better spirits than we were. We had had a hard march; we had made the longest and most successful cavalry raid of the war; we had fought a decisive battle; we had captured an entire army.[9]

Sheridan and his large mounted force, along with the Sixth Corps, would soon return to the Army of the Potomac and slowly strangle Lee's army in the siege lines around Petersburg.

The war rapidly moved toward its end phase, and Kidd was missing the excitement, much to his great displeasure. On March 6, his uncle wrote, asking him to find a billet for a young man from Grand Rapids named Louis Henry Jennings.[10] In mid-March, Kidd responded with a letter that showed great insight into what ultimately broke the Confederacy's will to resist.

> Mil. Comm. Rooms
> Hd Qrs Mid Mil Div
> Winchester Va March 19, 1865

Dear Uncle Rich

Yours with reference to young Jennings[11] is recd and I will see what can be done with him. He is not now with the regiment no more am I and do not know when I shall be. I was very reluctant to be kept on this kind of duty but cannot get off at present. It is far easier and more pleasant as well as less dangerous than duty in the field while at the same time I am learning something all the time, but notwithstanding this I shall go back with the regiment as soon as I possibly can get off.

General Sheridan is accomplishing much & I should like to share the honor.

I am President of a Military Commission for the trial of such offences as are not cognizable by Courts-Martial usually very important cases. There is a large number of men and officers here and at Remount Camp for our Cavalry.[12] When communication is opened again and horses supplied to mount them.

For the present you can consider me most emphatically safe not even subject to guerrilla hostilities.

I think the people of the south are ready to submit, and would gladly hail peace on the basis of reconstruction. They are only waiting for the leader to take the initiative. This opinion from my own observation, and conversation with disloyal citizens.

I have heard many *"good Southern men"* say if Sherman & Sheridan are allowed to go where they please they might as well submit at once, and others say, they wish Grant would capture Lee's army and bring the war to an end, as that must be the ultimate result.

The opinion seems to be the Southern Confederacy is gone up, and in that opinion everybody on our side seems to concur.

> Yrs very truly
> J H Kidd, Col.

WHEN HE WROTE his memoirs, Kidd had little comment on this unhappy period of his career. Part of his court-martial duties included the trial of a man accused of being a Confederate spy. Observing that a witness named Lemoss acted like a hardened criminal, Kidd wrote: "The case was on trial when the army moved. General Sheridan seemed to lay much stress on the matter for he refused the request of the president of the commission to be relieved in order to rejoin his regiment. A personal letter from General Merritt to General Forsythe, chief of staff, making the same request, was negatived and an order issued directing the commission to remain in session until that particular case was disposed of and providing that such members as should then desire it, be relieved and their places filled by others."[13]

It turned out there were two spies involved. One, who used the alias "Renfrew," was actually John Wilkes Booth, who eventually gained infamy as the assassin of Abraham Lincoln.[14]

At the end of March, the cavalry having arrived, Grant broke loose from the lines at Petersburg and, with Sheridan's large mounted force leading the way, began moving west, looking to cut off Lee's line of retreat. The months of attrition warfare had taken their toll on the Confederate forces; by the end of March, the once-proud Confederate cavalry could mount only less than five thousand men fit for duty.[15] The end was clearly in sight.

On March 29, a major fight occurred along the Weldon Railroad to the west of Petersburg that cut Lee's last remaining vital lifeline to the important port city of Wilmington, North Carolina. On March 31, Sheridan shattered what was left of the Confederate cavalry at Dinwiddie Court House. Then, on April 1, his cavalry assaulted the important crossroads hamlet of Five Forks, bagging a large force of Rebel cavalry and infantry and forcing Lee to abandon his lines at Petersburg or risk being surrounded.[16]

Thus began the final campaign of the war. Kidd remained trapped in Winchester, marooned in the war's backwater.

Mil Com Rooms
Winchester 29 March

Dear Father & Mother

I have written two or three times within a few days to you and others at home. Owing to the uncertainty in which I am, I do not expect to hear from you regularly. Although still in Winchester I may any day be ordered to City Point where the regiment is, as the business already before my Commission is nearly completed and nothing in prospective that I know of. When I leave this place I will inform you: until you hear from me suffer no uneasiness on my account. I am enjoying myself hugely here satisfying my conscience with the assurance that I can't help myself and am simply obeying orders as any soldier is obliged to do. Gen. Hancock[17] is in command here. Gen. Torbert is here, and much cavalry.[18] I anticipate orders for all the troops here to join Grant although of course I know nothing officially. Everything is in readiness. I shall not be surprised if I am with the old Army of the Potomac in the vicinity of Petersburg within the next week.

Rumor has it here that a general engagement is going on there. I shudder at the thought of it although I have no fears for the final result. If unsuccessful on our part, it will have a bad effect of course, if successful it will be the rebellion's death knell. In either case, the slaughter must be terrible. I sincerely hope this may be the last general engagement of this war: and "seems to me" "it must be so." Write often. Love to all.

Yours &c.
J. H. Kidd

Two DAYS LATER, as the Army of the Potomac advanced all along the lines, the long-awaited orders for Kidd to rejoin his Wolverines still had not arrived. Realizing that the war was ending, Kidd fretted about his future.

Mil Com Rooms
Winchester 31st March

Dear Father & Mother

Today is raining hard here. We have adjourned till Monday: and I am entirely out of business and hardly know what to do with myself. We have had constant rain now for over 48 hours, and still it pours. Today somebody stole my rubber coat and I am out in the wet.

Things are exceedingly quiet here and I am living so much after home style that I hardly know whether I am soldier or civilian. This kind of soldiering is something I never dreamed of and did not suppose I could ever put to work at it. But a few weeks of easy working may not be a bad thing after all, not much glory, but glory is a thing not so much sought after as formerly.

I recd a letter a few days ago from Kate who was then in Saginaw. I answered it at length. She wrote Sarah & Frank had joined the church. I am glad of it and congratulate them if they have made a profession of religion in good faith. Kate herself I thought was seriously inclined judging from the tone of her letter. Well I am glad of that too. She is a sort of a favorite with me, and anything for her *good* gives me satisfaction. She's a good girl and ought to be happy.

I hear but little about business at home lately. I hope it goes on well: I am sometimes at a loss to know what I am to go about after the war or when my time's up. I suppose there will be a corner for me to make my share of money somewhere and a place for me to enjoy my part in life and a way for me to make myself useful; I hope so, and should like to know when, where, and how; But sufficient unto the day is the evil thereof. I have got more will and more energy than I ever had credit for and may manage to take a creditable part in the drama of civil life as well as life military. Give my love to all the good people at home, & remember me with the rest to Grandfather Stevenson. Believe me as ever

Your son

J. H. Kidd

IN LATE MARCH, James's father made a trip to Detroit, where he paid for a new regimental standard for the 6th Michigan Cavalry and arranged to have it shipped to his son. This new flag was carried proudly by Kidd's regiment for the rest of its career in the field. The good citizens of Ionia had raised the money to purchase the flag, and Kidd's father was proud to forward it to his son. However, the father sounded an ominous note in a letter of April 2: "The hard times are beginning to come and I think this summer will be a hard one for all. . . . I will do my best this summer & hope to get out of debt but for 4 months to come I will be hard pressed for money."[19] Mr. Kidd was absolutely correct in his prediction that it would be a hard summer for his son in particular.

The war winding down, Kidd missed the excitement of the Cavalry Corps' greatest moments. He later noted, "On the 4th of April the regiment charged the enemy's line of battle near Beaver Mills, Va., losing in the charge Lieut. S. H. Finney, a gallant officer."[20] As word of the Army of the Potomac's successes filtered into Winchester, the frustrated colonel again pleaded to be sent back to his regiment.

Mil Com Rooms
Winchester 6th April 1865

Capt George Lee
A.A.A.G. M.M.D.

I have the honor to request that I be relieved from duty on the Military Commission of which I am President, for the following reasons.

My regiment is serving with the Army of the Potomac under General Sheridan and I am anxious if possible to be with it.

When I previously made application and when General Merritt applied to have me relieved General Sheridan refused the application on the ground that the case I was then trying was important to be concluded, and that it was therefore impracticable to permit to join my regiment *at that time*. That case as well as several others have been concluded and I respectfully ask that some officer whose command is doing duty in this department be assigned to the duty I am now performing and that I be ordered to rejoin my command with the Army of the Potomac.

Very respectfully
Yr obt servant
J. H. Kidd
Col 6th Mich Cavalry
Presdt. Mil. Comm.

ALTHOUGH THE COURT-MARTIAL was finally over, the request was once again denied. That same day, Kidd's father wrote, "In regard to your business after the war I cannot now advise other than for you to remain as quiet as you can doing your duty fully until your time expires at which time I hope the war will be fully over & an honorable peace established. Then you will find plenty to do and of such business as you are competent to perform at paying rates."[21] Kidd's reaction to these soothing words is not recorded.

In the interim, Grant's great army, divided into two huge, hungry pincers, raced west toward its date with destiny, seeking to trap the ragged remnants of Lee's army between its hungry jaws. The Michigan Brigade did more good service during the pursuit—Lts. Thomas W. Custer and Elliott M. Norton of the 6th Michigan were both awarded the Medal of Honor for capturing Confederate battle flags at the Battle of Sayler's Creek on April 6, 1865.[22] After several more brisk fights, Custer's Third Cavalry Division interdicted Lee's line of march at Appomattox Court

House, west of Richmond. There, faced with the prospect of annihilation, Lee had no choice but to seek a truce to discuss surrender terms.

When the Confederates offered the flag of truce, Lt. Col. George G. Briggs of the 7th Michigan received it. As Briggs rode off to find a superior officer, the joyous news spread like wildfire, with "cheer upon cheer" thundering along the line.[23] Seeking to honor his former commander, Colonel Briggs sought out George A. Custer and delivered the flag of truce to him. Not long after, Lee met with Grant and surrendered the proud veterans of the Army of Northern Virginia on April 9, 1865, which brought the war in Virginia to a close. The next day, Kidd reported the happy news to his family in Michigan.

> Headquarters Mid Mil Div
> Winchester Va
> April 10th 1865

Dear Father & Mother

Last night we heard that Lee had surrendered his army to Gen Grant. "Gloria in excelcis." This ends the war and at last we are certainly on the eve of peace. If God is not fervently thanked by every loyal citizen of our glorious country, we do not deserve such magnificent success.

Four years of war have not been in vain, and who cannot trace the hands of Providence in those four years of courage. So long as the Executive, the Congress and the people, stood aloof from a square toed determination to abolish slavery, we were unsuccessful and treason seemed promised success, but when the right was fully vindicated, the cause of Rebellion began to decline, and has been swift to collapse.

Thus end all conspiracies against the rights of man: and against the cause of truth and justice. From the time when Sherman began his triumphant march[24] I have not entertained a doubt of the result. Success has been speedier and more complete than the most sanguine could have hoped for, yet not more certain than we all expected.

When every rebel in arms has again owned allegiance to his flag. When law and order are again restored throughout the land. When calm reason has dispelled party bias and sectional prejudice, and the sun shines again upon our people once more, united, harmonious *free*, let us hope that no cause of estrangement may again arise to prevent the fraction of our glorious destiny among the nations. Let patriotism stifle prejudice, reason humble *pride* and sweet peace will ever smile upon our Union, "one and inseparable."

And I am here. Time and again have I tried to get away but cannot. Gen Hancock has at length promised to let me go when I have tried one more case. I get no mail and dare not tell you to send letters here not knowing when I shall leave; probably as I told you before in a week. At all events be not uneasy. I will let you know where I am. With love to all of you I am

Your son

J. H. Kidd, Col.

ON APRIL 11, Hancock's chief of staff sent a letter to John Singleton Mosby informing him of Lee's surrender and further telling him that Hancock was "authorized to receive the surrender of the forces under [his] command on the same conditions offered to General Lee." Hancock offered to send an officer of equal rank to treat with Mosby, the only condition being that the troopers swear the oath of loyalty to the Union.[25] The Union high command spent several anxious days waiting for the Gray Ghost's response. A few days later, word filtered in that Mosby was willing to meet with a Federal officer to negotiate the surrender terms. Torbert and Brig. Gen. George H. Chapman, accompanied by Chapman's brigade of cavalry and Kidd, were sent to meet with the raider. Chapman was to impress upon Mosby the need for partisan activities to cease.[26] Kidd recalled, "The bold and dashing partisan was . . . capable of doing much mischief and it was thought best by General Hancock to treat with him and see if he would not consent to a cessation of hostilities and, possibly, take the parole. Accordingly, an agreement was made to meet him at Millwood, a little town a few miles distant from Winchester and near the mountains."[27]

Chapman's contingent met with Mosby on April 18. Mosby asked for a forty-eight-hour extension in the agreed-upon truce so he could attempt to communicate with the remaining elements of the Confederate government, which forced a second meeting to be called for April 20.[28] Although the agreement was accepted by the Federal high command, Grant instructed, "If Mosby does not avail himself of the present truce, end it and hunt him and his men down. Guerrillas, after beating the armies of the enemy, will not be entitled to quarter."[29] Riding with the Federal force dispatched to meet with Mosby, Kidd was a bit uneasy about passing through the heart of Mosby's Confederacy.

Arriving at Millwood before Mosby, the Federals impatiently awaited his arrival. Not long after, Mosby and his whole command arrived, with the guerrilla commander attired for the occasion in his best uniform. Kidd was surprised to learn that the formidable opponent was a slight wisp of a man and asked Mosby how much he weighed. Mosby responded, "One hundred and twenty-eight pounds." Kidd replied, "Well, judging from your fighting reputation, I looked for a two hundred pounder at least."[30]

As the leaders conferred, Kidd and the others mingled with their foes, chatting amiably. Despite cordial discussions with the Federal commissioners, Mosby did not surrender his command. Growing suspicious of Federal motives when informed about the approach of a large Federal mounted force, Mosby gathered his troopers and left. A few minutes later, Kidd learned that Mosby intended to disband his command the next day at Salem, Virginia.[31] The war was now truly over, and the gravest threat to the Federal forces remaining in the Shenandoah Valley was removed. Kidd was eager to rejoin his regiment because he wanted to participate in the victory celebrations that were sure to come.

This time, the request was granted, and Kidd rejoined the 6th Michigan.[32] Kidd set off across Virginia for Richmond. Finding his regiment gone, he learned that it had marched off toward North Carolina, where it was to join Sherman's army, which was preparing to corner the remnants of Gen. Joseph Johnston's scratch force near Goldsborough.[33] The Federal cavalry made it as far as the North Carolina border before word of Johnston's surrender arrived, which caused them to turn around and begin marching back toward Richmond and Petersburg.[34]

Writing on a piece of captured Confederate writing paper, Kidd recounted his impressions of the former Confederate capital, so long the focus of the Union's attentions.

> Richmond VA
> Spotswood Hotel
> May 1, 1865

Dear Father & Mother

At length after nearly three years service I find myself in the Capital of the "Confederate States" and quartered in the first hotel in the city Spotswood. I have been here two days and have visited all the places of interest. Libby Prison, "Belle Isle,"[35] State capitol, Jeff Davis' house, etc. I succeeded finally in getting the order to join my regiment which I had so long sought and on my arrival at City Point found the command except that portion dismounted gone off so that I was unable to reach them, and not being able to report for duty, have concluded to spend my time sight-seeing. [Johnston] having surrendered, I anticipate no more fighting; and think my chance for getting home "after the war" pretty good. I came up the James River in a steamer, seeing [Maj. Gen. Benjamin F.] Butler's "Dutch Gap Canal," the obstructions in the river, Fort Darling and all the points made historical and of interest by the events of the war.

Richmond is a much more beautiful city than I supposed. No city I have ever visited is as much admired by me. The grounds around the State Capital [are] particularly fine. The equestrian statue of Washington, the bronze statues of Henry, Mason and Jefferson and the marble statue of Henry Clay,[36] and the fine Capital building itself lending an artistic charm to the artificial and natural beauty of the place. The city is situated on a succession of high hills overlooking the James River, is well laid out, and the residences uniformly fine. So many fine residences in so small a space is a peculiar feature of this city which I have scarcely met with elsewhere. But the entire business portion of the place or most of it was given to the flames by the criminal action of rebel officials.[37] It is a sad sight and illustrates the character of the men who controlled secession, willing to sacrifice the wealth and comfort of their own people rather than give us a chance to permit them to enjoy both. I have met and talked with a large number of rebel men and officers. They all express themselves subjugated, many of them manifest chagrin, and disappointment, many a continued inimical feeling towards the north, many are tired of the war and ready to welcome peace and its consequences. All admit the hopelessness of their cause. The deep gloom occasioned by the President's assassination I need not comment upon. It was felt in Michigan at the same time and in the same intense degree as in the army and that expresses a depth of *national* grief, which finds no parallel in history. I shall visit Petersburg if possible, though I shall join the command at the earliest practicable moment. I am well but have received no tidings from home in over six weeks. My letters were sent to Winchester after I left there and from there will be re-mailed to the regiment and I shall not receive them sooner than I join that.

Hoping that we may all be at home soon with love for all of you I remain

Yr affectionate son

J. H. Kidd

A few days later, Kidd finally found the 6th Michigan Cavalry near Petersburg. He rejoined his regiment and resumed command of it, after almost six months away.

Headquarters 6th Mich Cavalry
Petersburg Va May 7, 1865

Dear Father

Yours of April 2nd and April 6th were recd yesterday. My mail having been sent to the regiment was retained several weeks and was then re-mailed to Winchester just too late to reach there before I left, and thence was sent to the regiment again and has just found [me] having wandered around for a month in search of me. I wrote from Richmond where I spent a day or two. I am now here and find the command about as I left it. But one officer was killed. Lieutenant Finney[38] of my old company. He was a faithful, brave soldier, and his death, has caused no little sorrow in the regiment.

The war now being over I hope we may speedily be mustered out of service. Nothing can now make a longer continuance in the service desirable, or obligatory. We are to go to Washington soon; when I suppose we shall settle up and get our discharge papers.

In regard to the flag I did not intend nor wish you to pay for it. The officers of the regiment are able & willing to do it, but I thought perhaps the ladies of Ionia would be glad to do it, never having done anything for our regiment.[39] (I beg their pardon) (I believe they did present my new Co. E with "Housewives"[40]) I do not share your anticipation of hard times, entirely. I see no reason why we should not prosper beyond anything we have heretofore known. We have a sound currency. There will be plenty of labor. Articles of merchandise must come down and then with large stocks must lose, but their production will be cheaper, and on a larger scale. I think, business must be good.

Capt Tower is not well, but is not dangerously sick. I am well and everybody you know.

Hoping to hear from you often during the short time I have to remain in the army I am

Yr affectionate son
J. H. Kidd

NOT LONG AFTER Kidd wrote his letter, the 6th Michigan received orders to march to Washington to participate in a grand review of the Army of the Potomac. Kidd wrote home once he got settled in.

Headqrs 6th Mich Cav
Washington May 17 1865

Dear Father

Your last of 7th instant just received. We arrived here yesterday, having been six days coming overland from Petersburg.

That flag cannot be found in Washington. There must be some mistake about addressing or something.

I have time to write but a word at this time. Will write very soon. Love to all.

Your son
J. H. Kidd

THE WOLVERINES "went into camp on the hills near the city and busied ourselves in cleaning up the arms and accoutrements, brushing and mending clothes and fixing up to make as good an appearance as possible in the Grand Review."[41] President Andrew Johnson was to review the troops and a grateful nation would turn out to thank the men who had sacrificed so much to save the Union. Kidd issued the following orders for the coming review:

HeadQuarters 6th Mich Cav
May 19th 1865

Special Orders
No. 90

In anticipation of a review of the Command on Thursday the 22nd inst, the Col. Commanding requests Battalion, Squadron, and Company commanders to exert themselves to make the appearance of the Regiment on that occasion as creditable as possible. The following order will be complied with.

1st All commissioned officers will wear caps and sabres.

2nd All noncommissioned officers will wear chevrons and stripes.

3rd Caps and blouses must be provided for the men.

4th Straps will be worn on the Pants and Boots well blacked. Cross sabres and letters of companies will be worn on the caps. Such companies are not supplied with the necessary articles will immediately procure them.

No officer or soldier who fails to comply with this order will be permitted to appear at the review and the names of those who thus fail or of the Officer responsible will be published before the Regiment.

By order of

James H. Kidd

Col Comdg Regt[42]

THE MICHIGAN BRIGADE proudly led the march of the First Division, and James H. Kidd and the 6th Michigan Cavalry were at the head of the Michigan Brigade. It was a proud day for Kidd and his Wolverines.[43]

Huge throngs lined the crowded streets, prompting one veteran to write, "It really looked as if the whole North had emptied itself into Washington for the purpose of honoring us."[44] Lt. Robert C. Wallace of the 5th Michigan Cavalry later recorded, "The passing of [Maj. Gen. William T. Sherman's western theatre armies and the Army of the Potomac] in Review was something long to be remembered. They were no Sunday soldiers, but the real, weather beaten, war worn, hardened veterans, nothing bright about them but their arms."[45]

The review over, the Army of the Potomac melted away, most units leaving to go home. The Wolverines were not so fortunate. On May 21, as the Wolverines prepared for their triumphant march down Pennsylvania Avenue, the following order was issued to Maj. Gen. George Crook, who succeeded Merritt as chief of cavalry:

You will order the First Brigade, First Cavalry Division of your command, composed of the First, Fifth, Sixth and Seventh Michigan Regiments, to proceed at once with horse equipments and arms complete to report to Maj. Gen. John Pope at Saint Louis, Mo. The quartermaster's department will furnish transportation immediately.

By command of Lieutenant-General Grant.[46]

Instead of being discharged, the men of the Michigan Brigade were forced to complete their terms of service, which did not expire until the fall of 1865. Much to their consternation, they were to become reluctant Indian fighters. Their enlistment papers included a clause stating that their terms of service were three years, "unless the war ended first." It must have been very disheartening indeed for these proud men to watch their comrades in arms prepare to go home while they prepared to take the field again; indeed, many of them were "very much disgusted" by their new mission.[47]

Maj. Gen. Grenville Dodge, commanding the Department of Missouri and the Federal forces in the Kansas and Nebraska territories, was worried about increased activity by the area's Indians, who had launched a number of bloody attacks on Union outposts. He decided to launch a campaign consisting of seven columns that fanned out across the countryside in search of the hostile Indians. One column, to march from Fort Laramie directly north to the Powder River, was to be commanded by Brig. Gen. Patrick E. Connor, commander of the Department of the Plains. Connor had earned a reputation as an Indian fighter as a result of a victory over a force of Indians early in the Civil War. Kidd later described him as "evidently a very slow, taciturn, obstinate, determined man who has been accustomed to have his own way." By all appearances, and based on his prior record, however, Connor appeared to be the right officer to command this expedition.[48]

Connor's column was to "strike the Indians wherever found"[49]—a plan that depended on his men doing their duty in a prompt and efficient fashion. As we shall see, that did not occur. Kidd reflected the uncertainty felt by the men of the Michigan Brigade in a letter home on May 31.

Washington D.C.
May 31, 1865

Dear Father

I send enclosed a draft for $400, and also Osmond Tower[50] $50. Get his receipt, and dispose of the rest as you see fit.

I am well, and start for St. Louis today where the regiment has already gone. I can't say if we are to be mustered out or not. Nobody knows.

The flag came to hand at last and gives eminent satisfaction. Everybody says it is the handsomest flag in the army. Two or three dollars is due Buhloled[51] for exchange, but I have lost the account. I will try to ascertain what it is and will forward it to them. Get a receipt from him.

I will write from St. Louis.

Affectionately
J. H. Kidd, Col.
Tell Kate to write.

THE JOURNEY TO St. Louis was thoroughly unpleasant. The Wolverines took trains to Parkersburg, West Virginia, where they embarked on a small flotilla of steamboats. The weather was very hot, the train tightly packed, the drinking water "horrid," and rations scarce. Chaplain Stephen Greeley of the 6th traveled on a boat carrying the horses of both the 5th and 6th Michigan. The boats were terribly overcrowded, causing Greeley to conclude that "there seemed to be little care on the part of the managers of the concern, whether the men had any comforts or not."[52] When the boats finally made landfall, officers had stood guard to prevent the men from going ashore. Frustrated, the troopers simply dropped the impeding officers into the Mississippi River and went ashore anyway.[53]

Arriving safely in St. Louis after the unpleasant trip, Kidd spent a pleasant night. Stagg received orders to march his brigade without delay to Fort Leavenworth, Kansas. The quartermaster's department was to provide the necessary transportation for the men and to provide horses for those needing mounts upon arrival at Fort Leavenworth.[54]

On June 3, Kidd took passage on a steamer up the Missouri River. To pass the time he wrote lengthy passages in the diary that had sat dormant for more than a year. On June 8, Kidd arrived at Kansas City, Missouri, where the Wolverines mounted up and made the thirty-five-mile march to Fort Leavenworth, Kansas. He observed that his surroundings were "better land than I have seen on the river below. The banks are stiffer and not so easily washed away."[55] Many of the unhappy Wolverines saw an opportunity to go home and deserted in droves. Other men of the 6th Michigan spent several quiet days resting and refitting at Fort Leavenworth, which gave Kidd an opportunity to reflect on what the end of the war meant to him.

> Hd Qrs 6th Mich Cavalry
> Leavenworth Kansas
> June 12 1865

Dear Father

I wrote you from Washington sending a draft for $400. I wrote Kate on the steamer Paragon from St. Louis bound for this point.

I need not tell you of my delightful ride by rail from Washington, when I bade farewell to the scenes that have become so familiar. Virginia, where for three years I had been struggling against the main army of the rebellion, where so many thousands of our brave countrymen repose beneath the sod, where I had myself buried many of my most valued friends, whose soil had been the scene of bitterer feuds and savage strife than has fallen to the lot of any other state or country, and yet which I had learned to live in spite of its disloyalty and desolation. Farewell; and I can scarcely restrain the falling tear, as I say it. The first part of my journey lies through a part of Virginia rendered memorable by earlier scenes of the war. As I pass the "Relay House," the junction of the B & O RR and the "Washington Branch," dreamily the time four years and more ago is recalled when the telegraph announced to the country the important fact that "McClellan had arrived at the Relay House," and the shifting scenes of the war from that time to this were arrayed in misty panorama before my mind's eye. The defeats, the victories, the defeated ambitions, and blasted reputations, the vacillating impulses of the people, their loyal support, and their half disloyal opposition to the administration, their periods of victory, of hope and exultation, and their periods of despondency and doubt; periods when the best men trembled and feared. I saw the long array of great names produced by the war. Some comet-like blazed for a time and vanished. Some, the puppets of a nation's caprice were used for a while and then thrown away in disgust. Some struggling into notice, by modest merit alone, took the place of affixed stars, and shining with a steadfast and sterling brilliancy, led the populace back to notice after they had stayed long enough with rockets, and meteors.

I saw the President, with patience, modesty, and superhuman will, struggling to steer the almost unmanageable ship of state, saw him shape its course through the breakers and quicksand of war and anarchy into the quiet sea of peace and good order, then saw him murdered and through all I could see the form of "Liberty" watching the contest and cheering on the right.

I was rendered still more visionary by the sudden arrival of the train at "Harper's Ferry" when I saw "Col Lee"[56] at the head of a force of U.S. forces engaged in ferreting out one of the martyrs to public opinion, John Brown, and I saw that same Col Lee the chief of the conspiracy against the very government he then professed to serve, saw him lead armies against and plan expeditions against the Capitol of his own nation. Saw him through four bloody years, trying to uproot freedom and overthrow the right. Saw him as the actual head of a system of torture against Union prisoners, of well-considered plans of cruelty—of diabolical conspiracies. Saw for a long time successful, at length to fail. Saw him defeated, routed, fugitive. Saw him reluctantly submit to fate, and heard him congratulate rebels on the services they had done their country. Then I saw Northern toadyism, flatter this arch-traitor because great he was less a traitor, back on such toadies.[57] Well that'll do now. Whoa, Jim!

From Harper's Ferry to Cumberland and Grafton and Wheeling through the new State of Western Virginia and its magnificent scenery, went we following crooked streams over and through mountains, twisting around double curves, the engine curvetted and snorted. Sometimes coming straight back upon you, causing you to jerk your head into the car suddenly for fear the locomotive on your own train may run against it. Like a snake this road coils itself around the bases of these mountains. Wait till my next. Love to all.

Yr af. Son

J. H. Kidd

RECOGNIZING THAT HIS MEN were very unhappy with their circumstances and realizing that their morale was terrible, Kidd addressed his regiment. According to cavalryman Franklin P. Grommon, Kidd gave "a short but good speech . . . concerning the state of things. He says we will have to stay our time out now & he said that it was orders from the War Department that we should. it dont look right but we must stand it it seems for [a] few months longer. Then we hope they will be content to let us go home in piece. . . . [Kidd's speech] has made the boys feel a good deal better & I for one feel some better than at first."[58]

As the Wolverines prepared to march, their morale was only slightly better; some of their comrades of the 1st Michigan were discharged. Further, they did not like hearing that the Michigan Brigade would be broken up to serve in scattered detachments. Greatly discontented, the men prepared for their next expedition with a great deal of reluctance and uncertainty.

On June 16, Kidd noted in his diary, "Getting ready to move. Orders to move tomorrow."[59] The orders made it clear that the march would be a long one. As he prepared to march, Kidd again scribbled a letter, not knowing when he would be coming home.

Headqrs 6th Mich Cavalry
Fort Leavenworth, Dept. NW
Kansas
June 16th 1865

Dear Mother and Father

You last heard of me through the letter sent by Col Vinton in which I left myself at Wheeling. From that place I came via Columbus and Cincinnati and to St. Louis. A thousand incidents of the journey I would like to relate but have not time. From St. Louis I came by boat to this point where I found the regiment all well. We are under orders to march today. I go alone. The other regiments follow in a day or two. The following are my orders.

'Col J H Kidd
Comdg 6th Mich Cav,

Col, you will march with your Regt tomorrow morning for Julesburg, C.T.,[60] reporting to Brig. Gen. P. E. Connor commanding Dept. of the Plains. Thirty (30) days rations will be furnished you in the supply train and 5 days will be carried. Have your men carry 15 lbs of grain on their horses. A.A.Q.M. T Ballard[61] will order a forage train with one day supply to go out with you to where you encamp the first night. You will procure a supply of ammunition this evening, 200 rounds per man, 40 to be carried by the men and the remainder in the squadron wagons. You will report your arrival at Fort Kearny to Genl Dodge and Genl Connor by telegraph.'

You will use your own discretion about the distance you march each day, but Genl Dodge is anxious that you get through as soon as possible. I will follow you in two or three days.

Very respectfully
Yr Ob servt
P Stagg
Brvt Brig. Gen. Commdg

Julesburg[62] is about 500 miles west of here and, in the n.e. corner of Colorado T. I recd your letter urging me to resign but have concluded to wait and be mustered out with the old men whose time expires October 11th, 1865. We shall perhaps go through as far as Salt Lake City if not further. You may however expect me home if alive in the fall. Col Vinton has gone home on 10 days leave. Expects to see you. I will write often. I expect a pleasant trip.

I met on the boat Wm. Buts, formerly of Chicago, now connected with the army. Said he knew my father *"intimately"* and came a long distance on purpose to visit me. Please write and tell me all about him. What manner of man he is. Says he was in lumber business etc.; and promised to write you. I am working hard to equip the command and get off today. Will tell you more next time. Love to all.

Your aff. son

J. H. Kidd

INSTEAD OF GOING home, Kidd was starting a new chapter of his military career as a reluctant Indian fighter. It was not a duty he relished.

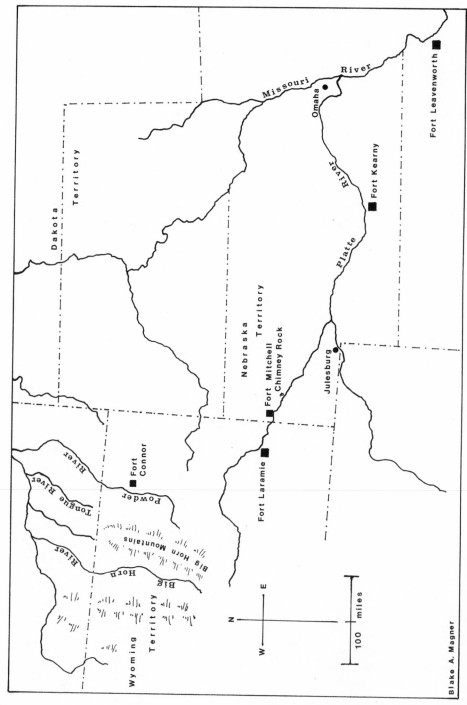

The Powder River Indian Expedition.

Blake A. Magner

7

Reluctant Indian Fighter

The fact cannot be disguised that there was and is a bitter feeling among us against the authors of this wild goose chase.

Kɪᴅᴅ ʟᴇᴅ ᴛʜᴇ ʟᴇꜰᴛ ᴄᴏʟᴜᴍɴ out of camp as ordered. His force consisted of ninety officers and men of the 7th Iowa Cavalry, ninety officers and men of the 11th Ohio Cavalry, two hundred officers and men of the 6th Michigan, and ninety-five officers and men of the Pawnee Scouts, an Indian force friendly to the Federal government—altogether a total of approximately 475 officers and men.[1] They headed north-northwest toward Fort Laramie, on the North Platte River. The march was scenic; one trooper observed that it was "a delightful country" and that "everything here is wild, romantic, picturesque."[2] Kidd's friend and tentmate, Capt. Benjamin F. Rockafellow, kept a diary of the march. When the march began, Rockafellow raved about "the splendid prairie country" and "the finest rolling prairie in the world." Just a week later, his tune changed, and he complained of bears and rattlesnakes and "nothing but prairie, prairie" in the "most worthless country" he had ever seen.[3]

On July 2, Kidd noted his own boredom in his diary: "Today being Sunday I concluded to remain in camp, merely moving to a more convenient camp for water. Slept all the forenoon and finished my letter to Kate in the afternoon. . . . Had a dress parade in the evening. Storm intervened and stopped it. . . . No services, having no chaplain."[4] On July 4, the column reached Fort Kearny, where the Wolverines found the garrison drunkenly celebrating the holiday. Later that day, Kidd received telegraphed orders from Connor to report to Fort Laramie.[5]

Kidd observed and evaluated the garrison at Fort Kearny during his short stay there. He noted in his diary, "The 1st Neb. Cav. is on duty here. Do not consider this a first class regiment."[6] Kidd had no idea how accurate his assessment was; only a few days later, the men of the 1st Nebraska mutinied. On July 21, Connor reported to Dodge that "part of the First Nebraska Cavalry stationed at Kearny claim, as the war is over, that they are entitled to discharge, and have mutinied. I have ordered Colonel Heath to suppress it with grape and canister, and bring the leaders to trial."[7] Capt. Palmer, the quartermaster officer for the expedition, recorded in his diary that it was "a lively little matinee" and that the men of the 1st Nebraska believed that "they had not lost any red devils and were not disposed to hunt for any." Faced with "two howitzers, double shotted," and orders to allow the grape and canister to do the talking for it, Heath's force gave the mutineers five minutes to surrender, which they wisely did. Seven ringleaders of the mutiny were arrested and the unhappy balance of the regiment set off on "the dismal, unprofitable, inglorious hunt for 'scalp lifters.'"[8]

Kidd's column moved out on the morning of the 6th. The march was tedious and unpleasant, as he recounted in his diary: "Trouble with knats, a sort of an infinitesimal atom of life, which tickles the nostrils inserts itself into the ears and inflames the eyes. Coming in swarms from which escape is impossible."[9] He continued to complain about the gnats for days. The gnats were soon joined by mosquitoes and buffalo flies. The combination of insects, dust, and scorching heat made the march miserable for all involved. On July 7, Kidd's father sent unwelcome news: "My own health [is good] except I have to much to do am very thin and weak am not fully able to do portions of the laborious business I am obliged to run."

He continued, "I hope this will find you well and in good spirits and that you may have a good time . . . and return home as soon as your time is out."[10] On July 11, more unpleasant news arrived:

> Headquarters Mich Cav Brig
> Cottonwood
> July 11th 1865

Col. J. H. Kidd
Comdg 6th Mich Cav.
Col,

You will proceed with all dispatch to Fort Laramie reporting to Genl.

Connor at that place. Draw sufficient store at Julesburg to take you through. Genl. Connor is anxious to get you there as soon as possible.

Very respectfully

Yr obdt Servt

P. Stagg

Bvt. Brig. Gen. Commanding

KIDD MARCHED twenty-eight miles the next day, his little force joined by sixty-five men led by Capt. Rockafellow. On July 13, arriving at the Rising Sun Ranch, about fifty miles from Julesburg, Kidd met the owner, C. C. Mann, who invited Kidd and his officers to join him for a champagne dinner, which included oysters, cake, and strawberries.[11]

Kidd and his troopers arrived at Julesburg early on the afternoon of July 15; the next day, he received orders from Connor to leave Julesburg and march for Laramie. The troopers were unhappy and demoralized. Kidd noted in his diary, "Everybody wants to go home and these plains are consigned in the curses of men and officers to a worse place than any of them covet for themselves." To try to cheer himself, Kidd and Don Lovell rode off in search of antelope and saw several herds. The relief was brief; the march went on.[12]

During Kidd's march to Julesburg, the Michigan Brigade was broken up. On July 18, Stagg was ordered to report for duty at headquarters at Fort Laramie, and the regiments of the brigade scattered. The 1st Michigan Cavalry was sent to Camp Collins, Colorado, and the 7th Michigan ordered to report to Fort Laramie. The days of the Wolverines serving as a cohesive unit were over.[13]

Capt. Rockafellow, Kidd's messmate and friend, recorded in his diary on July 20, "As Regt. moved out Col Kidd and several officers went ahead and planted our Regt. Colors . . . on pinnacle of Court House Rock. We were lustily cheered by boys." The regiment went into camp that evening, prompting Rockafellow to recall, "Had fine time playing whist with Col., Capt. Lovell & Lt. Moon. Moved my 'bed' to Cols tent. Sport plenty this evening and kept up until late hour."[14] On July 21, the column arrived at Chimney Rock, "a still more singular freak of nature" than Kidd had seen to date. He described it as "a pyramid shaped mound risen perhaps 300 feet from the shoots of a perpendicular rock a hundred feet higher resembling nothing more than a chimney."[15] He climbed part way up the rock and "planted Regt. colors on highest point which could be reached."[16] Camping near Chimney Rock, Kidd wrote a long letter home.

> On the N. Branch of the Platte River
> About 113 miles from Julesburg, C.T.
> On the road to Fort Laramie, In
> camp

Friday July 21st 1865

Dear Father

Your letter of the 23rd ultimo was received but a day or two since: and was none the less acceptable because I had not heard from you in a long time. Your surmise that I would soon be off across the plains, as you of course are already aware has proved true. I have written twice since we left once the 19th June and once the 1st July, both times I believe to Kate. I ought to have written oftener and supposed I had but time flies with such amazing swiftness that I did not keep a diary. I should not know the day of week or month; one almost before I was aware of it nearly a month has elapsed.

My last was mailed at Fort Kearny but written a day or two before my arrival there. At that place I spent the 4th of July and a duller, more unenthusiastic 4th I never saw. Far away from everybody except ourselves and the few officers on duty at the Fort, with melancholy & bitter feelings we recalled the events of that day in years past and thought of the celebrations that jubilant and over-flowing patriotism would indulge in at the north, on the first anniversary of our independence after the downfall of the great rebellion. Thought of gay and festive scenes, of a grand gala-day everywhere, thought of the ovations to the returning soldiers, of the praises of their gallantry, the greetings of friends and relatives long-separated. Of our fathers and mothers, sisters, brothers, that *we* were precluded from participation in all this, shut out from the enjoyment of what was granted to those who had served their Country no more faithfully nor longer in the field. Many a tear was seen to fall, and many a muttered curse was heard, as we ruminated in the solitude of the boundless western prairies upon the fickleness of *justice* the heartlessness of intrigue. The fact cannot be disguised that there was and is a bitter feeling among us against the authors of this wild goose chase, and the men are not slow to say that had I refused to come with them they would have suffered the consequences of open mutiny rather than have stirred a step. I have had no trouble. My men are attached to me and if we are allowed to go home when our time expires there will be no trouble, otherwise I anticipate it. If the Gov. of Mich. and the friends of the regiment at home would make the exertion they ought to with the authorities at Washington, this can be brought about. Enough of this. I could write a volume about the incidents of our journey that would probably be interesting to you, but must restrict myself to the space. Fort Kearny, where I was July 4th is about 300 miles from Leavenworth in Nebraska Territory. It is like Fort L. simply a collection of barracks, answering for quarters for troops and a depot of supplies. Here is where the two great routes, from Omaha and Leavenworth converge. At this point we strike the South Fork of the Platte River, along which we found plenty of grass for our stock. This stream in some places bet 2 & 3 miles wide, is very shallow and were it not, for the quicksand bottom, fordable at any point. It is of course not navigable: A river 2 or 3 miles wide, so shallow that a man can wade across it is a phenomenon. After leaving the Little Blue we were obliged to march 35 miles without water or rest, on a hot and dusty day. Starting at 6 o'clock in the morning we pushed our way, blinded by dust and choked with thirst, across a barren plain, until 3 o'clock in the afternoon when our eyes were gladdened with a sight of the woods fringing the banks of the Platte yet 8 miles distant and after reaching it, we found our visions of comfort only half-realized, for the wood was across the river, out of reach the grass poor and the river water muddy, and no other for the horses or ourselves. We camped near a dirty little burg of *"Adobe"* huts (huts built of turfs) dignified by the name of Dogtown. For the first time we were restricted to *"Buffalo chips"* for fuel. This novel kind of fuel answers very well in dry weather as a substitute for wood.

The next day we reached the Fort and I have already told you of that. We went in with flying colors but met with no reception, though afterwards the officers about the Fort were very hospitable, invited us to their 4th of July ball in the evening, and gave us of the good things that they had. Here I recd a telegram from Brig. Gen Conner to proceed without delay to Fort Laramie which would be 200 miles beyond Julesburg, where to thence I know not. We are all decidedly disinclined to further locomotion in this direction. The question is very pertinently asked how we are to get back this fall. Please write. Give my love to all the folks out home and remember me to friends.

Yr affectionate son
J. H. Kidd

THE NEXT DAY, in atrocious weather, the column reached Fort Mitchell, a post only fifty miles from their destination at Fort Laramie. Kidd felt ill and spent a couple of days riding in the back of an ambulance, shielding himself from the effects of the weather. On July 23, Kidd noted in his diary, "Gen. Stagg passed us today in an ambulance. Men in trains are said to have groaned him. I did not hear it."[17] The men's morale continued to deteriorate as they marched; on the 24th, Kidd observed, "Don't want to see any more of this God-Forsaken vicinity. Would be grateful to see a flood sink the whole area."[18]

The next day, thirty-eight days after leaving Fort Leavenworth, the column finally arrived at Fort Laramie, where they found "a dirty, ill-regulated post, situated on the banks of the Laramie a beautiful stream, deep and rapid. The country is barren as Grand Haven sand hills." The 6th Michigan arrived there "half armed" and "no arms here for them." Connor reported that "Much dissatisfaction exists in the Sixth Michigan. . . . They demand their discharge. I will manage them."[19] Waiting for Kidd were orders to lead the left column of the Powder River Indian Expedition, in retaliation for Indian attacks at Platte Bridge Station, approximately 128 miles from Fort Laramie.[20] When Kidd announced orders to the men, they did not receive the news well. Kidd recorded, "Officers at a mutiny appointed a committee consisting of Capts Rockafellow, Lovell and Creevy to confer with General Connor. Nothing accomplished except an 'assurance doubly sure' that we can go out when time expired." Mollified, the men agreed to continue.[21]

On July 27, headquarters learned that a war party of Sioux and Cheyenne, numbering more than one thousand, was attacking the Federal outpost at Platte River Bridge and that the garrison there was nearly out of ammunition. As a result, Connor ordered Kidd to "proceed immediately with the four squadrons ordered to report to you and the five squadrons under commande of Capt. Creevy by forced marches to Platte bridge for the relief and assistance of that garrison."[22] That same day, Rockafellow noted in his diary, "Whiskey was the cause of trouble last night. Col sent Rigby, Corpl. Brannan & Kennedy back to Fort under arrest."[23] In obedience to Connor's orders, Kidd issued the following instructions to his command: "Companies B, C, D, E, F, H, I, L & M will be in readiness to move at 3 o'clock in the afternoon. Five days rations & eighty (80) rounds of carbine or fifty (50) rounds of pistol ammunition will be issued by the Quartermaster and two days forage. The surplus forage and subsistence stores heretofore ordered will be carried in the wagons. Company desks and Regimental HdQtrs will be left in camp. Capt. J. O. Probasco will assume command of the Regiment."[24]

The 6th Michigan marched from Fort Laramie on July 28. Sunday, July 30, was an especially boring day. Kidd noted that he spent a "very dull" day "playing chess and whist whiling away the time to the best advantage possible."[25] He also wrote a letter to his parents.

> "Past Labonte" Dacotah Territory
> 65 miles west of Fort Laramie
> on the Pacific Telegraph route
> About 200 miles E of South Pass in
> the Rocky Mountains on the Platte R.
> Sunday July 30th 1865

Dear Father & Mother

When I left Fort Laramie Thursday evening last I requested Lieutenant Simonds[26] regimental clerk to write you, not expecting to be within mail communications of home for some time. A large party of Sioux and Cheyenne Indians had attacked the post at Platte Bridge, 128 miles west, and killed 27 men wounding 8. I was ordered to their relief. Before reaching this point however it was ascertained that they had gone north towards Powder River and I have recd orders to wait here until orders.

I was booked for the command of a column in the expedition to start yesterday against the Indians in the Powder River country, to take 4 companies of this regiment a company of Artillery a company of Pawnee Indian Scouts and other detachments.

I am so far on the route to be taken by the column which will cross the Platte River 18 miles west of here and leaving the telegraph and mail routes. Will strike off into the interior for a point several hundred miles distant near the boundary line between Dacotah and Montana territories. This expedition is to be commanded by Brig Gen Connor, and will consist of four columns. The left column is the one assigned me. The right column which started out from Omaha is commanded by Col. Cale 2nd Missouri Artillery. The Center by Lt Col of 10th Kansas Cav and another one still by an officer of the 2nd California Cavalry.[27] The Indians have been exceedingly troublesome of late and it is proposed to take vigorous measures against them. But this whole department has undoubtedly been mis-managed not so much perhaps by the officers who have commanded here as by the Government which has heretofore indicated by its policy, the belief that any sort of troops and the fewest no positional supplies could easily vanquish all the Indians in the Northwest. To give you some idea of how the thing runs first understand that Fort Laramie is about 700 miles from Leavenworth, that all supplies are hauled from there by wagons. This wagon transportation has come to be a great business and although the grass is as luxuriant for nearly the whole distance that the cost of keeping the teams is a mere nothing. The Government pays these transporters such enormous prices that they frequently make fortunes of $30,000 and $40,000 a year. And while the Government is selling off immense numbers of splendid teams of mules and horses at Washington for half of what they are worth they are paying $30 a hundred for transporting corn to Fort Laramie, or buying up mules that are so small or young as to be worthless, making forage cost about $20 a bushel, and while so many troops are still in the service 150 men are expected to guard a telegraph line 300 miles long with thousands of Indians ready to pounce upon every small party that goes on the road. After we leave Laramie there is no grass for our horses, and having a very little of the $20 corn I know not what we shall do.

If a full division of Cavalry, had been sent here under a good commander with enough of the Government's superfluous transportation to convey forage to supply the command until the expedition was over. The roads are good, and the corn would simply have cost what it's price was at Leavenworth, and we would have had enough, and could have accomplished something. As it is we have a few men scattered from Dan to Beer Sheba with forage enough to keep about one horse. I predict the expedition will be a failure and ought to be. Our horses and mules will starve unless we find some grass as we progress.

The Government is commencing this Indian war just as it commenced the Rebellion and until it has had experienced enough to see the folly of exposing a few men when it has men enough it will not be finished. 1500 Indians attacked a party of 20, and of course killed them, and 128 miles off [I] am ordered to help them by forced marches without forage over a country where there is no grass and of course the Indians would be gone when I got there anyway.[28] But now about coming home. I have got the promise that we can be mustered-out when our time expires the 11th of October and for that matter we shall come then anyway. It is supposed that these difficulties will be settled by that time and you may safely expect to see me by December. I do not hear from home often. Kate has not answered my two last. With love to all I am

Yrs. Affectionately
J. H. Kidd

Lt. Simonds wrote to James M. Kidd on August 1, "In compliance with a request from your son, Col. Kidd, I have the pleasure of announcing to you the safe arrival of himself and Regiment at this post on the 25th ult. after a journey of some thirty-eight days from Fort Leavenworth, Kan." Simonds reported the formation of the Powder River Indian Expedition and informed James M. Kidd of his son's role in the coming campaign. Simonds concluded: "There has been but little sickness in the regiment since we left the Missouri River and the men enjoyed the trip very well, but *home* is quite a consideration with them now that the war is over & some felt that there was great injustice, and justly too, at being ordered so far from home when having but a short term to serve. However they moved out cheerfully with the Col. knowing that he had done all in his power to comply with their wishes to see their homes."[29]

On August 1, Connor joined Kidd's little force and assumed personal command. Connor's arrival gave Kidd the opportunity to discuss his concerns with the general, prompting Rockafellow to note, "Col. Kidd talked very plainly to [Connor]. I expect we will have considerable hard work, receive no credit for the men we may lose and do as well as we may receive finally an unfavorable report."[30]

Connor's operational orders, which were eventually countermanded by Maj. Gen. John Pope, the commander of the Department of the Missouri, were: "You will not receive overtures of peace or submission from Indians, but will attack and kill every male Indian over twelve years of age." Pope responded by directing General Dodge, "These instructions are atrocious, and are in direct violation of my repeated orders. You will please take immediate steps to countermand such orders. If any such orders as General Connor's are carried out, it will be disgraceful to the government, and will cost him his commission, if not worse."[31]

The column marched on July 31, Kidd observing that the expedition "promises anything but a pleasant trip. We are all discouraged and demoralized. Have no heart in the work. Our only ambition being to 'worry about the time' until the 11th of October."[32] Two days later, he wrote to his sister Kate during a break in the march.

Dakota Territory
Hd Qrs Left Column
Powder River Ind. Expedition
Wednesday Aug 4, 1865

Dear Kate

My diary says that tonight we have been constantly on the march west-
ward and northwest fifty three (53) days since leaving Leavenworth. That
we have marched 850 miles in that time. The particulars of that march
are imperfectly recorded in that diary. I have in past given you in the letters I have written home (perhaps you have not recd them all) the last was
written from Labonte on the 31st ultimo. Mail communications are so
irregular and remote that I do not expect you to receive half of what I
write. In what I have written I have attempted to give you an idea of this
to me entirely-new kind of life, the continually shifting scenes—the
country—its inhabitants, its products and characteristics. A thousand and
one things have of course been omitted. To fully appreciate it you must
yourself be present. When I left Julesburg and crossed the Platte where
our horses had to swim I thought I left civilization behind, but not till
after marching to Fort Laramie did I bid farewell with all intercourse with
the world. I told you in my letter from Labonte to Father and Mother of
my departure from Laramie and the reasons therefor; I went only to that
point when I was ordered to Labonte crossing 50 miles from Laramie the
rendezvous of my column of the P.R. Ind. Expedition and commencing
at that point I shall endeavor to make my letters home more a diary of
the occurrences of each than otherwise and as they will always be written
after marching you will excuse absence of rhetorical flourishes etc. If you
do not receive such diaries you may rest satisfied that they are lost in trans-
mittal. Since I *had* to come off west I am glad I am sent so far for I shall
see things that few who have not dared much have ever seen; we shall visit
country unknown except to the hunter and trapper or explorer and of late
undisturbed by them; a country where no road marks the passage of previous parties. We are to pioneer our way through a region but imperfectly
represented in the geographies, where Indians alone make their home,
and where buffalo and antelope will reward the hunter; where the hostile
bands of Indians falling back before the progress of civilization still implac-
able and untameable make war upon each other hunting, plan robbing
and murdering expeditions upon the remote lines of communication
between east and west. We shall see many strange, new things, shall in-

crease our find of useful information, and perhaps may undergo something of danger and hardship, and enjoy much of adventure and sport. I'm glad thrice glad I was not left to linger away my time around some fort or post. Two months of something new, romantic, adventurous, perhaps perilous and if perchance the fates do not oppose us. "Richard's himself again."

Over yonder is Company "A" of the "Pawnee Scouts," a co of about 100 Pawnee Indians a tribe which is friendly and fights on our side unless they can catch a white man a long ways from home when they amuse themselves by scalping him and attributing it to Sioux. They are going down to fight their inveterate enemies the Sioux into whose country they have never before penetrated so far. They are commanded by Capt North,[33] a very gentleman who talks Pawnee as fluently as his own tongue. These Indians are armed with bows and arrows, guns & pistols and mounted on ponies a hardy animal which goes up or down hill with equal facility and lives on cottonwood bark when grass can't be had. They are very much like white men *and women.* Some are handsome, some are *not,* some comb their hair and wash their faces, others do not. They are of fine *physique,* long, straight, black hair, the color of your tea kettle and have splendid teeth. They all wear the U.S. uniform decorated in some instances with cross grills, hen-feathers, corn stalks and other fantastic gur-gows characteristic of "ye poor Indian." They are inveterate gamblers and the bravest of all the tribes of Indians.

For fear that if I resume here to the last that either I shall have exhausted my powers of description (which at the best are inadequate) or that I shall forget him entirely, I'll throw Capt Marshall's Company [F 11th Ohio Cavalry] "into line just here." A company of 80 good well-armed men commanded by a certain Marshall whose surname is Capt a man with a great deal of whiskers very little sense and no brains who says, "I ken jest take that air company o men then can bring 'em down yer and throw em into line up yonder I ken jest lick any number o men you ken bring agin em." One of those meddlesome officers, self-conceited, ignorant men who are always successful in making themselves ridiculous—and their neighbors uncomfortable. You may hear of him hereafter. Then there is a small detachment of the signal corps, two officers Lieutenants Brown and Richards[34] in charge. They like us here, come down from Washington to do duty in the *Wilderness,* nice fellows sort of cultured and refined and pleasant companions *"du voyage."* I must not omit mention of O'Bryan's battery.[35] Its Capt O'B is a good sort of a person who walks very straight, deeply impressed with his own importance and responsibility but well-meaning and brave, what shall I say of his battery—a motley assortment of pieces all sorts and calibres, a three inch rifled gun, a brass ten pounder, a howitzer, several guns designated by the euphonious appellation "Jacksons," all in wretched order, drawn by poor horses, badly managed, sort of a burlesque on the name of artillery, but good enough probably to *scare Indians.* Here comes our train 100 wagons loaded with 150,000 rations to feed the command and to supply a post to be established somewhere in the Powder River Country: rations of moldy flour petrified hard tack and bacon. Ten sutlers wagons loaded with goods to swindle any one of us who finds it necessary or convenient to submit to process. Last and not least our General and his staff. Gen Connor whose real name I suppose is Patrick O'Connor, is an Irishman who in respect to national characteristics out-Herods Herod. A man of perhaps 40 or 45 years who has a wife and two children at Laramie. He was in the Mexican War and was wounded at Buena Vista. Originally col of the 2nd Cal Cav he was promoted to Brig Gen for an affair with Indians in which his regt was engaged. Some knowing ones maliciously assert that for what one of his subordinates (now serving on the staff) did he himself took the credit and hence his promotion, but malice assails everyone and this never be not true. He has for a long time been in command of the Dept of the Plains embracing near Fort Kearny and the country north and has in some way earned the sobriquet of Connor the Indian fighter although never I believe engaged with them since the affair alluded to. He appears to be a strict disciplinarian and not an unpleasant man to be with although not sociable at all. He accompanies this column. A little modest man with black mustache, who signs himself C G Laurent AAG[36] runs the Adjutant General's office. He came up from St. Louis to take this position. He never talks, and minds his own business. Two originals are Capt Robins, Chief Engineer, and Lieut Jewett ADC,[37] standing each over six feet, and well proportioned. They are physically immense men. They have been to California in the mines, have roughed it, fought Indians and all that, carry gold watches, with heavy chains, are shrewd, well educated, and thorough sharpers, and will take the spin chargers out of any fellow who is fool enough to bet on cards. Our Quartermaster who wears a red shirt[38] and here I will leave us and for the events of the subsequent march wait. Give my love to all. I do not hear from you any more.

Before I start you off on the P.R. Expedition let me give you an idea of our *"outfit,"* the name they give in this country to everything from a lady's wardrobe to a Brig General's command. Let me tell you what and who it was that, assembled on the banks of the Platte at Labonte Crossing, Tuesday the 1st day of August 1865 constituted the "left" column of the Powder River I.E. and trust me: I will attempt to be neither facetious nor critical in my description. In the first place four companies of our regiment, F, H, I and M commanded by Capt Rockafellow, small companies well-worn, good companies and not ill mannered; assuming, perhaps, a little of the swagger and devil-may-care air characteristic of men whose time's about out and who think they are near enough citizens to enjoy that prerogative which allows a civilian to do what he has a mind to, but who submit with a quiet good grace to the order which compels them to still serve their "beloved country" for the benefit of the Government, its Generals, or contractors, or "any other man." These are scattered around upon the bank, some fishing, some cooking, some washing, sleeping, eating & what not the usual picture of a camp with nothing to do waiting for orders to move. The officers with us are Lovell, Rockafellow, Cole, Kellogg, Dr Johnson, Curtiss, Moon, Stone, Gould,[39] good fellows all.

About our *"mess,"* four of us, Lovell, Rockafellow, Dr J and your servant, Don, Goodfellow, Doc and Col for short: all sleep in one tent, if not under one blanket, for I have "raised myself from the ground" at night in spite of the rattlesnakes. We all gather around the stove festive board, mealtimes. We have provided ourselves with say 10 lbs sugar, ditto coffee, 20 lbs apples, 50 lbs bacon and hams, 10 lbs "consecrated" (desiccated) potatoes (sort of a cross between corn-meal and saw-dust), a few cans of peaches, plenty of smoking tobacco pipes and matches. "Don" looks healthy but homesick. "Good fellow" very pale on account of the reflection from his mustachios. Doc has his hair cropped short and looks like a candidate for Congress, after he has made the necessary pledges to his *"friends"* to secure his election, i.e., as though all sold but the ears. As for myself as purposeless and useless as ever, the same except that I have taken to wearing long hair and reading novels, also eat pork and smoke (that same meerschaun you coveted so much from when I was at home on furlough). Good tobacco and cigars however I ignore entirely, like beefsteak (because they can't be had). Then I am not so handsome as formerly. I am getting old-looking and I fear positively ugly. My hair is coming out and I shall soon be bald. That crook in my nose, you will recollect of, is becoming too palpable and lends a wry and unseemly expression to features that were it not for this and somewhat too red an appearance would not be positively unattractive. However do not get alarmed about me nor think of me as one dead.

[The balance of the letter is missing.]

THINGS DID NOT IMPROVE. On August 7, Kidd recorded, "Capts. Rockafellow, Lovell Cale and myself played 7 games of whist yesterday before we discovered that it was Sunday, and feel not a little ashamed of it. Today, Capt Lovell & Dr. went out with Pawnees and had a buffalo hunt. Had a fine time and came in full of stories of their exploits. 3 buffaloes were killed by the party and as they fired their revolvers at them, hitting as they were claiming a share of the honor."[40]

Despite these pleasant respites, the march continued, the column moving farther to the north and west of Fort Laramie, proceeding up the Powder River, finding evidence that the Indians had fled the area. On August 9, Captain Palmer described the column's first look at the Big Horn Mountains: "The sun so shone as to fall with full blaze upon the southern and southwestern sides of Cloud Peak, which is about ten thousand feet above sea level, and the whole snow-covered range so clearly blended with the sky as to leave it in doubt whether all was not a mass of bright cloud."[41]

On August 12, the column went into camp again. Twenty-five members of the 6th Michigan under command of Connor's aide, Lt. Oscar Jewett, went up river to look for a location for the construction of a new military post. They marched twenty-five miles up river and back the same day.[42] The next day, Kidd observed, "Took a bath in the morning and 'rugged out' in our best. With due respect for the day refrained from card playing and all improper exercises. In the utter absence of chaplains, had no services."[43] On August 15, Connor and Kidd laid out a fort to be established on the east side of the river. Kidd was assigned command of the new post.

Head Quarters Left Column
P. R. Ind. Expedition
Powder River Dacotah Territory
Aug. 15, 1865

General Order
No. 1

I. In pursuance of instructions from Brig General P. E. Connor comdg District of the Plains, a military post is hereby established at this point to be known as *Fort Connor.*

II. The following is declared the military reserve pertaining to this post, commencing at a point ten (10) miles due north of garrison Flagstaff, running thence east in ten (10) miles thence south twenty (20) miles thence west twenty (20) miles, thence north twenty (20) miles and thence east ten (10) miles to the place of starting.

> J. H. Kidd
> Col 6th Mich Cav
> Comdg

THE NEXT DAY, Kidd moved his command to the site of the new fort, and construction began. The task gave the men something to do, and "every soldier and all the teamsters who could be urged to work were supplied with axes and the men seemed to enjoy the exercise, chopping trees and cutting stockade timber."[44] Connor reported to Dodge that the post was a "splendid location" and that the men were "now building block-houses and stockades. The post is about eighty miles from Deer Creek Station."[45] Another observer noted, "The site has been described as an unusually fine one, the only serious drawback being an almost total absence of good hay land. Crude buildings stood on the mesa which rose more than one hundred feet above the river and extended to a line of white bluffs over five miles to the west."[46] The location was not the greatest. One newspaper correspondent called the river "the filthiest stream in America or elsewhere." Another described it as "too thick to drink and too thin to plow," and also as "four hundred miles long, a mile wide, and an inch deep." In its upper reaches, it is a stream of "deep and narrow canyons fringed with cottonwood, ash, and various kinds of berry bushes which give fine protection against the winds of winter and made it another favorite camping place of the Sioux."[47]

Connor periodically visited the site to check on the progress of the construction and apparently confided in Kidd, prompting Kidd to comment, "General Connor down occasionally to blow off. Think his Irish spleen is somewhat out of repair. Self contemplation alone seems to ease him."[48]

On August 17, the Pawnee scouts had an engagement with Cheyenne warriors. That night, Kidd, accompanied by Capts. Rockafellow, Lovell, Tubbs, and Kellogg and Lts. Stone, Moon, and Curtiss went to the Pawnee camp to see the scouts' war dance. As Rockafellow recorded, it was quite a spectacle:

> Was quite dark. They had large fire built and Indians dressed in squaw traps they captured were dancing inside ring with the trophies of chase

about them, carried scalps which they had tattooed or rather stretched on small round hoops and colored flesh very red with their Tanning process. Had them on same sticks were brought in on. Other Indians were dancing around circles and striking sort of drum, shaking bells, whooping and singing.

All of a sudden old Indian commenced a sing song announcement which was about punishing the braves and telling what they did. . . . The dancing at once stopped and they gave strictest attention though the responses were less prompt and enthusiastic. One buck had belt of Cheyenne woman which was five inches wide and ornamented with silver brooches and brass buttons.[49]

On August 20, Kidd led a scout after a band of Indians. Taking twenty-five men, Kidd "struck the Indian trail and followed it about 12 miles coming onto a party estimated at 500 or 1000. Concluded that discretion was the better part of valor as I was a long way from reinforcements and returned without a fight."[50] As a consequence, the next day Connor sent the entire force after the Indians, who had fled. Once again, his efforts yielded nothing but frustration. The following day, Kidd recorded that "General Connor moved with left column P.R.E. this morning. 'Adieu: Adieu: Adieu. And If forever then forever fare-thee-well.' Had a bit of spicy conversation respecting relieving us on time. Did not get much satisfaction, and told him he would have no right to keep us over our time. He asked if I would abandon this post if not relieved."[51]

That same day, Kidd's father wrote a long letter, stating, "Sorry you were ordered off so far, but hope it will come out all right." He continued, "In regard to your Expedition the time is so short I would try and carry it out to the end of your time without a complaint. . . . Your Michigan Brigade has earned for its self by its industry & hard work a name that must not now be spoiled by any misstep. . . . I advise you to do all you can to retain your honor, already obtained." Kidd's father then reported on his efforts to secure the discharge of the 6th Michigan and concluded that he was confident that its men would be released from service upon expiration of their terms.[52]

Happy news finally arrived at Fort Connor on August 25. That day, Kidd received orders to send an armed guard to Little Horn to escort an officer to Fort Connor to relieve Kidd and then to "proceed with that portion of the regiment under my immediate command to Fort Laramie and report . . . for further orders. This gives highest satisfaction."[53] Rockafellow noted in his diary that Kidd had been given the name Chi-to-tak-kah, or "White Man," by the Indians traveling with the column.[54]

On August 28, without Kidd or the men of the 6th Michigan participating, the Powder River Indian Expedition climaxed. Connor led his forces in a surprise attack on an Arapaho village on the Tongue River, north of the Powder River. After a five-hour fight, Connor's troopers and their Pawnee allies destroyed 250 Indian lodges, killed 50 inhabitants including women and children, and confiscated all of the village ponies and horses. Connor pushed north and then doubled back along the Powder River, continuing to engage small bands of Indians along the way. The expedition was a failure, with the leaders of the two columns, Cole and Walker, fumbling their way along the line of march. Ironically, George Custer later lead a similar expedition over much of the same ground eleven years later and lost his life in the process.[55]

One modern historian has noted, "It was a case of the blind leading the blind; the reconnaissance of the troops was so poor that they actually passed between a large camp of hostiles—some fifteen hundred to two thousand lodges—on the Powder River, and the Uncpapa camp of Sitting Bull and Black Moon—which was even larger—on the Little Missouri without being aware of the existence of either camp, and without seeing a hostile Indian."[56] Later in September, warriors seeking revenge for Connor's depredations on the Tongue River ambushed him. Connor's prestige was greatly diminished by these ambushes, and his expedition ended in failure a few days later. Connor was stigmatized for killing women and children and his army career was over within a year.[57]

Dodge blamed the failure of the expedition on the column commanders. He wrote, "The failure on the part of General Connor's column commanders to join him at the point designated no doubt prevented him from carrying out his plans fully and successfully."[58] Presumably, this did not apply to Kidd, because Connor rode with Kidd's column. Ironically, Kidd's idol, George A. Custer, died twelve years later, leading another doomed expedition against the Sioux over much of the same ground. However, unlike Connor's failure, Custer's failure cost him his life, as well as the lives of more than 250 members of the 7th U.S. Cavalry.

Because Connor also failed, Kidd's small command suffered. In mid-August, Connor ordered an escort of twenty men of the 6th Michigan Cavalry, under command of Capt. Osmer F. Cole, to escort a party of civilian prospectors to the gold fields of Montana. Three days after the attack on the Tongue River village, angry warriors attacked Cole's party and killed Cole, who had been scouting in advance of the civilians. When his men found his body, it had five arrows in it. A friend of Cole's wrote, "He was a young man of fine talents, brave and genial in his manners, and was much lamented by the command."[59] Two of Cole's men, Sgt. William Hall and Pvt. Henry E. Evans, escaped to bring word to the nearest garrison. They covered fifty miles on foot, "through a wild and to them an unknown country, swarming with hostile Indians,"[60] and led a rescue party to find the remaining civilians and bring them to safety.

In the interim, Kidd wrote little in his diary other than reiterating his utter boredom and his wish to go home. Kidd received a gift on September 2, when the post sutler presented him with a smoking pipe belonging to Swift Bear, a chief of the Ogalala Sioux.[61] On September 4, Rockafellow eloquently recorded in his diary the efforts that he and Kidd took to break the tedium: "Col and I took a walk and obeying divine injunction (for be it understood the life we live at a Fort is a sluggard kind, rise at 8 A.M. and breakfast. Dinner 4 P.M.) went 'to the Ant to consider her ways & gain wisdom.' We placed pieces of fruit cake about their hill. This pleased them and with great energy they set to work to secure their prise and add to their stock for wintry days. A gun cap, match, tooth pick, piece of saltpeter & lead pencil all displeased them and they worked with equal energy to rid themselves of the nuisances."[62]

While waiting for the regiment to be relieved, Kidd "entered into a solemn obligation with Capt. R[ockafellow] to stick to our temperance or total abstinence for 10 years. Ale excepted."[63] The reasons for taking this solemn oath were not disclosed, but Kidd gave some sense of the reason in an article written years after the war. While recuperating from the wound he received at Falling Waters, Kidd attended a temperance lecture in Michigan, wherein he learned of the evils of using alcohol and its effects on the body.[64]

On September 5, Kidd recorded, "Have concluded to start tomorrow with 20 or 25 men on a hunting expedition to Big Horn Mountains. Making my details cleaning up arms and getting ready today. . . . Dispatch from Norton states 1st 6th and 7th to be consolidated, the old men going home. Men are wanted to make out the papers."[65] Kidd also wrote home just before departing on the hunting expedition.

Fort Connor Dakota Terr.
September 6 1865

Dear Father,

As I am about to send a party to escort an official communication to the mail-route. I will write a line, informing you of the condition of our affairs. The 1st, 6th and 7th Mich Cav regts are to be consolidated into one regiment, all men whose terms of service does not expire prior to Feby 1st 1866, remaining in the service. One Captain, and 2 Lieutenants to each one hundred men. The papers preparatory to the consolidation are to be in by the 15th instant. I hope there will be no delay in effecting this arrangement for I am anxious to get home and shall do so as speedily as possible. I am going out today with a few men on a three days hunt into the bear, elk and buffalo country and expect. Capt Lovell[66] who went with the escort to Big Horn will be here when I return, in which event I shall start immediately for Laramie. I have not been very well for a few days. Attribute it to the inactivity of post life. Expect that the exercise and excitement of hunting will cure me.

I get very little news from Michigan. If you send any papers they are purloined from the mail before reaching me for I have not seen one since I came into this country, and your letters are few and far between. The weather which has been very hot has moderated and the nights are now quite cold. A rain storm is a novelty which we have not seen. Everything parched, dust intolerable.

I hope to have the entire regiment mustered out but those men who enlisted late getting large bounties cannot complain if they are required to carry out their contracts with the Government.

There are many however who enlisted two years ago who have done good service and did not receive large bounties, and who have earned an honorable discharge but the loss of too many men would deprive somebody of a commission and a good fat sinecure. As for me nothing could induce me to remain longer in the service. I want to get on a suit of citizen's clothes and proclaim myself a free man once more. I want to get into some sort of business and not be dependent on Uncle Sam. If I am not mistaken I shall never trouble the government for place, preferring some employment which shall owe its recompense to my own exertions. With love to all I am

Yours affectionately,
J. H. Kidd

THE HUNTING EXPEDITION almost met disaster soon after its start. Taking his small force of men into the hills, Kidd spotted heavy smoke rising on the other side of the mountains. Riding ahead to investigate the source, Kidd spotted a large Indian village and wisely turned back the next day, with no game to show for his efforts.[67]

Arriving back at camp, Kidd was met by General Dodge and a party of dignitaries. A lengthy discussion about the discharge of the men of the 6th Michigan took place. Evidently, the discussion went well, for Kidd commented, "Everything is satisfactory about going home. Gen. D. is very courteous, and I have now no fear."[68] Two days later, Kidd wrote his father again.

Fort Connor, D.T.

Sept 9, 1865

Dear Father

An opportunity offers to send a letter through to Fort Laramie, and I write to say that we are all right here, and I have no reason to change my mind in reference to the time I shall be at home. General Dodge came here yesterday with a small escort. I gave him a grand reception. He took dinner with me, and everything is arranged satisfactorily so far as the old men are concerned. We are to proceed in a few days to Leavenworth whence I suppose to Detroit before being mustered out. We shall probably not be dismounted till we get to Leavenworth. Capt Terrell[69] who went to Little Horn has not returned, expect him today or tomorrow.

Capt Kellogg who went 14 days ago with an escort of 15 men to Gen Connor with mail has not returned, and I am somewhat apprehensive for his safety as I have seen signs of Indians, and he would have to come 200 miles through their country. I hope to see him today. With Gen Dodge here, Mr Kusson Representative in Congress from Iowa, Gen Williamson[70] and several others. We had a pleasant time. We are having the first rain storms since we came here. Weather very cold, which accounts for my irregular penmanship. My fingers in absences of stoves are number. The buffalo have all disappeared from our vicinity. I went 25 miles up the river the other day and saw none. Had plenty of them coming out. Buffalo meat supplying the place of beef but buffalo retreat like the Indian before white men.

All are well here. Hoping to be with you soon. With love to all I am

Yours affectionately

J. H. Kidd

KIDD AND ROCKAFELLOW had an encounter with a grizzly bear on the morning of September 13. A sentry reported the bear's approach, and Kidd and Rockafellow, accompanied by three Pawnee scouts, rode out after the bear. Kidd rode bareback and could not stop his horse as the bear approached. Rockafellow "at once halted & dismounted and as the old fellow came bounding along gave him a shot which fortunately passed through his heart. He only went about twenty rods when one of the Indians fired & bear fell."[71] On September 15, Kidd and Rockafellow went hunting for wolves but did not find any.

On September 17, three days before Connor's forlorn column returned to Fort Connor, the long-awaited orders to leave to go home were finally issued. Kidd promptly marched the 6th Michigan to Fort Laramie as ordered. On the 20th, the column reached Labonte, where the post commander fed the officers a hearty dinner and shared "choice cigars for those who use them." Alcohol also flowed at the dinner. Rockafellow proudly noted his abstinence in his diary, passing the first test of the vow of temperance sworn by him and Kidd. There is no mention of whether Kidd also passed the test. The men continued their leisurely march, finally arriving at Fort Laramie a few days later. On October 7, even more welcome news arrived.

> Head Quarters District of the Plaints
> Office of Assistant Adjutant General
> Fort Laramie D.T. Oct 7th 1865

Special Order

12

In conformity with Paragraph II of Special Field Orders No. 11 Head Quarters U.S. Forces Kansas and the Territories of Sept. 17th 1865 Colonel J. H. Kidd 6th Michigan Cavalry will proceed without delay to Fort Leavenworth Kansas in command of that portion of the Michigan Brigade whose term of service expires prior to February 1st 1866 for muster out.

The proper staff Department will furnish the necessary supplies for the prompt execution of this order.

> By Order of
> Bvt. Major General Wheaton
> Jno. Lewis
> A.A.A. Genl.

CONTINUING THE LONG MARCH east and reaching Fort Kearny in October, Kidd got the unwelcome news that men of the 6th Michigan whose terms of service were *not* about to expire were to be sent to Utah for further service, until their terms finally expired in the spring of 1866. The remaining troopers were consolidated into a single unit, the 1st Michigan Veteran Cavalry. One officer of the 7th Michigan Cavalry echoed the disappointment of those not going home: "Disappointment on October 5th, when an order from the War Department was received, ordering a portion of our command to return East to be mustered out, while a part of the command was ordered to remain in the service and march farther West."[72] These unfortunates were not discharged until March 1866. Then, they discovered that the government allowance granted for travel would not cover the cost of transportation home; it took a special act of the Michigan Legislature to compensate these unhappy men for their inconvenience.[73] The debate went on for months; in the spring of 1866, the *Ionia Sentinel* reported:

> Why an exception should be made in the case of these regiments, we never could comprehend. Already Michigan regiments, recruited in 1862, were on their way to their homes, receiving warm receptions, after nearly three years of service, while these three regiments, which had fought so gallantly and earned an enviable reputation under Custer, were doomed to set their faces towards the setting sun, and march thousands of weary miles; to be scattered in small numbers at intervals of many miles, and, thus placed at the mercy of the ruthless savage, to see many of their noblest comrades pierced by the arrow and left scalpless on the Plains.[74]

Kidd vented his frustration in a letter to his father.

Fort Kearny N.T.
Oct. 24 1865

Dear Father

I arrived here yesterday, resume the march again today. Expect to be 12 days going through not more than 15 at the outside.

We have had lovely weather so far until day before yesterday, since which it has been cold and unpleasant. My health is improving: have been quite out of sorts for a number of weeks, only weigh 119 lbs. but if I continue to improve shall reach a higher figure before I get home. Col Vinton got sick and after we left Laramie got transportation by stage, playing gentleman while I am doing the work as usual.

Indians are already at work on the road. The P.R. Expedition has been a fizzle only equalled by the way in which we are all humbugged in this country.

My men who have some of them less than 8 months to serve have been sent to Utah, while troops who have 18 months to serve and never have done anything are on the road two days in my rear to be mustered-out. Kansas and Missouri troops whose duty is to protect their own frontier, all through political influence and the cause our Generals have their headquarters in those states.

It is an outrage: I am yet in the service and *mum* is the word, but were I out here a profane man I am afraid I should say something that could never be forgiven.

There has been a big tussle for officers in the new regiment. Some portions of my own command I report to say have been as greedy for position as though *shoulder straps* were the acme of all human ambition. Vinton and Drew[75] have both been talked up for Lt Col. I suppose Drew will get it. I am sick of service, also am getting Brevets out here who never heard a bullet whistle. I have for a long time wished to get out but am disgusted with the pertinacity with which some men cling to it.

I hope to be home for Thanksgiving but *may not*. Give my love to all and believe me

Your affectionate son
J. H. Kidd

FINALLY ARRIVING AT Fort Leavenworth, Kidd happily signed his discharge papers on November 7.[76] The wait, however, was not over.

Headquarters 6th Mich Cav
Near Fort Leavenworth
November 14 1865

Major J. W. Barnes[77]
Asst Adj General
Major

I have the honor to state that certain men are here belonging to my regiment, who in compliance with instructions from Brevt Maj Gen F Wheaton,[78] having been recommended for discharge, on account of physical disability were sent from the hospital at Laramie for muster-out here. These men do not come under "Par 2, Special Orders No 79." I respectfully ask if they shall be placed on the muster out rolls as though of the class whose time will expire prior to Feb 1/66, or whether they shall be mustered out on separate rolls. I need specific instructions on this point, to enable company commanders to comply with the required forms in making the muster-out rolls.

I have the honor to be

> Very respectfully
> Yr obdt servant
> J. H. Kidd
> Col 6th Mich Cav

DESPITE HAVING SIGNED his discharge papers, Kidd remained on active-duty status at Fort Leavenworth, waiting orders to go home. In September, as the discharge papers of the men of the 1st, 6th, and 7th regiments came through, Pope ordered that the remaining men be consolidated into a single regiment, the 1st Michigan Veteran Cavalry. Troopers with less than two years to go on their terms of service would be discharged immediately. However, General Dodge was worried that the release of most of the brigade at once would seriously deplete the strength of his garrisons. He dragged out the consolidation process through the end of November, and those eligible to go home were held in service until mid-December. The men considered Dodge's actions in ignoring his superior's order an "unwarrantable and inexcusable" exercise of power, even though they were powerless to act. Their unhappiness, already deep, simply grew deeper.[79]

On November 16, James M. Kidd wrote to his son, "Glad to hear that there is a prospect of your being home with us again soon and permanently and hope no accident will happen to prevent the full confirmation of our anticipations." James M. Kidd teased his son, laying out some preliminary but incomplete ideas for the future of the family business. The reader is left to wonder what those ideas were, because no written record has survived.[80] Kidd's anticipation of going home comes through in his final surviving letter home, written on November 20.

Headquarters 6th Mich Cavalry
Near Fort Leavenworth
Nov 20, 1865

Dear Father

I wrote for you to send any papers you might receive from Washington for me to this place. I write now to tell you not to send them, unless you have already done so. If you have recd any and have sent them please telegraph (payable here) to me at once informing me of the fact. Our rolls are nearly ready for examination and the prospect is quite favorable for getting out this week or next. There are now orders to Detroit for final discharge and payment. Weather here lovely. All well. Kindest remembrances to everybody I know. I'll let you know when we will be at Detroit.

Yours affectionately
J. H. Kidd

FINALLY, THE WEEK before Christmas, eight months after the end of the war, James Harvey Kidd boarded a steamer to take him home to Michigan.[81] The greatest adventure of his life was finally over.

Conclusion

His record as a soldier was one to be proud of . . .

Finally released from his military service, James H. Kidd "returned to Ionia laden with honors and with the consciousness of having served his country well and faithfully."[1] Settling back into familiar surroundings, he went into the family business, the name of which was changed to J. M. Kidd and Son.[2] In 1867, Kidd was appointed register of the land office at Ionia, a position he held for eight years, but resigned on July 1, 1875.[3] That same year, he was appointed secretary of Michigan's deep waterways commission, headquartered at Detroit, a post he held for three years. In August 1897, he was reappointed to the same commission by his old friend, Russell A. Alger, at that time secretary of war under President William McKinley.[4]

On June 30, 1866, Representative Thomas W. Ferry, the congressman representing the district that included Ionia, wrote to Kidd, "In reference to my recommendation I have the pleasure to enclose you an Official Notice from the War Department of your deserved promotion to the rank of Brig. General by brevet."[5] Despite being issued on June 27, 1866, the promotion was made retroactive to March 13, 1865.[6] The belated promotion finally recognized Kidd's long and gallant service during the Civil War.

Restless with his career and not entirely happy being in his father's manufacturing business, Kidd longed to return to journalism. T. G. Stevenson and J. C. Taylor started the *Ionia Sentinel* on May 1, 1866, and Kidd became a regular contributor, writing periodic articles that recounted his service in the Michigan Brigade. He purchased a one-third interest in the newspaper in 1870, and in 1887 became its sole owner. Daily and weekly editions of the paper were published. A local historian noted, "The *Sentinel* has always been a Republican paper in politics and is a widely read county newspaper occupying first rank. With the largest circulation in the county it is a well-patronized advertising medium."[7] Kidd spent the rest of his life publishing the *Sentinel*, as well as writing and lecturing about his wartime experiences. He later wrote, "His forte as a newspaper man, if he has any, is editorial writing."[8]

In January 1868, the *Weekly Standard*, sister paper to the *Sentinel*, ran a brief piece about bachelors of Ionia County. The profile of Kidd read, "A bachelor of 27; good looking; sports side whiskers . . . not engaged; lots of stamps; don't want to marry; splendid chance for some one; income for two."[9] It took three more years for him to change his status as a bachelor. On December 25, 1871, the thirty-one-year-old Kidd took the plunge, marrying eighteen-year-old Florence S. McConnell of New York City. The wedding took place in Ionia and was performed by Rev. T. F. Hildreth.[10] It was the first wedding ceremony performed in Ionia's Methodist Church.[11] The marriage was a long and happy one that produced a son, Frederick McConnell Kidd, born on April 28, 1881.[12] James H. Kidd's political patron, Representative Ferry, wrote, "Congratulating you upon an union that brings you more happiness than that for which you tendered your life, I very heartily say long may you be undivided."[13]

Not long after his wedding, Kidd constructed a home on Washington Street in Ionia. It was "of the Franco-Italian style of architecture, about 40 feet by 50 feet on the ground and will present an elegant appearance. Such buildings always add very largely to the attractiveness of any town."[14] Kidd lived in this handsome home for the rest of his life.

Life in Ionia was quiet but fulfilling. Around Christmas 1876, an "Old Folks Concert" was held. Dressed in colonial-style costumes, the attendees performed several songs, including one by a quartet of Mr. and Mrs. L. H. Thayer and the Kidds, who sang "My Mountain Home" and "Old Folks at Home." Kidd soloed with "Deacon Jones' Lament," and Kidd's wife with "One Hundred Years Ago."[15] In June 1866, he was elected president of "The Custer Base Ball Club of Ionia" and helped organize the team, predictably called the Wolverines. Bob Kidd also periodically served as an umpire for the team's games and enjoyed their frequent victories.[16] He acted as the first president of the Ionia Horse Breeders Association and served as secretary of the Ionia Horticultural Society.[17] In 1870, he served as an assistant marshal for the City of Ionia's Independence Day festivities.[18] Despite his enjoyment during these activities, Kidd longed for the excitement and camaraderie of his years in the military.

In 1876, Kidd reentered the military as first captain of the Ionia Light Guard, a position he held until 1879. Then, in 1879, he was appointed colonel and brigade quartermaster of the Michigan National Guard when it was organized into a full brigade. In 1882 and 1883, he served as brigade inspector, and, in 1885, he was appointed inspector general under his old friend Russell A. Alger, who had become governor of Michigan. In 1895, Kidd was appointed quartermaster general on the staff of Governor John T. Rich, and in 1901, he held the same position on the staff of Governor A. T. Bliss. By that time, young Fred Kidd also served in the Michigan National Guard, commanding the Ionia Light Guard as its captain. James Kidd received an appointment as quartermaster general on the staff of Governor Fred M. Warner, holding that position from 1905 until Kidd's retirement in 1911 with the rank of brigadier general.[19] A staff officer of the Michigan National Guard later paid him a high compliment, stating, "[to] General Kidd more than . . . any other member . . . does the Michigan National Guard owe its present high standing, being developed along the most approved and latest lines by that gentleman during his term of office."[20]

Kidd also was active in the Masonic Order, holding the rank of eminent commander of the Masonic Order in Ionia and junior warden of the grand commandery. He participated in Republican politics in Michigan for the rest of his life.[21] In 1868, he drafted a fervent call to "the Boys in Blue of Ionia County" to vote for the national Republican ticket, topped by Ulysses S. Grant, who was running for the White House his first time. Wrote Kidd:

We ask you . . . by the memory of our departed comrades, slain on battlefields, dying of lingering disease in hospitals, and starved in rebel prisons; in justice to our living brothers who ask the right to live upon American soil, which, by a common bravery with yours, they helped to regain and repossess; as you adore and idolize that glorious flag—the Stars and Stripes—the banner that floated so proudly over you in camp, that was pushed by you so fearlessly into the glare and smoke of a hundred battle-fields; to come out in force that day. Come singly or in companies from every town in the country, and we of Ionia will meet you.[22]

Some of Kidd's friends attempted to persuade him to run for governor of Michigan in 1897, which prompted a newspaper reporter to write:

> The fact that no less than a dozen republican patriots have already placed themselves in the hands of their friends and cast a longing glance in the direction of the gubernatorial nomination, has had no deterring effect on the friends of Quartermaster-General James H. Kidd, who are quietly taking up his qualifications for the office. They point to his most excellent record both in military and civil life, and dwell with not a little force on the fact that western Michigan has yet to supply an occupant of the executive chair. Gen. Kidd has never made any declaration of his intentions in this regard, but if his numerous friends in this section of the state have their way about it, he will cut quite a figure in the canvass.[23]

Kidd never made the run, for unknown reasons. Perhaps more important to Kidd was his work with various veterans organizations. As early as the summer of 1866, he helped form the Ionia County Soldiers' Union and served as president of the Officers' Association of the 6th Michigan Cavalry, whose meetings he always closed with the dramatic toast, "The Sixth Michigan Cavalry." Kidd belonged to the Michigan Commandery of the Military Order of the Loyal Legion of the United States, and commanded the Department of Michigan, Grand Army of the Republic. He attended many reunions and ceremonies around the country and joined the Michigan delegation to the funeral of Ulysses S. Grant in 1885.[24] In June 1882, Kidd led the Second Division in a procession at a reunion of the Army of the Potomac in Detroit. Kidd rode his beloved old warhorse, Billy, then twenty-six years old and a survivor of combat wounds received at Winchester and Cedar Creek.[25] "Bay Billy" finally died in December 1888, at the age of thirty-three, and was buried in Kidd's yard.[26]

In 1892, Kidd's *Sentinel* reported the passing of his old friend and commander, Col. George Gray, who had served as general counsel for the Northern Pacific Railroad Company for many years. Kidd wrote, "A short article . . . announcing the death of Col. George Gray was sad news to many Ionians. . . . As an officer and as a man he was highly esteemed by the regiment."[27] His old comrades in arms from the 6th Michigan were passing from the scene one by one, and Kidd must have sensed his own mortality.

Much respected for his writing and lecturing on the role of the Union cavalry in the Civil War, Kidd gave the keynote address at the dedication of the Michigan Cavalry Brigade monument on East Cavalry Field at Gettysburg in 1888. He gave the principal address at a Memorial Day celebration in Ionia in May 1885 and another at Port Huron in 1899. Among the many papers written by Kidd describing his war years was a study of the role of the Michigan Cavalry Brigade in the Wilderness Campaign and another entitled "Michigan at Andersonville." He also served on the committee to plan a celebration of the fiftieth anniversary of the Battle of Gettysburg in 1913.

In 1907, Governor Warner appointed a committee consisting of Kidd, Col. George C. Briggs of the 7th Michigan Cavalry, and Lt. Frederick A. Nims to oversee the erection of an equestrian monument to George Armstrong Custer in his hometown of Monroe, Michigan.[28] The handsome monument, which cost the then princely sum of $24,000, was dedicated not long after, with Kidd giving the keynote speech at the dedication. Paying tribute to his hero, Kidd wrote, "No higher tribute can be paid. It fully justifies the opinion often expressed by the writer that George Armstrong Custer was the foremost cavalry officer of his time, not excepting any, Federal or Confederate. His fame is the common heritage of all patriots of the reunited republic, and deserves to be jealously treasured and perpetuated."[29] Kidd's stirring speech outlined the life and career of Custer, including the Boy General's unfortunate and untimely death at the Little Big Horn. A few days later, a letter arrived from Custer's widow, Libbie, who wrote, "It does me such good to hear a voice brave enough to refute the charge of recklessness that my husband's enemies constantly make. I thank you sincerely."[30]

Also in 1907, Kidd applied for a veteran's pension and began receiving monthly stipends of $12 to compensate him for the wound suffered at Falling Waters. In 1910, the payment was increased to $15 per month. His widow, Florence, continued to receive the pension until her death.[31]

In 1910, the University of Michigan finally conferred a degree upon Kidd, albeit an honorary one. The letter from the president of the University stated, "It gives me great pleasure to inform you that the Board of Regents of the University of Michigan at a meeting held on May 25th, 1910, voted to confer upon you the degree of Doctor of Laws on the occasion of the Commencement exercises to be held June 30th."[32] Ever modest, Kidd immediately demurred, claiming that he did not deserve such an honor. Several people encouraged him to accept and finally persuaded him that the honorary degree was "most worthily and fittingly bestowed."

He had "achieved much in his lifetime" and his "achievements would have received fuller and louder recognition than they have, had not [his] exceeding modesty stood in the way."[33] Kidd finally consented, and the degree was bestowed as scheduled.[34]

Kidd's "greatest pleasure during the late years of his life was writing a history of the Michigan Cavalry Brigade in the Civil War, and this work was completed several years ago entitled *Personal Recollections of a Cavalryman with Custer's Michigan Cavalry Brigade in the Civil War*." The *Sentinel* published the book in 1908. It took Kidd twenty-two years to complete his memoirs. Afterward, he wrote, "It may have been but yesterday, so deep and lasting were the impressions then produced."[35]

Arguably the finest single brigade of cavalry attached to the Army of the Potomac, the Wolverines left their mark on many battlefields. William O. Lee, compiler of a history of the 7th Michigan Cavalry, proudly observed that the Michigan Brigade "was organized and will ever be known in history as Brigade, still it was more like a large Regiment. Almost invariably, where one Regiment was, the balance of them were in immediate vicinity; if one Regiment or more were on the skirmish line, or in a skirmish or battle, the balance of the Brigade was there as reserve to do and did their part when called upon."[36] A Michigan newspaper described the brigade in 1864 as "the pride of [the] country, and the terror of its foes."[37] One trooper proudly told his loved ones that the Rebels called the Wolverines "the flying devils of Michigan."[38] Seven members of the brigade, including three members of the 6th Michigan, were awarded Medals of Honor, Lt. Thomas Custer of the 6th Michigan being one of only two men to be awarded two such medals during the Civil War.[39]

In addition, many of the brigade's officers achieved high rank: George A. Custer was promoted to major general of volunteers, and Copeland held the rank of brigadier general of volunteers. Further, counting Kidd and his rival Peter Stagg, seven of the brigade's officers received brevets to brigadier general.[40] Luther S. Trowbridge of the 5th Michigan Cavalry, one of those brevetted to brigadier general, wrote to Kidd, "The truth is that, while I performed no service with the old brigade worth mentioning, I have a genuine pride in its history and in having once belonged to it."[41] The veterans were proud to say that they had served under Custer, and Kidd's memoirs provided a rallying point for them to do so.

The memoir got good reviews. One early reviewer, Edward Cahill, wrote, "The bare statement of the opportunities General Kidd had for knowing, is enough to attract the interest of every student of the war. The style in which the story is told enlivens and holds that interest to the end of the nearly five hundred pages." Cahill continued, "I have enjoyed this book so much myself that I cannot withhold my personal tribute to Gen. Kidd for his valuable contribution to the history of the war, in which he played so gallant a part."[42] Today, modern historians consider Kidd's memoirs a classic. They are an essential part of the library of any student of the Army of the Potomac's Cavalry Corps.

As the fiftieth anniversary of the Battle of Gettysburg approached, Kidd eagerly looked forward to attending the scheduled veterans' reunion to be held there in July 1913. However, this fond wish was not granted. On January 11, 1913, Kidd suffered a stroke. He "was at the time of his sickness at his desk getting out a circular, postponing a dinner arranged for January 17 in Detroit. He could not finish the task and went home. He is holding his own and although in a critical condition, his recovery is hoped for," the *Sentinel* reported.[43] After a few days, his condition indeed improved, which permitted him "to be up and around the house, but a second and then a third attack greatly weakened him," reported the *Sentinel* on March 18, "and for the last two weeks he has been confined to his bed and growing weaker. His condition today is very uncertain."[44] He died the next day, at the age of seventy-three. He was survived by his wife Florence and his son Frederick.

A huge crowd thronged to his funeral, held at the Presbyterian Church in Ionia. Fittingly, Kidd's casket was draped with the flag of the Michigan Cavalry Brigade. Old comrades from the 6th Michigan, including Luther G. Kanouse, George W. Barbour, and Charles E. Storrs, attended the funeral. Dr. W. K. Spencer, the pastor at the church, eulogized Kidd:

I have . . . learned from those outside the immediate circle of relations that he reserved his best for his dearest at home. We do not always act this way. We go home and put on jacket and slippers and often with them our careless manners. Not every one is most considerate, courteous, gentle and affectionate to his. Yet we recognize this thing as one of the marks of a gentleman and Christian. The Savior never did a more wonderful thing then when on the cross he gave His love and care to His mother. And this friend of ours had caught His spirit in his constant display of loving courtesy and thoughtful care for those he loved best in his home.

He was justly proud of having lived in the nation's heroic times and having done his part to maintain right and freedom. His history as a soldier was very dear to him. His personal relations with his fellow soldiers in the sixties were ever cherished. None of his old comrades ever thought him cold or distant. I well remember when in 1910 Michigan University granted him the honorary title of Doctor of Laws, how pleased he was to find written down upon the parchment, as one of the reasons for conferring such an honor, that he was "Miles Fortissimus," "a very brave soldier."[45]

Another eulogizer wrote that Kidd "bore his distinction in military and civil life with manly modesty; he performed the duties of an official position with dignity and high intelligence; his integrity was never questioned. His record as a soldier was one to be proud of, and was probably the most distinguishing part of his public career—made him the most widely known, gave him the most prestige, and attached to him some of his most valued friends."[46]

With those loving words echoing, James Harvey Kidd was laid to rest in the family plot, Section 4, Lot 130, of the Highland Cemetery in Ionia. Thus ended the long and productive life of one of Custer's Wolverines, a man who made great contributions to the memory of the sacrifices made by those who fought to save the Union.

Appendix A

Itinerary of the 6th Michigan Cavalry

The 6th Michigan Cavalry was mustered into service in Grand Rapids, Michigan, on October 13, 1862, for a three-year term of service. Congressman Francis W. Kellogg organized it. The regiment was immediately ordered to Washington, D.C. Its original commander was Col. George Gray, who served until 1864, when illness forced his resignation from the regiment. Lt. Col. Russell A. Alger, the next senior officer of the 6th Michigan, was assigned command of the 5th Michigan Cavalry in 1864. James H. Kidd, who assumed interim command of the regiment as a major in the fall of 1863, served as colonel of the regiment from the middle of 1864 until the regiment was mustered out of service in November 1865. On December 10, 1862, the new regiment left Grand Rapids and traveled to Washington, where it encamped at Camp Gray, on Meridian Hill, located in the northwest quadrant of the city.

From the time of its arrival in Washington until June 1863, the regiment served with Brig. Gen. Julius Stahel's independent division of cavalry, which was assigned to the defenses of the city. In June 1863, the regiment was attached to the Cavalry Corps, Army of the Potomac, where it served until the summer of 1864 as the 2d Brigade, Third Division, under command of Brig. Gen. Judson Kilpatrick. In 1864, it became 2d Brigade, First Division, under command of Brig. Gen. A. T. A. Torbert. In August 1864, Maj. Gen. Philip H. Sheridan was given command of the newly formed Army of the Shenandoah. From August 1864 until March 1865, the 6th Michigan served in the First Division of the

Cavalry Corps of the Army of the Shenandoah. From March to June 1865, the regiment served in the First Division of the Cavalry Corps of the Army of the Potomac. In June 1865, the Michigan Brigade, including the 6th Michigan Cavalry, was assigned to the District of the Plains, where it remained until mustered out of the service in November 1865.

At all times, the regiment was armed with sabers and repeating weapons. It was one of two units armed with Spencer repeating rifles in 1863. In 1864, it traded the Spencer rifles for Spencer repeating carbines. Throughout its tenure of service, the regiment was proficient in fighting dismounted, making good use of its repeating weapons.

The following is an itinerary of the raids and battles in which the 6th Michigan Cavalry participated. Routine reconnaissances and scouting missions are not included in this list.

1863

December 1862–February 1863: On duty at Camp Gray, in the defenses of Washington, D.C.

March–April: Expedition to Freedom Hill, Virginia.

March 26: Expedition to Fairfax Court House, Virginia.

March 27: On picket duty near Chantilly, Virginia.

April 3–8: Expedition to the Loudoun Valley of Virginia, to pursue Capt. John S. Mosby's raiders.

The regiment remained on picket duty until June 20.

June 20: Crossed the Potomac River into Maryland and joined the Army of the Potomac's Cavalry Corps.

June 27: Reconnaissance to Sharpsburg, Maryland.

June 30: Battle at Hanover, Pennsylvania.

July 2: Battle at Hunterstown, Pennsylvania.

July 3: Battle at Gettysburg, Pennsylvania.

July 4: Battle at Monterey Pass, Pennsylvania.

July 5: Battle at Smithsburg, Maryland.

July 6: Engagements at Hagerstown and Williamsport, Maryland.

July 9: Battle at Boonsboro, Maryland.

July 12: Battle at Hagerstown, Maryland.

July 14: Affair at Falling Waters, Maryland.

July 20: Engagement at Ashby's Gap, Virginia.

July 24: Engagement at Battle Mountain, Virginia.

August 7: Affair at Waterford, Virginia.

September 13: Battle at Culpeper Court House, Virginia.

September 14–16: Engagement at Somerville Ford, Virginia.

September 21: Engagement at Madison Court House, Virginia.

September 22: Engagement at Liberty Mills, Virginia.

October 10: Engagement at James City, Virginia.

October 11: Battle at Brandy Station, Virginia.

October 19: Battle at Buckland Mills, Virginia ("Buckland Races").

November 7: Engagement at Stevensburg, Virginia.

December 1: Winter encampment at Brandy Station, Virginia.

The regiment remained on picket duty at Brandy Station along the Rapidan and Rappahannock Rivers until May 4, 1864.

1864

February 28–March 4: Participated in the Kilpatrick/Dahlgren Raid on Richmond.

March 5–May 5: Engaged in picket duty along the Rappahannock River until the beginning of General Grant's spring campaign.

May 6: Battle of the Wilderness, Virginia.

May 9–13: Sheridan's Raid on Richmond, Virginia.

May 9: Engagement at Beaver Dam Station, Virginia.

May 10: Sheridan's raid on Richmond, Virginia.

May 11: Battle of Yellow Tavern, Virginia.

May 12: Engagement at Meadow Bridge, Virginia.

May 19: Expedition to Bottom's Bridge, Virginia.

May 20: Skirmish at Milford Station, Virginia.

May 27: Engagement at Hanovertown, Virginia.

May 28: Battle of Haw's Shop, Virginia.

May 30–31: Battle of Cold Harbor, Virginia.

May 30: Skirmish at Old Church, Virginia.

May 31: Skirmish at Bottom's Bridge, Virginia.

June 8–21: Sheridan's Trevilian Station Raid.

June 11–12: Battle of Trevilian Station, Virginia.

June 21–August 1: On picket duty with the Army of the Potomac near Petersburg, Virginia.

June 21: Skirmish at White House Landing, Virginia.

July 27–28: Engagement at Deep Bottom, Virginia.

August: Assigned to the Cavalry Corps, Army of the Shenandoah.

August 10: Skirmish at Berryville Pike, Virginia.

August 12: Engagement at Winchester, Virginia.

August 15: Skirmish at Fisher's Hill, Virginia.

August 16: Skirmish at Front Royal, Virginia.

August 21: Skirmish at Summit Point, Virginia.

August 25: Skirmish at Shepherdstown, Virginia.

August 28–29: Expedition to Smithfield, Virginia.

September 3–4: Engagement at Berryville, Virginia.

September 19: Battle of Opequon Creek, Virginia.

September 19: Battle of Winchester, Virginia.

September 22: Battle of Fisher's Hill, Virginia.

September 24: Skirmish at Luray, Virginia.

September 26: Engagement at Port Republic, Virginia.

October 2: Engagement at Waynesborough, Virginia.

October: Participated in the destruction of the Shenandoah Valley known as "The Burning."

October 8–9: Battle at Woodstock, Virginia ("Woodstock Races").

October 9: Battle of Tom's Brook, Virginia.

October 19: Battle of Cedar Creek, Virginia.

November 22: Engagement at Rood's Hill, Virginia.

November 28–December 2: Participated in the burning of the Loudoun Valley.

December 8–28: Sheridan's Raid on Gordonsville, Virginia.

December 20: Battle at Madison Court House, Virginia.

December 23: Engagement at Jack's Shop, near Gordonsville, Virginia.

December 29: Into winter quarters near Winchester, Virginia, where the regiment remained on picket duty until February 28, 1865.

1865

February 27–March 25: Sheridan's Raid into central Virginia.

March 1: Battle of Waynesborough, Virginia.

March 10: Regiment marches to Petersburg, Virginia, to rejoin
Army of the Potomac's Cavalry Corps.

March 30–31: Battle of Dinwiddie Court House, Virginia.

April 1: Battle of Five Forks, Virginia.

April 6: Battle of Sayler's Creek, Virginia.

April 6: Battle of the Ridge, Virginia.

April 9: Action at Appomattox Court House, Virginia.

May 15: Regiment ordered to march to Washington, D.C.

May 23: Participated in the Grand Review, Army of the
Potomac, Washington, D.C.

June 1–November 1: Assigned to the Department of the Plains,
Colorado and Dakota Territories. Marched to Forts Leaven-
worth and Laramie in June. Participated in Powder River
Indian Expedition, June and July. Served at Fort Connor,
Dakota Territory until mustered out.

November 1: Regiment mustered out at Fort Leavenworth,
Kansas.

The 6th Michigan Cavalry mustered in 1,624 officers and men. During its term of service, it lost 10 officers, 8 sergeants, 8 corporals, and 97
men listed as killed in action or dead of wounds, for a total of 121. Sixty-
five other members of the regiment died at Andersonville prison in Geor-
gia, and another 42 died in other places as prisoners of war. An additional
132 men died of disease during the course of the war; 214 were wounded
in action; and another 150 were discharged for disability, for total dead
and wounded numbering 724. There are no statistics available for the number of men taken prisoner during the course of the war.

The 6th Michigan Cavalry left behind a rich legacy as a hard-fighting
regiment with good leadership.

Appendix B

James H. Kidd's Report for the Year 1864

Headquarters Sixth Michigan Cavalry
First Brigade, First Division, Cavalry
   Corps
Army of the Shenandoah
Winchester, VA.
Dec. 17, 1864

Brig-Gen John Robertson,
Adjutant General of Michigan,
General:

I have the honor to submit the following brief resume of operations of this
   command for the year embraced between the dates November 1st, 1863, and
   November 1st, 1864.

Except a skirmish with Wade Hampton's Division of Cavalry at Stevensburg in the
   early part of November, and three or four demonstrations upon the enemy's
   lines on the Rapidan, at Raccoon, Summerville, and Morton's Fords, no active
   duty was assigned to the regiment, from November 1st until the expiration of
   the year 1863.

The regiment was engaged in the fight at Morton's Ford, on the 1st of December,
   and went into winter quarters at Stevensburg soon after; and continued to do its
   proportionate amount of picket duty until the month of February, 1864, when
   General Kilpatrick made his celebrated Richmond raid, when it accompanied
   him and participated in all the dangers and privations of that bold but unsuc-

cessful movement.

On the night when the enemy attacked the camps of the Third Division near Richmond, the Sixth, or a portion of it (Troops A, E, and G), under my immediate command, together with one battalion of the First Vermont Cavalry, brought up the rear when the Division retreated.

After returning to our old camps at Stevensburg nothing of importance (except the transfer of the Michigan Brigade to the First Cavalry Division), occurred until the 4th of May, when the spring campaign opened. I will here remark that on the 3rd, companies (troops) I and M, which, under the command of Major C. W. Deane for a year had been operating in the Shenandoah Valley, returned to the regiment for duty.[1]

On the 4th and 5th of May the First Division, having the rear, did not become engaged. On the 6th, the Michigan Brigade, having the left, connecting with the Second Corps of Infantry, was attacked with great impetuosity by the rebel generals, Rosser and Fitz Lee. The charge was met by the Sixth in conjunction with the First. The regiment was engaged all that day—repulsing the first charge made by the enemy—and holding the right of the Brigade line against a greatly superior force. Among the casualties were Lieut. Cortez P. Pendill[2] of K and Lieut. B. F. Rockafellow of M, both severely wounded while leading their men. Lieut. Pendill when wounded was far in advance of everybody, in pursuit of a rebel officer. The casualties among the enlisted men were numerous, but as I have already forwarded the aggregate of casualties for the year I will not encumber this report with details of that character.

Seventh, 8th and 9th occupied with slight skirmishing, and guarding the flank of General Meade's army.

Tenth, Sheridan's raid commenced. This regiment had the advance of the entire Cavalry Corps during a portion of the day, and was the second regiment to reach Beaver Dam Station, assisting in the capture and destruction of a large amount of rebel stores there accumulated, and in recapturing about 350 Union soldiers who had been captured in the Wilderness.

The 11th was fought the battle of Yellow Tavern. This regiment being dismounted, made several charges on the left of the line occupied by the Fifth Michigan Cavalry, succeeding each time in driving the enemy from strong positions in woods and behind fences, finally driving the enemy so far that pursuit with dismounted men was useless. Our casualties were large.

Twelfth, reached Meadow Bridge, on the Chickahominy, found the bridge gone and the crossing disputed by the enemy's dismounted cavalry with strong breastworks and artillery.

From the swampy nature of the ground it was impossible to bring artillery to bear upon them. "The stream must be crossed at all hazards" was the order, and the Fifth and Sixth were assigned the duty. Dismounting, the two regiments crossed on the ties of a railroad bridge, one at a time, in the face of a galling fire of musketry and artillery, and succeeding in gaining a foothold on the opposite bank, subsequently charged and drove the enemy from their works, killing and capturing many. This, one of the most desperate fights the regiment was ever engaged in, was attended with very few casualties. Lieut. Thomas A. Edie of Troop A,[3] one of our bravest and most efficient officers, was instantly killed by a shot through the head.

Twelfth, 13th, 14th, marched over the historic grounds of McClellan's seven days' battles, reaching Malvern Hill on the 14th, where we remained until the 17th, when we broke camp and marched to Charles City Court House, thence to Baltimore Crossroads, reaching that point on the 18th.

On the 19th, pursuant to orders from General Custer, I went with my command to Bottom's Bridge, which I destroyed, together with the extensive railroad bridge across the Chickahominy near that point, meeting with but slight opposition from small parties of the enemy who were easily dispersed.

Twentieth, marched via Newcastle to Hanover Courthouse, General Custer in command. The Sixth, having the advance, charged the town, driving out a force of the enemy stationed there, cut the wires and destroyed the track, burning several bridges on the Virginia Central railroad.

Twentieth to twenty-fifth, marched, via White House, to Chesterfield Station, where we rejoined the Army of the Potomac. From the 4th of May till the 26th, the regiment marched 300 miles.

Twenty-seventh, having marched all night, crossed the Pamunkey at Hanovertown, at daylight. I was ordered by General Custer to proceed in the direction of Hanover Courthouse, which I did and soon became engaged with Gordon's Brigade of Rebel cavalry.[4] All of the Michigan Brigade, as well as General Devin's Brigade, became engaged, and the enemy was routed in great confusion. Our losses in killed and wounded were considerable.

On the 28th fought the battle of Hawes' Shop. Gregg's men were falling back. This Brigade was ordered to support him. The Brigade was dismounted. The Sixth had the right of the road, its left on the road. The enemy was in the woods. We formed in the open field. General Custer ordered three cheers and a charge. The cheers were given and the order to charge obeyed. In a minute the fight was hand to hand. The rebels fought with desperation, but were routed. They left their dead and wounded in our hands and many prisoners. In ten minutes out of 140 men I had engaged 33 were killed or wounded. Twelve were killed outright, four died before morning. The ground where the regiment fought was covered with rebel dead and wounded. The trees were riddled. Infantry officers who saw the fight spoke of it as one of the most desperate they ever witnessed. It is not boasting to say that the gallantry displayed by the men of the Michigan Brigade in that fight was extraordinary, unexampled.

Twenty-eighth, marched to Newcastle Ferry, on the Pamunkey river. Thirtieth at the battle of Old Church, the Brigade being dismounted, this regiment was held in reserve mounted, but for some reason was not ordered to charge as was expected.

Thirty-first, the Brigade being about the advance on Cold Harbor by the direct road, I was sent with the regiment by an unfrequented road to threaten the flank of the enemy's position. This I succeeded in doing, by driving in the enemy's pickets on the New Kent road, where I formed, afterwards, a junction with the Second Brigade, commanded by Colonel Devin. By a vigorous attack made on the rebel front and this threatened attack in flank the enemy was routed. During the night we were engaged in throwing up breastworks, having received a notice that the Cavalry were ordered to hold the position (Cold Harbor), until the Infantry could come up. On the morning of the 31st the enemy's infantry made a furious assault upon our position, but were repulsed, failing in every attempt to drive us from our works. About 12 o'clock, M, we were replaced by the First Corps, to our great relief, for officers and men were worn out with incessant marching and fighting by night and day.

During the month of June, General Sheridan with the First and Second Divisions of the Cavalry Corps, made his raid toward Gordonsville.[5] The enemy's entire Cavalry force was encountered on the 11th of the month at Trevillian Station on the Orange and Alexandria railroad.[6] This regiment was engaged the entire day, fighting both mounted and dismounted, charging and counter-charging. Not less than one hundred prisoners were captured by the regiment, but being surrounded for several hours, many men were necessarily lost. On the 12th, the enemy having been reinforced by Infantry, confronted and opposed our advance.[7] Having the advance, I was ordered by General Custer to go toward Gordonsville, but had proceeded less than a mile when I encountered and drove in the rebel pickets upon the main reserve, which was nothing less than their whole force posted in formidable entrenched positions. In the bloody work of that day we were the first regiment engaged, and one of the three last to leave the field. Among the casualties was Sergeant M. E. Avery of Troop E,[8] killed by a cannon ball. One of the bravest of the brave, I must pay him the tribute of admiration due to every soldier who was always found at his post, bravely and conscientiously discharging his duty. Had his life been spared, a commission would have before this rewarded him for his conspicuous gallantry. Capt. Don G. Lovell and Lieut. Luther Canouse[9] were among the wounded.

From Trevillian Station we returned, via White House, Jones' bridge on the Chickahominy, etc., to the Army of the Potomac, which had found a resting place on the south side of the James river. Terribly jaded, men and horses needed rest, but were immediately ordered off to find Wilson's Cavalry, which had been cut off in the vicinity of Reams' Station.

The residue of the month of June and the month of July was occupied in recuperating, reorganizing and remounting. When General Hancock made his feint on the north side of the James river the Cavalry corps accompanied him. We were only slightly engaged. Picketing, we had plenty of it, little else. From the 26th of May to the 1st August the regiment marched not less than 400 miles.

On the 3rd of August the regiment embarked on transports at City Point, arriving at Washington on the 6th, and marched thence via Poolesville and Harper's Ferry to Halltown, reaching the latter place on the morning of the 10th, in time to join in the advance of the new army of the Middle Military Division, under its new commander.

On the morning of the 11th marched at daylight, took up a position beyond the Opequan Creek, towards Winchester. A section of Ransom's battery was charged upon by the enemy. Captain James Mather,[10] with one battalion of the Sixth Michigan Cavalry, happening to be at hand, repulsed the charge and saved the battery, at the sacrifice, however, of his own life. He was instantly killed while urging his men forward.

Twelfth, was ordered by General Custer to reconnoitre the enemy's position beyond Cedar Creek. Found him in strong force and no attack was made by the cavalry upon the position.

Thirteenth, in camp. Fifteenth, moved to Cedarville. On the 16th the First Cavalry Division was attacked in its camp near Front Royal by Kershaw's Division of Infantry[11] and Fitz Lee's Division of Cavalry. In the bloody repulse given the enemy, only one battalion of this regiment participated, the others being several miles distant at the time guarding a ford. The Second Battalion, commanded by Captain H. H. Vinton[12] (subsequently Major and now Lieutenant Colonel), constituting the skirmish line in front of the Brigade, repulsed the first attack made by the enemy's cavalry, and afterwards made two charges, capturing many prisoners.

The time from the 16th to the 25th was consumed in a retrograde movement, finally bringing up at Shepardstown.

Twenty-fifth, fought the battle of Kearneysville and Shepardstown, when the Michigan Brigade, cut off from all support and surrounded by the enemy's infantry and cavalry, was rescued by the genius of its commander, and the intrepidity of its men. Of the men of this regiment, who, of course, came under my immediate notice, not a man left the ranks, or betrayed a sign of weakness or fear, when the enemy were assailing us in front and on both flanks, with a river in rear, the fords of which were supposed to be in possession of the enemy. So unflinchingly did they face the danger that the enemy dared not charge our line, but suffered us slowly to retire to a ford, the existence of which was known to General Custer alone. That officer afterwards said that if he had found the enemy at the ford, as he apprehended, he had determined to break through their lines in the direction of Shepardstown. From this perilous position we escaped without the loss of a man captured, and our wounded were all brought off.

From the 25th August to the 18th September, the regiment was engaged in the fights at Leetown and Smithfield, made three reconnaissances, encountered the enemy each time, and being under fire, acted once as escort for General Sheridan, and had one chase after Mosby's guerrillas, wounding an officer of his command, who was captured, and was with General Sheridan during all the marchings and counter marchings which characterized the earlier part of the Shenandoah Campaign.

On the 19th of September this regiment, at Sevres Ford on Opequan Creek, was dismounted and ordered by General Custer to dislodge the enemy from their position on the opposite bank and open the way for the Brigade to cross. The enemy was strongly posted behind breastworks of rails, in such a manner as to completely command the ford. For an eighth of a mile before reaching the ford the country was open. Across this space the regiment charged, exposed to a galling fire, when reaching temporary shelter a halt was made to reform the lines. When the advance was again ordered the enemy fell back precipitately, a force having come up from another direction to threaten his flank.

Having effected a crossing the Brigade pushed on to Winchester, reaching which point we soon became engaged with rebel cavalry and infantry. Three charges were made by the regiment. In the first we assisted in routing the rebel cavalry. In the second, we were repulsed by rebel infantry, and in the third charge made by that portion of the Brigade which had rallied, led by General Custer in person, this regiment alone captured more prisoners than it had men engaged. Seven officers had their horses shot under them on the field.

From the 19th to the 23rd, in pursuit of Early's army. Twenty-fourth overtook Wickham's Brigade[13] of Rebel Cavalry in the Luray Valley and charged on the left of the Brigade line, assisting in routing the enemy.

Twenty-sixth, crossed the Shenandoah at Port Republic. The regiment charged on a rebel wagon train near Brown's Gap, but finding itself confronted by Early's entire army, very judiciously failed to capture the train.

From the 26th September to the 26th October the regiment was commanded by Major Charles W. Deane. During that time the regiment made several reconnaissances, acted as escort for General Sheridan three times, and fought three battles. On the evening of the 8th October, I was ordered by General Merritt to drive the force which had been harassing our rear in the retrograde movement from Harrisonburg back to Woodstock, a distance of six miles. Giving the Sixth Michigan the advance, I succeeded in doing this. The enemy were driven at a run the entire distance. They made several attempts to charge the regiment but were repulsed each time. On the 9th I was ordered to open the ball by attacking the flank of a very strong cavalry force which confronted General Custer. The attack was made with great impetuosity by the Sixth and Seventh Michigan, but as this report has only to do with one regiment I will omit all mention of the very gallant part taken in the fight by the Seventh Michigan and the splendid gallantry of the Fifth Michigan in the fight of the 8th.

The Sixth Michigan charged and scattered a mounted and dismounted line of the enemy, made the first impression that was made upon the enemy's lines in the action of the 9th October, charging and routing everything that opposed them, until they found themselves two miles in advance of the other two brigades of the First Division, who were being at the same time driven back by another portion of the same force engaging us, and until ordered by the Division commander to halt.

On the 19th of October the regiment behaved with such coolness in the face of the defeat which threatened our arms as to win complimentary notice of all its com-

manders.[14] It made two charges upon the lines of infantry, in both of which it
succeeded in breaking the enemy's lines. In the second charge many prisoners
and a battle flag were the trophies. The enemy was utterly routed.

During the year the regiment has been in twenty-three pitched battles, besides
innumerable skirmishes, has captured more prisoners than it has ever had men
for duty, has participated in the dangers and shared all the honors of the Michigan Cavalry Brigade.

> Very respectfully,
> Your obedient servant,
> J. H. Kidd, Colonel Commanding

Notes

Introduction

1. John S. Schenck, *History of Ionia and Montcalm Counties, Michigan, with Illustrations and Biographical Sketches of Their Prominent Men and Pioneers* (Philadelphia: J. B. Lippincott, 1881), 110.

2. *Portraits Biographical Album of Ionia and Montcalm Counties, Michigan* (Chicago: Chapman Bros., 1891); Schenck, *History of Ionia*, 145.

3. 1860 United States Census for Ionia, Michigan, Kiddville Post Office, 233.

4. James H. Kidd obituary, *Ionia (Michigan) Sentinel*, Mar. 20, 1913; Schenck, *History of Ionia*, 146.

5. *Portraits*, 335.

6. James H. Kidd, *Personal Recollections of a Cavalryman in Custer's Michigan Brigade in the Civil War* (Ionia, Mich.: Sentinel Printing, 1908), 5–6, 10.

7. *Catalogue of the Officers and Students of the University of Michigan for 1862* (Ann Arbor: Univ. of Michigan, 1862), 32.

8. Ibid., 36.

9. Ibid., 68.

10. Ibid., 61.

11. James H. Kidd, "Reminiscences of a Volunteer, No. XXXIV," *Ionia (Michigan) Sentinel*, date unknown, Kidd Papers, University of Michigan, Bentley Historical Library, Ann Arbor, Mich.

12. *Ionia Souvenir of 1907* (Ionia, Mich.: n.p., 1907), 8.

13. Richard Kidd to James M. Kidd, Nov. 9, 1861.

14. Kidd, *Personal Recollections*, 20–21.

15. James H. Kidd, "Memorial Address, Delivered in the Rink at Ionia, May 30,

1885, by Gen. James H. Kidd," Kidd Papers, University of Michigan, Bentley Historical Library.

16. The 4th Michigan Cavalry did not serve in the eastern theater of the Civil War. It served with Maj. Gen. William T. Sherman's Army of the Tennessee and played an important role during Sherman's magnificent Atlanta campaign in the spring and summer of 1864.

17. Originally the lieutenant colonel of the 1st Michigan Cavalry, Copeland assumed command of the 5th Michigan upon its formation. He was later promoted to brigadier general and become the first commander of the Michigan Cavalry Brigade. Copeland was relieved of command on June 28, 1863, upon the promotion of George A. Custer from captain to brigadier general.

18. Kidd, *Personal Recollections*, 32.

19. James H. Kidd Pension File, National Archives.

20. Kidd, *Personal Recollections*, 39.

21. "Funeral Held for Gen. Kidd," *Ionia (Michigan) Sentinel*, date unknown, Kidd Papers, University of Michigan, Bentley Historical Library.

1. The Organization of the 6th Michigan Cavalry

1. The 2d Michigan Cavalry was originally commanded by a young regular army officer named Gordon Granger, who achieved fame as an infantry corps commander in the Western theater. Col. Philip H. Sheridan, who gained undying fame as a cavalry commander later in the war, succeeded him. Bvt. Brig. Gen. Robert H. Minty, who commanded what was perhaps the finest brigade of cavalry in the West, also served with the 2d Michigan.

2. J. K. Lowden, "A Gallant Record: Michigan's 5th Cav. in the Latter Part of the War," *National Tribune*, July 16, 1896.

3. Kidd, *Personal Recollections*, 35.

4. Cyrus Lovell was one of the owners of the Ionia House, a tavern located in Ionia. He was also an attorney-at-law and later served as a judge. One of the company commanders of the 6th Michigan Cavalry was named Don G. Lovell. It is possible that the two men were related. Don G. Lovell has not been identified, but he was presumably a prominent member of the Ionia community. Abel Avery, who owned a tavern in Ionia called the Grand River Eagle, was one of Ionia's prominent early merchants.

5. Kidd, *Personal Recollections*, 37.

6. Ibid., 44, 40.

7. Charles Lanman, *The Red Book of Michigan: A Civil, Military and Biographical History* (Detroit: E. B. Smith, 1871), 236.

8. Ibid., 46.

9. Ibid., 52.

10. *Mecosta County (Michigan) Pioneer*, Oct. 23, 1862.

11. William D. Mann, "Organization of the Seventh Michigan Cavalry," in *Personal and Historical Sketches and Facial History of and by Members of the Seventh Michigan Cavalry, 1862–1865*, William O. Lee (Detroit: Ralston-Stroup, 1904), 24.

12. Lt. Col. Russell A. Alger succeeded Gray as the regiment's lieutenant colonel. Alger was later transferred to the 5th Michigan Cavalry and became its commanding officer. Alger served as secretary of war in 1898, during the Spanish-American War.

13. Henry E. Thompson of Grand Rapids, Company A; John Torry of Saginaw, Company L; George A. Drew of Detroit, Company G; Charles W. Deane of Pentwater, Company I; Peter A. Weber of Grand Rapids, Company B; John F. Andrews of Thornapple, Company K; Wesley Armstrong of Lapeer, Company C; John M. Pratt of Saranac, Company M; David G. Royce of Burns, Company D; William Hyser of Plainfield, Company F; Henry L. Wise of Caledonia, Company H.

14. Kidd, *Personal Recollections*, 68.

15. *Mecosta County (Mich.) Pioneer*, Oct. 3, 1862.

16. Unidentified.

17. A battalion consisted of two squadrons, and a squadron two companies.

18. This refers to Company M being the regiment's twelfth and final company.

19. *Mecosta County Pioneer*, Oct. 23, 1862.

20. Ibid., Nov. 6, 1862.

21. *Record Sixth Michigan Cavalry, 1861–1865* (Kalamazoo, Mich.: Ihling Bros., 1905), 3. George A. Custer was criticized for adopting this practice in the postwar 7th U.S. Cavalry.

22. Kidd, *Personal Recollections*, 70–71.

23. Ibid., 74.

24. Ibid., 75–76.

25. Joseph T. Copeland to J. C. Kelton, July 9, 1863, Gratz Collection, Historical Society of Pennsylvania.

26. Louis H. Carpenter, "Sheridan's Expedition Around Richmond May 9–25, 1864," *Journal of the United States Cavalry Association* 1 (1888): 301.

27. *Record Sixth Michigan*, 3.

28. Isaac R. Hart of Orleans. Hart was captured on July 28, 1863, at Newby's Crossroads, Virginia, and died a prisoner of war at Andersonville prison. He is buried there in the National Cemetery. George and James W. Brown came from Kidd's hometown of Ionia. George was eventually promoted to sergeant and served out the war. James was also promoted to sergeant—in January 1864—but lost his life in action at the Battle of Hawes Shop, May 28, 1864.

29. Second Lt. Ambrose L. Soult of Lyons. Soult remained in this position for the balance of his term of service with the 6th Michigan Cavalry.

30. Maj. Gen. Henry Wager Halleck, the general in chief of the Union armies; Brig. Gen. Montgomery Meigs, the quartermaster general of the Union armies; Secretary of War Edwin M. Stanton; and Secretary of the Navy Gideon Welles.

31. Maj. Gen. Silas Casey, commander of the defenses of Washington.

32. The 5th Michigan Cavalry, commanded by Col. Joseph T. Copeland.

33. Kidd refers to the Spencer repeating rifle, which was not technically a revolving weapon but rather had a seven-shot magazine. The Ballard carbine was a .52 caliber single-shot carbine.

34. David M. Cooper, *Obituary Discourse on Occasion of the Death of Noah Henry Ferry* (New York: John F. Trow, 1863), 21.

35. William Ball to parents, Jan. 31, 1863, Ball Papers, Waldo Library, Western Michigan University, Kalamazoo.

36. Kidd, *Personal Recollections*, 87.

2. *In Pursuit of Mosby's Raiders*

1. *Mecosta County Pioneer*, Jan. 15, 1863.

2. Apparently a sutler serving the needs of the regiment.

3. Randall S. Compton of Ionia served as a private in Company E. The regimental muster rolls show no soldier named Charles Axtell. They do, however, show a private in Company E named John S. Axtell, also of Ionia.

4. Capt. John Pratt of Saranac commanded Company M. First Sgt. Angelo E. Tower of Ionia was Kidd's childhood best friend. Tower was eventually commissioned as an officer and achieved the rank of captain before being discharged as a consequence of disability in the summer of 1864. Second Lt. Ambrose L. Soule of Lyons also served in Company E.

5. First Lt. Edward L. Craw, also of Lyons, was Kidd's second in command in Company E.

6. Edward G. Longacre, *Custer and His Wolverines: The Michigan Cavalry Brigade 1861–1865* (Conshohocken, Pa.: Combined Books, 1997), 108.

7. Kidd, *Personal Recollections*, 87–88.

8. Sgt. William H. Robinson of Muir, who died March 4, 1863, at Washington, D.C.

9. Levant W. Barnhart of Ypsilanti served as 1st sergeant in Company E and was later commissioned an officer. He eventually achieved the rank of brevet major and stayed in the regular army after the war.

10. Col. Sir Percy Wyndham, an Englishman, commanded the 1st New Jersey Cavalry. The 6th Michigan was assigned to Wyndham's command for this expedition.

11. Neither Barden nor Frank Wilson appear in the roster of the 6th Michigan.

12. Maj. Gen. Joseph Hooker, commanding the Army of the Potomac.

13. The cavalry division of Brig. Gen. William Woods Averell, commanding the Second Division of the Army of the Potomac's newly formed Cavalry Corps. The fight Kidd refered to here was the Battle of Kelley's Ford, fought on March 17, 1863, arguably the federal cavalry's first victory.

14. Maj. Gen. J. E. B. Stuart, commander of the Confederate cavalry forces attached to the Army of Northern Virginia.

15. Brig. Gen. Julius Stahel, a Hungarian-born officer assigned command of the division of cavalry attached to the defenses of Washington, D.C.

16. First Division, First Army Corps, Army of the Potomac.

17. Kidd had received a letter from his younger brother, William.

18. Kidd, *Personal Recollections*, 90–91.

19. Edward G. Longacre, "Sir Percy Wyndham," *Civil War Times Illustrated* 8 (Dec. 1968): 12, 14.

20. Samuel Harris, *Personal Reminiscences of Samuel Harris* (Chicago: Rogerson, 1897), 14.

21. Walter S. Newhall to My Dear George, Oct. 2, 1863, Newhall Family Papers, Historical Society of Pennsylvania.

22. Hugh C. Keen and Horace Mewborn, *43rd Battalion Virginia Cavalry: Mosby's Command*, 2d ed. (Lynchburg, Va.: H. E. Howard, 1993), 9.

23. Ibid., 11.

24. Robert C. Wallace, *A Few Memories of a Long Life* (Fairfield, Wash.: Ye Galleon Press, 1988), 24.

25. Keen and Mewborn, *43rd Battalion*, 24.

26. *The War of the Rebellion: A Compilation of the Official Records of the Union and Confederate Armies*, 128 vols. (Washington, D.C.: GPO, 1880–1901), ser. 1, vol. 25, 1:38–39 (hereafter cited as *OR*, and unless otherwise noted, all future references will be to series 1).

27. Ibid., 39. In January 1863, Maj. Gen. George Stoneman was appointed to command the newly formed Cavalry Corps of the Army of the Potomac. Wyndham referred to the Army of the Potomac's Cavalry Corps in his reference to Stoneman's cavalry forces.

28. Ibid., 40.

29. Ibid.

30. Ezra W. Warner, *Generals in Blue: Lives of the Union Commanders* (Baton Rouge: Louisiana State Univ. Press, 1964), 469.

31. Kidd, *Personal Recollections*, 97.

32. Edward G. Longacre, *The Cavalry at Gettysburg: A Tactical Study of Mounted Operations During the Civil War's Pivotal Campaign, 9 June –14 July 1863* (Lincoln: University of Nebraska Press, 1986), p. 61.

33. Kidd refers to Maj. Gen. James Ewell Brown Stuart, Robert E. Lee's chief of cavalry.

34. This was actually the 1st West Virginia Cavalry. Along with the 5th New York, 18th Pennsylvania, and 1st Vermont, this unit rendered excellent service throughout the coming months of campaigning.

35. Maj. Gen. Ambrose Everett Burnside commanded the Army of the Potomac from November 1862 to February 1863. The "great battle-field" refers to the site of Burnside's disastrous defeat at the Battle of Fredericksburg, fought on December 13 and 14, 1862.

36. John S. Mosby, *The Memoirs of Colonel John S. Mosby* (New York: Little, Brown, 1917), 172–74; Keen and Mewborn, *43rd Battalion*, 32–35.

37. Longacre, *Custer and His Wolverines*, 10. The 1st Michigan Cavalry was utilized primarily for mounted fighting as well. Its proficiency with the saber was well known. The 7th Michigan was armed with single-shot Burnside carbines—not with Spencer repeating rifles, as were the 5th and 6th Michigan. As a result, the 7th Michigan was

considered an "understudy to the 1st Michigan," even though the 7th Michigan was also capable of fighting effectively while dismounted. These two regiments are best known for their crucial roles in two of the most famous mounted charges of the Civil War on the East Cavalry Field at Gettysburg on the afternoon of July 3, 1863. On that day, the 5th and 6th Michigan fought effectively while dismounted.

38. Joseph T. Copeland to J. C. Kelton, July 9, 1863, Simon Gratz Collection, Historical Society of Pennsylvania.

39. Longacre, *Custer and His Wolverines*, 114–15.

40. Virgil Carrington Jones, *Ranger Mosby* (Chapel Hill: Univ. of North Carolina Press, 1944), 72–73.

41. Lt. Col. Russell A. Alger, second in command of the regiment.

42. A squadron typically consisted of two companies. For a new regiment such as the 6th Michigan, which had not yet suffered many casualties, a squadron probably included close to two hundred men.

43. This probably refers to the rest of Stahel's division, which was another brigade consisting of the 5th New York, 1st Vermont, 1st West Virginia, and 18th Pennsylvania cavalry regiments.

44. *OR*, vol. 25, 1:72.

45. Ibid., 78.

46. Lee, *Personal and Historical Sketches*, 221.

47. Brig. Gen. Fitzhugh Lee, nephew of Gen. Robert E. Lee and commander of a Confederate cavalry brigade attached to Stuart's command.

48. *Detroit Free Press*, Apr. 15, 1863.

49. Longacre, *Custer and His Wolverines*, 115.

50. Jeffry D. Wert, *Mosby's Rangers: The True Adventures of the Most Famous Command of the Civil War* (New York: Simon and Schuster, 1990), 55.

51. Freedom Hill is also known as Independence Hill, located just to the west of Tyson's Corner.

52. First Lt. Edward Craw and 2d Lt. Ambrose L. Soule, both of Lyons, Michigan.

53. Kidd probably refers to a stream near this site called Difficult Run.

54. The area that Kidd described was the theater of operations for the 2d Bull Run campaign, which took up much of the summer of 1862. Maj. Gen. John Pope, commander of the Federal Army of Virginia, gave strict orders for his army to live off the land, and his large force virtually denuded the area.

55. This was the Loudoun Valley of Virginia, which saw a great deal of fighting during the second half of June 1863 when the Confederate Army of Northern Virginia made its advance into Pennsylvania.

56. Kidd refers to the Emancipation Proclamation, issued by Abraham Lincoln on January 1, 1863, which freed those slaves held in states still in rebellion against the Union at that time.

57. Drainesville is in the heart of Mosby's Confederacy and was often considered one of the more staunch bastions of support for his efforts.

58. A week before the great cavalry battle at Brandy Station, it was known that the Confederate cavalry was concentrating near Culpeper. Most observers speculated that the concentration of force was preparatory for a massive raid into Pennsylvania.

59. Kidd accurately predicted Lee's precise line of march into Pennsylvania.

60. Kidd, *Personal Recollections,* 107.

61. *OR,* vol. 27, 3:18.

62. Ibid., 31.

63. *Mecosta County Pioneer,* July 2, 1863.

64. Wert, *Mosby's Rangers,* 66.

65. *OR,* vol. 27, 1:44.

66. Pleasonton to Farnsworth, June 28, 1863, Pleasonton Papers, Library of Congress.

67. Luther S. Trowbridge, "The Operations of the Cavalry in the Gettysburg Campaign," Military Order of the Loyal Legion of the United States, *Michigan War Papers,* vol. 1 (Oct. 6, 1888), 7–8.

68. John S. Mosby, *Stuart's Cavalry in the Gettysburg Campaign* (New York: Moffat, Yard, 1908), 66.

69. Frank L. Klement, ed., "Edwin B. Bigelow: A Michigan Sergeant in the Civil War," *Michigan History* 38 (Sept. 1954): 218–19.

3. Campaigning with the Army of the Potomac: Gettysburg and After

1. Stahel's division was not assigned to the Army of the Potomac. Rather, it formed part of the forces specifically assigned to the defenses of Washington, D.C. Late in June, the division was temporarily attached to the Army of the Potomac. That assignment soon became permanent. Maj. Gen. William H. French commanded the Federal garrison at Harpers Ferry during most of the Gettysburg campaign, but later assumed temporary command of the Army of the Potomac's Third Corps after its commander, Maj. Gen. Daniel E. Sickles, was severely wounded at Gettysburg. The ranking division commander of the First Corps, Maj. Gen. Abner Doubleday, was entitled to corps command after Reynolds assumed command of the army's right wing.

2. The army's senior corps commander, Maj. Gen. John F. Reynolds, regularly commanded the First Corps, but assumed wing command as the Army of the Potomac moved north. This passage actually refers to the left wing of the Army of the Potomac; Hooker abandoned the "grand division" concept in February 1863.

3. On June 17, a brutal cavalry fight took place near Aldie in the Loudoun Valley of Virginia. In this passage, Kidd should have referred to the Battle of Upperville, fought on June 21.

4. Located in Culpeper County, Virginia, Kelly's Ford was a major point of passage across the Rappahannock River. The ford had already been the scene of several major mounted engagements during the war. Maj. Gen. Alfred Pleasonton assumed command of the Army of the Potomac's Cavalry Corps when Hooker relieved Maj. Gen. George Stoneman of command after the Battle of Chancellorsville.

5. Capt. Peter A. Weber of Grand Rapids.

6. Guidons are swallow-tailed pennons used to distinguish cavalry from infantry units. Guidons often had unique appearances.

7. The Union army had two pontoon bridges at this crossing, over which much of the Army of the Potomac crossed on the way to Gettysburg.

8. Maj. Thaddeus Foote, second in command of the regiment, and Maj. Simeon B. Brown, its third ranking officer.

9. Kidd, *Personal Recollections*, 116.

10. Linda G. Black, "Gettysburg's Preview of War: Early's June 26, 1863 Raid," *Gettysburg: Articles of Lasting Historical Interest* 3 (July 1990): 5.

11. Walter Kempster, "The Cavalry at Gettysburg," Military Order of the Loyal Legion of the United States, *Wisconsin War Papers*, vol. 4 (Kidd read October 1, 1913), 399.

12. Joseph T. Copeland to J. C. Kelton, July 9, 1863, Simon Gratz Collection, Historical Society of Pennsylvania.

13. Edward G. Longacre, "Judson Kilpatrick," *Civil War Times Illustrated* 10 (Apr. 1971): 10.

14. James H. Wilson, *Under the Old Flag: Recollections of Military Operations in the War for the Union, the Spanish War, the Boxer Rebellion, Etc.* (New York: D. Appleton, 1912), 1:370–71.

15. Worthington C. Ford, ed., *A Cycle of Adams Letters 1861–1865* (Boston: Houghton-Mifflin, 1920), 2:44–45.

16. Theodore C. Lyman, *Meade's Headquarters 1863–1865: Letters of Colonel Theodore Lyman from the Wilderness to Appomattox*, ed. George R. Agassiz (1922; reprint, Lincoln: Univ. of Nebraska Press, 1992), 76.

17. James A. Connolly, *Three Years in the Army of the Cumberland: The Letters and Diary of Major James A. Connolly* (Bloomington: Univ. of Indiana Press, 1959), 348.

18. *OR*, vol. 27, 3:376.

19. There is some dispute as to whether Custer's promotion from lieutenant to captain came through prior to his promotion to brigadier general.

20. Kidd, *Personal Recollections*, 128.

21. Samuel Harris, *Michigan Brigade of Cavalry at the Battle of Gettysburg, July 3, 1863, Under Command of Brig.-Gen. Geo. A. Custer* (Cass City, Mich.: privately printed, 1894), 7.

22. Kidd, *Personal Recollections*, 129.

23. *OR*, vol. 27, 1:992.

24. Kidd, *Personal Recollections*, 134.

25. *New York Times*, Aug. 6, 1863. The author of a recent article on the role of the 18th Pennsylvania Cavalry in the Gettysburg Campaign contends that this charge was actually made by the 18th Pennsylvania, not the 6th Michigan. There is some authority to support his position, but his position is not supported by the traditional interpretations of this action and is at odds with most of the surviving primary source accounts. See Harold A. Klingensmith, "A Cavalry Regiment's First Campaign: The 18th Penn-

sylvania at Gettysburg," *Gettysburg: Articles of Lasting Historical Interest* 20 (Dec. 1998): 61n. 79. This author does not accept Klingensmith's interpretation of these events.

26. Kidd, *Personal Recollections*, 134.

27. Paul Shevchuk, "The Battle of Hunterstown, Pennsylvania, July 2, 1863," *Gettysburg: Articles of Lasting Historical Interest* 1 (July 1989): 93–104.

28. Longacre, *Custer and His Wolverines*, 140.

29. Shevchuk, "Battle of Hunterstown," 100.

30. *Michigan at Gettysburg: Proceedings Incident to the Dedication of the Michigan Monuments Upon the Battlefield at Gettysburg, June 12th, 1889* (Detroit: Winn and Hammond, 1889), 142.

31. The Third Division, Cavalry Corps, Army of the Potomac, commanded by Brig. Gen. Hugh Judson Kilpatrick. The Michigan Brigade was the Second Brigade of the Third Division.

32. Small towns near Hanover, Pennsylvania.

33. First Lt. Seymour Shipman of New Haven, Michigan; Kidd's close friend, Henry E. Thompson; and 1st Sgt. Charles W. Cox of St. Clair, who was mortally wounded at Hunterstown on July 2 and died the next day.

34. Monterey Pass ran through South Mountain, near Greencastle, Pennsylvania, not far from the Mason-Dixon Line. For more details about the fight at Monterey Pass, see Eric J. Wittenberg, "The Midnight Fight in the Monterey Pass, July 4-5, 1863," *North and South* 2.6 (May 1999): 44–54.

35. By then, the regiment was known as the 1st West Virginia Cavalry.

36. Maj. Noah Ferry of the 5th Michigan Cavalry.

37. Luther W. Hopkins, *From Bull Run to Appomattox: A Boy's View* (Baltimore: Fleet-McGinley, 1908), 105.

38. Longacre, *Custer and His Wolverines*, 160.

39. Longacre, *Cavalry at Gettysburg*, 262–65.

40. Kidd, *Personal Recollections*, 164–65.

41. Ibid., 110–11.

42. Ibid., 185.

43. *New York Times*, Aug. 6, 1863.

44. John Watts DePeyster, *Decisive Conflicts of the Civil War, or Slaveholders' Rebellion* (New York: MacDonald, 1867), 149.

45. See Garry L. Bush, "Sixth Michigan Cavalry at Falling Waters: The End of the Gettysburg Campaign," *Gettysburg: Articles of Lasting Historical Interest* 9 (July 1993): 109–16.

46. Ibid., 187–88.

47. The division of Maj. Gen. Henry Heth, assigned to Lt. Gen. A. P. Hill's Third Corps of the Army of Northern Virginia.

48. Capt. David G. Royce of Burns, 2d Lt. Charles E. Bolza of Grand Rapids, and 1st Lt. Edward Potter of Burchville.

49. Second Lts. James H. Kellogg of Grand Rapids, and George W. Crawford of Plainfield.

50. Unidentified.

51. First Lt. Manning D. Birge of Grand Rapids.

52. Second Lt. Stephen H. Ballard of Grand Rapids.

53. First Lt. Daniel H. Powers of Grand Rapids.

54. Capt. William Hyser of Plainfield.

55. Capt. Henry L. Wise of Caledonia.

56. Capt. John F. Andrews of Thornapple.

57. First Lt. Peter Cramer of Woodland.

58. Capt. John Torry of Saginaw.

59. Kidd, *Personal Recollections*, 162–63. For more on Farnsworth's gallant charge and heroic death, see Eric J. Wittenberg, *Gettysburg's Forgotten Cavalry Actions* (Gettysburg, Pa.: Thomas Publications, 1998).

60. Capt. Harvey H. Vinton of Vergennes.

61. Alexander C. M. Pennington to Jacob L. Greene, Aug. 2, 1863, in *Supplement to the Official Records of the Union and Confederate Armies*, 100 vols. (Wilmington, N.C.: Broadfoot Publishing, 1990), ser. 1, vol. 5: 288.

62. William H. Rockwell to wife, July 27, 1863, Rockwell Letters, Waldo Library, Western Michigan University.

63. Jeffry D. Wert, *Custer: The Controversial Life of George Armstrong Custer* (New York: Simon and Schuster, 1996), 102.

64. George A. Custer to sister, July 26, 1863, Custer Collection, Monroe County Library System, Monroe, Michigan.

65. *OR*, vol. 29, 1:142–43.

66. Hammond to wife, Sept. 29, 1863, in *In Memoriam: John Hammond* (Chicago: P. F. Pettibone, 1890), 72.

67. The Second Division, Cavalry Corps, Army of the Potomac, commanded by Brig. Gen. David M. Gregg.

68. Gray never returned to the regiment. His injuries prevented him from sitting in the saddle for any extended period. He resigned his commission in May 1864.

69. George A. Drew of Detroit.

70. Levant W. Barnhart of Ypsilanti, Cortez P. Pendill of Prairieville, and Albert T. Henshaw of Bowne.

71. Schuyler F. Seager of Lansing was a supernumerary, unassigned to any specific company.

72. Capt. Daniel H. Powers of Grand Rapids.

73. Capts. Harrison N. Throop of Owosso, Company K; and Philip G. Cory of Galesburg, Company L.

74. James H. Kidd, "Reminiscences of a Volunteer, Part XXXIV," *Ionia (Michigan) Sentinel*, date unknown, Kidd Papers, University of Michigan, Bentley Historical Library.

75. Kidd, *Personal Recollections*, 205.

76. J. F. S., "At Brandy Station: Graphic Description of One of the Greatest Cavalry Battles of the War," *National Tribune*, Jan. 14, 1892.

77. Judson Kilpatrick, "Lee's Campaign in October, '63. Wise in Conception, but in Execution a Failure," *Philadelphia Weekly Times*, date unknown.

78. Longacre, *Custer and His Wolverines*, 187; *OR*, vol. 29, 1:390–91.

79. J. Allen Bigelow, "Custer's Michigan Cavalry Brigade: It Has a Brisk October Day on the Banks of the Robinson River; One of its Famous Charges," *National Tribune*, July 24, 1919.

80. Kidd, *Personal Recollections*, 212.

81. *OR*, vol. 29, 1:391.

82. William D. Henderson, *The Road to Bristoe Station: Campaigning With Lee and Meade, August 1–October 20, 1863* (Lynchburg, Va.: H. E. Howard, 1987), 201.

83. *OR*, vol. 29, 1:391.

84. Brig. Gen. Fitzhugh Lee commanded a veteran brigade of Confederate cavalry.

85. Brig. Gen. Henry E. Davies commanded a brigade of Federal cavalry.

86. Maj. John E. Clark of Ann Arbor, second in command of the 5th Michigan Cavalry; and Capt. Edwin M. Lee of Port Huron, of the 5th Michigan Cavalry.

87. *OR*, vol. 29, 1:383.

88. Henry B. McClellan, "With Stuart in October '63: A Campaign Brimful of Successful Service and Stirring Incidents," *Philadelphia Weekly Times*, June 7, 1879.

89. Longacre, *Custer and His Wolverines*, 191.

90. Kidd, *Personal Recollections*, 222.

91. Ibid., 226.

92. Maj. Gen. Winfield Scott Hancock normally commanded the Second Corps. However, Hancock was badly wounded on the final day of the Battle of Gettysburg and had not yet recovered sufficiently to resume command in the field. Warren's permanent assignment, at this time, was as chief engineer of the Army of the Potomac, although he was later assigned to command the Fifth Corps.

93. Kidd, *Personal Recollections*, 210.

94. Stevensburg is a hamlet about five miles southeast of Brandy Station, near Kelley's Ford on the Rappahannock River.

95. Charles H. Patten of Grand Rapids.

96. James H. Kidd to Dear General, Nov. 17, 1864, Adjutant General's Reports, Michigan State Archives, Lansing.

4. Grant's Overland Campaign

1. Wallace, *A Few Memories*, 31.

2. George W. Hill Diary, Jan. 25, 1864, Allan and Rita Losh Collection, Cedar Falls, Iowa.

3. William Ball to Dear Father, Feb. 5, 1864, Ball Papers, Waldo Library, Western Michigan University.

4. Kidd, *Personal Recollections*, 229.

5. Ibid., 232.

6. Ibid., entries for Jan. 15, 17, and 18.

7. Presumably, this was the father of regimental quartermaster Charles H. Patten of Grand Rapids.

8. The "fortunate young lady" was Elizabeth Clift "Libbie" Bacon of Monroe, daughter of prominent Judge Daniel S. Bacon.

9. Kidd, *Personal Recollections*, 235, 239.

10. Lt. Gen. James Longstreet, commander of the Army of Northern Virginia's First Corps.

11. During the winter of 1863, Longstreet's corps advanced upon and besieged the Federal garrison at Suffolk, Virginia. The expedition was a failure, but it created a great deal of consternation in the Army of the Potomac's high command.

12. Fortress Monroe is a large masonry fort located at the entrance to Hampton Roads. Its presence is a major reason why Hampton Roads' excellent harbor was never closed to the United States Navy during the course of the Civil War. Fortress Monroe was a major point of embarkation and debarkation for Federal troops being sent to various locations on the Peninsula.

13. Custer commanded a diversionary raid of five hundred handpicked troopers on Albemarle County, Virginia.

14. Kidd, *Personal Recollections*, 243.

15. Ibid., 240.

16. A. C. Litchfield, "Battle Near Richmond, March 1, 1864," in Lee, *Personal and Historical Sketches*, 29.

17. Stephen Z. Starr, *The Union Cavalry in the Civil War* (Baton Rouge: Louisiana State Univ. Press, 1981), 2:63.

18. Charles S. Wainwright, *A Diary of Battle: The Personal Journals of Colonel Charles S. Wainwright, 1861–1865*, ed. Allan Nevins (1962; reprint, Gettysburg, Pa.: Stan Clark Military Books, 1990), p. 325.

19. Kidd, *Personal Recollections*, 245.

20. Kidd's good friend, Henry E. "Hank" Thompson.

21. Ulysses S. Grant, *Personal Memoirs of Ulysses S. Grant* (New York: Charles L. Webster, 1886), 2:480–81.

22. Kidd, *Personal Recollections*, 298.

23. Philip H. Sheridan, *Personal Memoirs of P. H. Sheridan, General, United States Army* (New York: Charles L. Webster, 1888), 1:354–56.

24. George B. Sanford, *Fighting Rebels and Redskins: Experiences in Army Life of Colonel George B. Sanford, 1861–1892*, ed. E. R. Hagemann (Norman: Univ. of Oklahoma Press, 1969), 224.

25. Kidd, *Personal Recollections*, 261.

26. James H. Kidd, *The Michigan Cavalry Brigade in the Wilderness* (Detroit: Winn and Hammond, 1890), 4.

27. Sheridan, *Personal Memoirs*, 1:352–53.

28. Wert, *Custer*, 149.

29. J. K. Lowden, "A Gallant Record: Michigan's 5th Cav. in the Latter Period the War," *National Tribune*, July 23, 1896.

30. George Armstrong Custer and Elizabeth Bacon Custer, *The Custer Story: The Life and Letters of General George A. Custer and His Wife Elizabeth*, ed. Marguerite Merington (New York: Devin-Adair, 1950), 89.

31. *OR*, vol. 36, 1:787.

32. Special Order No. 4, Mar. 23, 1864, Regimental Order Books, 6th Michigan Cavalry, RG 94, National Archives.

33. Special Order No. 4, Apr. 16, 1864.

34. Maj. Gen. Alfred Pleasonton was relieved of command of the Army of the Potomac's Cavalry Corps and sent to Kansas, a backwater of the war. Although Grant never said why he relieved Pleasonton of command, Pleasonton was not the sort of commander to lead from the front—he was the sort to let others lead from the front. Further, Grant was dissatisfied with the accomplishments of the mounted arm.

35. Command of the Third Division went to another very young cavalryman, Brig. Gen. James H. Wilson, a favorite of Grant. Wilson did not perform well in command of such a large body of veteran troopers.

36. Thomas White Ferry, U.S. senator from Michigan and formerly congressman responsible for the district that including Ionia. Ferry was the father of Maj. Noah H. Ferry, of the 5th Michigan Cavalry, killed during the melee on the East Cavalry Field at Gettysburg on July 3, 1863.

37. Custer and Custer, *The Custer Story*, 92.

38. Col. Thomas Casimir Devin of New York City, formerly commanding officer of the 6th New York Cavalry. Devin had commanded a brigade of cavalry for almost a year by the time of Kidd's letter home. By war's end, Devin was a major general commanding a division of cavalry.

39. For more details about the Wilderness campaign, see Gordon C. Rhea, *The Battle of the Wilderness, May 5–6, 1864* (Baton Rouge: Louisiana State Univ. Press, 1994).

40. Gordon C. Rhea, *The Battles for Spotsylvania Court House and the Road to Yellow Tavern, May 7–12, 1864* (Baton Rouge: Louisiana State Univ. Press, 1997), 213.

41. Ibid., 69.

42. Kidd, *Personal Recollections*, 286.

43. Sheridan, *Personal Memoirs*, 1:371.

44. Kidd, *Personal Recollections*, 289.

45. George W. Hill Diary, May 11, 1864, Allan and Rita Losh Collection, Cedar Falls, Iowa. Hill was captured the same day and spent most of the balance of the war as a prisoner of war in Richmond's notorious Libby Prison.

46. Robert S. Hudgins, *Recollections of an Old Dominion Dragoon: The Civil War Experiences of Sgt. Robert S. Hudgins II, of Co. B, 3rd Virginia Cavalry*, eds. Garland C. Hudgins, and Richard B. Kleese (Orange, Va: Publisher's Press, Inc., 1993), 89–90. Sgt. John Huff served with the 2d U. S. Sharpshooters before enlisting in the 5th Michigan. He had won first prize for sharpshooting and was known as a crack shot. Huff watched one of his comrade's shots miss Stuart and his staff, and Huff commented, "Tom, you shot too low and to the left." Huff turned to Col. Russell A. Alger and said, "Colonel, I can fetch that man." Alger responded, "Try him." He then took deliberate aim across

a fence and fired; Stuart fell, mortally wounded. Huff proudly proclaimed to Alger, "There's a spread-eagle for you." Huff himself was killed in action at the battle of Haw's Shop, on May 28. This account is somewhat suspect; Alger is the only source for the specific identification of Huff as the soldier who shot and mortally wounded Stuart. John Robertson, comp., *Michigan in the War* (Lansing: W. S. George, 1882), 597.

47. Robertson, *Michigan in the War,* 597.

48. *OR,* vol. 36, 1:790.

49. Custer and Custer, *The Custer Story,* 97.

50. Kidd, *Personal Recollections,* 306.

51. Lyman, *Meade's Headquarters,* 125.

52. Moses Harris, "The Union Cavalry," *War Papers Read Before the Commandery of the State of Wisconsin, Military Order of the Loyal Legion of the United States,* vol. 1 (1891), 365.

53. *OR,* vol. 36, 1:801.

54. Longacre, *Custer and His Wolverines,* 223; Wert, *Custer,* 159.

55. James H. Kidd, *Historical Sketch of General Custer* (Monroe, Mich: Monroe County Library System, 1978), 23.

56. *OR,* vol. 36, 1:804.

57. Custer and Custer, *The Custer Story,* 100.

58. Cpl. Seth Carey of Ionia, who served in Kidd's Company E, was killed in action at the Battle of Haw's Shop on May 28, 1864. He is buried in the National Cemetery at Yorktown, Virginia.

59. Miles E. Hutchinson of Otisco, who also served in Kidd's Company E. Kidd was wrong about Hutchinson's prospects for recovery, because he died of his wounds.

60. Brig. Gen. David M. Gregg's Second Division of the Army of the Potomac's Cavalry Corps.

61. The brigade of Brig. Gen. Matthew Calbraith Butler of South Carolina.

62. The publisher of the *Ionia (Michigan) Sentinel.*

63. George Gray to Edwin M. Stanton, May 14, 1864, in *Record Sixth Michigan Cavalry,* 5. This letter played a critical role in Kidd's future as a soldier. As a consequence of his poor health, Gray resigned his commission as colonel on May 14, 1864: "in consequence of injuries received while temporarily in command of a Brigade, which rendered me wholly unfit for any duty. . . . [T]he effect of the injuries I received incapacitates me for the saddle, and renders me permanently unfit for active service. . . . Under these circumstances, [I feel] it to be most unjust to my very excellent Field Officers, on whom devolve the labors and responsibilities attending the command of the regiment, that I should retain my rank, while they perform the services corresponding thereto."

64. Kidd's friend Angelo E. Tower finally resigned his commission, as a consequence of disability, on August 15, 1864.

65. Special Order No. 49, June 12, 1864, Regimental Order Books, 6th Michigan Cavalry, RG 94, National Archives.

66. Wallace, *A Few Memories,* 59.

67. James M. Kidd to James H. Kidd, June 5, 1864, Kidd Papers, University of Michigan, Bentley Historical Library.

68. Francis W. Kellogg to James H. Kidd, June 5, 1864, ibid.

69. The list represents all company commanders of the 6th Michigan, as well as several of the staff officers.

70. Capt. Robert F. Judson of Kalamazoo, 5th Michigan Cavalry, served as the Michigan Brigade's Assistant Inspector General until he was discharged on October 7, 1864, as a result of disability that resulted from battle wounds.

71. Sheridan, *Personal Memoirs*, 1:417.

72. Kidd, *Personal Recollections*, 354.

73. Ibid., 363.

74. Kidd, *Historical Sketch*, 30.

75. The Virginia Central Railroad connected Lynchburg and Richmond.

76. The cavalry divisions of Maj. Gens. Wade Hampton and Fitzhugh Lee—the two largest Confederate cavalry divisions—were sent from the main Confederate defensive lines to intercept Sheridan's force of raiders.

77. Francis E. Heitman, *Historical Register and Dictionary of the United States Army* (Washington, D.C.: GPO, 1903), 1:596.

78. Kidd, *Personal Recollections*, 372.

79. *OR*, vol. 36, 1:799.

80. Kidd, *Personal Recollections*, 370.

81. *Detroit Free Press*, July 21, 1864.

82. Heitman, *Historical Register*, 1:914.

83. *Detroit Free Press*, July 21, 1864.

84. James M. Kidd to James H. Kidd, June 14, 1864, Kidd Papers, University of Michigan, Bentley Historical Library.

85. Capt. Don G. Lovell of Grand Rapids, commanding Company F. Lovell was wounded in action on June 12, 1864, at the Battle of Trevilian Station. He was eventually commissioned major on June 21, 1865.

86. Confederate lieutenant general Jubal A. Early took his Second Corps, Army of Northern Virginia, into the Shenandoah Valley and joined with other forces there that were rechristened the Army of the Valley. Defeating a scratch force under Maj. Gen. Lew Wallace at Monocacy Junction on the Baltimore and Ohio Railroad near Frederick, Maryland, Early advanced on the federal capital. He was rebuffed when elements of the Sixth Army Corps arrived just in time to repulse his planned attack at Fort Stevens, near modern-day Chevy Chase. Early then turned north, sending elements on a raid into Maryland and Pennsylvania.

87. Unidentified.

88. Uncle Rich to James H. Kidd, July 14, 1864, Kidd Papers, University of Michigan, Bentley Historical Library.

89. Unidentified.

90. Kidd probably refers to the lengthy cavalry raid of Confederate Brig. Gen. John Hunt Morgan, who spent nearly a month riding through Indiana and the southern portion of Ohio.

91. Actually, a large force of clerks and convalescents from the Veteran Reserve Corps came out of Washington's defenses to man various forts ringing the city when Early's

raid threatened to take the thinly defended Union capital. The reservists manned the city's defenses until infantry of the 6th Infantry Corps of the Army of the Potomac arrived on July 12, just before Early's planned assault on Fort Stevens, which helped form the city's defenses. Kidd's criticism is a bit unfair to the men who answered the call.

92. Kidd, *Personal Recollections*, 371.

93. Douglas Southall Freeman, *R. E. Lee: A Biography* (New York: Charles Scribner's Sons, 1934), 3:398.

94. *OR*, vol. 36, 1:802.

95. The sketch itself is missing.

96. Kidd refers to one of the many fights that marked Maj. Gen. William T. Sherman's advance on Atlanta, which occupied most of the summer of 1864. Although it is unclear which battle Kidd refers to, it was either the Battle of Peachtree Creek, fought on July 20, or the Battle of Atlanta, fought on July 22. Not enough information has been provided in this letter to enable identification of the specific engagement to which Kidd refers.

5. Sheridan's Shenandoah Valley Campaign

1. Jeffry D. Wert, *From Winchester to Cedar Creek: The Shenandoah Campaign of 1864* (Carlisle, Pa: South Mountain Press, 1987), 7.

2. *OR*, vol. 37, 2:572.

3. Ibid., vol. 43, 1:697–98.

4. Kidd, *Personal Recollections*, 374.

5. Ibid., 376–77.

6. Ibid., 380–81.

7. Adm. David Farragut had recently won a major naval battle in Mobile Bay, Alabama, which closed a major port to the Confederate blockade runners.

8. *OR*, vol. 43, 2:104.

9. Ibid., 1:455.

10. Kidd, *Personal Recollections*, 385.

11. Ibid., 387.

12. *Ionia (Michigan) Sentinel*, June 5, 1866.

13. *OR*, vol. 43, 1:498.

14. Col. Charles R. Lowell, of the 2d Massachusetts Cavalry, now commanded the reserve brigade.

15. Kidd, *Personal Recollections*, 390–91.

16. *OR*, vol. 43, 1:444.

17. Maj. Charles W. Deane of the 6th Michigan recorded that Torbert was opposed to this charge until Custer's leading charge forced Torbert to approve it at the head of the Michigan Brigade.

18. Wallace, *A Few Memories*, 49.

19. *Ionia (Michigan) Sentinel*, June 5, 1866.

20. Kidd, *Personal Recollections*, 392.

21. Ibid., 458.

22. Kidd, *Personal Recollections*, 394.

23. *OR*, vol. 43, 1:458.

24. Ibid., 428.

25. Gregory J. W. Urwin, *Custer Victorious: The Civil War Battles of George Armstrong Custer* (New Brunswick, N.J.: Associated Univ. Presses, 1983), 190.

26. Kidd, *Personal Recollections*, 236.

27. Ibid., 408.

28. Thomas W. Custer Medal of Honor Citations, Medal of Honor Citation Files, National Archives. The first was awarded for Custer's capture of a Rebel battle flag at the Battle of Namozine Church in May 1863. Custer received the second for capturing another battle flag at the Battle of Sailer's Creek, Virginia, on April 6, 1865.

29. George M. Neese, *Three Years in the Confederate Horse Artillery* (1903; reprint, Dayton, Ohio: Morningside House, 1988), 317.

30. *OR*, vol. 43, 2:269.

31. Wert, *From Winchester to Cedar Creek*, 147–56.

32. Kidd, *Personal Recollections*, 399.

33. *Ionia (Michigan) Sentinel*, June 5, 1866.

34. John L. Heatwole, *The Burning: Sheridan in the Shenandoah Valley* (Charlottesville, Va.: Rockbridge Publishing, 1998), 190.

35. *OR*, vol. 43, 1:30–31.

36. Ibid., 442.

37. Ibid., 2:327.

38. Wert, *From Winchester to Cedar Creek*, 160–65.

39. Theodore C. Mahr, *The Battle of Cedar Creek: Showdown in the Shenandoah, October 1–30, 1864* (Lynchburg, Va.: H. E. Howard, 1992), 55.

40. *OR*, vol. 43, 1:339.

41. Sheridan, *Personal Memoirs*, 2:59.

42. *OR*, vol. 43, 1:559.

43. Mahr, *Cedar Creek*, 177–80.

44. Kidd, *Personal Recollections*, 411.

45. Mahr, *Cedar Creek*, 136.

46. Ibid., 413–14.

47. Ibid., 421–23.

48. *OR*, vol. 43, 1:450.

49. Thomas L. Rosser, *Riding With Rosser*, ed. S. Roger Keller (Shippensburg, Pa.: Burd Street Press, 1997), 51–52.

50. Kidd, *Personal Recollections*, 424–25.

51. Maj. Gen. Horatio G. Wright, commander of the Sixth Army Corps.

52. Although Wright was caught off guard at Cedar Creek, this author has been unable to find any other references to his intoxication during the battle. Indeed, such conduct would have been very much out of character for Wright, who was known as a steady and reliable officer.

53. Rosser, *Riding With Rosser*, 52.

54. *OR*, vol. 43, 1:54.

55. Ibid., 461.

56. Ibid.

57. Uncle Rich to James H. Kidd, Nov. 3, 1864, Kidd Papers, University of Michigan, Bentley Historical Library.

58. James M. Kidd to James H. Kidd, Nov. 5, 1864, ibid.

59. Catherine Kidd to James H. Kidd, Nov. 12, 1864, ibid.

60. Longacre, *Custer and His Wolverines*, 260.

61. Special Order No. 14, Oct. 29, 1864, Regimental Order Books, 6th Michigan Cavalry, RG 94, National Archives.

62. Rix Diary, Jan. 5, Feb. 6, 18, 1865, Clarke Historical Library, Central Michigan University.

63. Unidentified.

64. Longacre, *Custer and His Wolverines*, 264.

65. Uncle Rich's wife to James H. Kidd, Dec. 5, 1864, Kidd Papers, University of Michigan, Bentley Historical Library.

66. James M. Kidd to James H. Kidd, Dec. 7, 1864, ibid.

67. Special Order No. 42, Dec. 6, 1864, Regimental Order Books, 6th Michigan Cavalry, RG 94, National Archives.

6. Missing the End of the War

1. *Detroit Advertiser and Tribune*, June 17, 1865.

2. Longacre, *Custer and His Wolverines*, 263.

3. James M. Kidd to James H. Kidd, Jan. 4, 1865, Kidd Papers, University of Michigan, Bentley Historical Library.

4. *Ionia (Michigan) Sentinel*, June 5, 1866.

5. Bvt. Brig. Gen. James W. Forsyth served as Sheridan's chief of staff.

6. Gregory J. W. Urwin, "Custer: The Civil War Years," in Andrew Paul Hutton, ed., *The Custer Reader* (Lincoln: Univ. of Nebraska Press, 1992), 22.

7. Asa B. Isham, *An Historical Sketch of the Seventh Regiment Michigan Volunteer Cavalry from Its Organization, in 1862, to Its Muster-Out, in 1865* (New York: Town Topics Publishing, 1893), 77–78.

8. *Detroit Advertiser and Tribune*, Apr. 4, 1865.

9. Harlan Lloyd Page, "The Battle of Waynesborough," in Hutton, *The Custer Reader*, 80–81.

10. Rich Kidd to James H. Kidd, Mar. 6, 1865, Kidd Papers, University of Michigan, Bentley Historical Library.

11. Louis H. Jennings of Grand Rapids enlisted in Company H of the 6th Michigan Cavalry on February 28, 1865, and was discharged in Washington, D.C., on June 3, 1865.

12. At the end of July 1863, just after the conclusion of the Gettysburg campaign,

a Cavalry Bureau was created and given the primary task of providing adequate mounts for the very large cavalry forces of the Union. The bureau provided mounts for new regiments that still filtered into Federal service and established several remount camps. At these camps new horses were trained to serve as proper cavalry horses, a process that took time. One large camp was located at Pleasant Valley, near Winchester, at the northern end of the Shenandoah Valley. Undoubtedly, this is the camp Kidd referred to in his letter.

13. Kidd, *Personal Recollections*, 435.

14. Ibid.

15. Fitzhugh Lee to Osmun Latrobe, Mar. 27, 1865, Lee Headquarters Papers, Virginia Historical Society.

16. For a detailed examination of the fight at Five Forks, see Ed Bearss and Chris Calkins, *The Battle of Five Forks* (Lynchburg, Va.: H. E. Howard, 1985).

17. Maj. Gen. Winfield Scott Hancock, former commander of the Army of the Potomac's Second Corps, received a very serious wound on the third day of Gettysburg. It had never fully healed, and the continuing problems were serious enough to prevent Hancock from performing his duty in the field, so he was sent to take command of the Middle Military District during the war's waning days.

18. When the First and Third Cavalry Divisions returned to the Army of the Potomac in March, Torbert was assigned to command the remaining Federal cavalry forces in the Shenandoah Valley.

19. James M. Kidd to James H. Kidd, Apr. 2, 1865, Kidd Papers, University of Michigan, Bentley Historical Library.

20. Lanman, *Red Book*, 264.

21. James M. Kidd to James H. Kidd, Apr. 6, 1865.

22. Thomas W. Custer and Elliott M. Norton Medal of Honor Citations, Medal of Honor Citation Files, National Archives.

23. John A. Clark, "The Final Push to Appomattox: Captain Clark's Account of the Seventh Michigan Cavalry in Action," ed. Frances R. Reece, *Michigan History Magazine* 28 (1944): 463.

24. Sherman's March to the Sea.

25. *OR*, vol. 48, 3:714, 774.

26. Ibid., 804.

27. Kidd, *Personal Recollections*, 444.

28. *OR*, vol. 48, 3:830.

29. Keen and Mewborn, *43rd Battalion*, 271.

30. Kidd, *Personal Recollections*, 448.

31. *OR*, vol. 48, 3:897.

32. Special Order No. 98, Apr. 20, 1865, Kidd Papers, University of Michigan, Bentley Historical Library.

33. Isham, *Historical Sketch*, 86. On April 22, Grant ordered his chief of staff, Maj. Gen. Henry W. Halleck, to "move Sheridan with his cavalry toward Greensborough as soon as possible. I think it will be well to send one corps of infantry with the cavalry.

The infantry need not go father than Danville unless they receive orders hereafter." Halleck ordered Meade to "put a corps at the disposition of General Sheridan." The Sixth Army Corps, which had been an integral part of success for the Army of the Shenandoah, was assigned to this task. *OR*, vol. 46, 3:888–89.

34. Wallace, *A Few Memories*, 65.

35. Libby Prison held Federal officers, whereas Belle Isle was the principal Confederate prison for enlisted men. Both prisons had similar reputations for brutality and pestilence.

36. Kidd refers to some of the many handsome statues lining Richmond's famous Monument Boulevard, which today also includes monuments to most of the Confederacy's heroes.

37. As the Confederate army pulled out of Richmond, the troops set many warehouses and stores aflame to keep the contents from falling into the hands of the enemy.

38. Lt. Solon H. Finney of Lyons. Finney enlisted in Company E as a sergeant in September 1862 and was commissioned second lieutenant in May 1864. He served until mortally wounded in action at Beaver Mills on April 4, 1865, and died on the 9th. He is buried in the Poplar Grove National Cemetery in Virginia.

39. This handsome flag survived and is on display in the Michigan State Historical Museum in Lansing.

40. A "housewife" was the soldier's sewing kit—carried in his pack and complete with a small rolled bit of fabric with needles, pins, thread, extra buttons, all the little bits and pieces a soldier needed to mend his own gear.

41. Wallace, *A Few Memories*, 67.

42. Special Order No. 10, May 19, 1865, Regimental Order Books, 6th Michigan Cavalry, RG 94, National Archives.

43. *OR*, vol. 46, 3:1191.

44. Wert, *Custer*, 228.

45. Wallace, *A Few Memories*, 68.

46. *OR*, vol. 46, 3:1191.

47. Longacre, *Custer and His Wolverines*, 279.

48. Kidd Diary, Aug. 14, 1865, Kidd Papers, University of Michigan, Bentley Historical Library

49. *OR*, vol. 48, 1:331.

50. It appears that this was the younger brother of Kidd's childhood friend, Angelo Tower.

51. Unidentified.

52. *Grand Rapids Daily Eagle*, June 19, 1865.

53. Victor C. Wattles to Jasper, June 11, 1865, University of Michigan, Victor C. Wattles Letters, Bentley Historical Library.

54. *OR*, vol. 48, 2:735.

55. Kidd Diary, June 8, 1865, Kidd Papers, University of Michigan, Bentley Historical Library.

56. At the time that John Brown seized the Federal armory at Harpers Ferry in 1859, the commander of the Federal forces sent to capture him was Lt. Col. Robert E. Lee.

57. Kidd proved remarkably accurate in his analysis of how future historians would view Lee. Not long after Lee's death, his former subordinates became his staunchest, most strident defenders. Former Lt. Gens. Jubal A. Early and John Brown Gordon principally led this faction, which seemed intent on canonizing Robert E. Lee. Their strident advocacy of Lee as sainted figure largely demonized James Longstreet. This school of thought was capped off with its crowning accomplishment, Douglas Southall Freeman's mammoth four-volume biography of Lee, wherein nary a critical word was written. Modern historians have taken a much more balanced view of Lee, with some recent efforts taking a far more revisionist view. The two leading examples of this approach are Thomas J. Connelly's *The Marble Man: Robert E. Lee and His Image in American Society* (New York: Knopf, 1977), and Alan T. Nolan's *Lee Considered: General Robert E. Lee and Civil War History* (Chapel Hill: Univ. of North Carolina Press, 1991). Some more balanced views of Lee are emerging, such as Emory Thomas's recent book, *Robert E. Lee: A Biography* (New York: W. W. Norton, 1995).

58. Grommon Diary, June 15, 1865, University of Michigan, Bentley Historical Library.

59. Kidd Diary, June 16, 1865, Kidd Papers, University of Michigan, Bentley Historical Library.

60. C.T. was a common abbreviation for the Colorado Territory, which encompassed most of the modern state of Colorado.

61. Unidentified.

62. Actually, Julesburg in the Colorado Territory.

7. Reluctant Indian Fighter

1. *OR*, vol. 48, 2:1129.

2. *Grand Rapids Daily Eagle*, Sept. 5, 1865.

3. LeRoy R. Hafen and Ann W. Hafen, eds., *Powder River Campaigns of 1865* (Glendale, Calif.: Arthur H. Clark, 1961), 154, 157, 169.

4. Kidd Diary, July 2, 1865, Kidd Papers, University of Michigan, Bentley Historical Library.

5. Ibid., July 4, 1865.

6. Ibid., July 5, 1865.

7. *OR*, vol. 48, 2:1112.

8. Hafen and Hafen, *Powder River*, 107.

9. Kidd Diary, July 7, 1865, Kidd Papers, University of Michigan, Bentley Historical Library.

10. James M. Kidd to James H. Kidd, July 7, 1865, Kidd Papers, University of Michigan, Bentley Historical Library.

11. Hafen and Hafen, *Powder River,* 161.

12. Kidd Diary, July 17, 1865, Kidd Papers, University of Michigan, Bentley Historical Library.

13. *OR,* vol. 48, 2:1092.

14. Hafen and Hafen, *Powder River,* 164–65. Lt. Robert A. Moon of Big Rapids. Moon was also held as a prisoner of war for more than a year and also returned to the regiment for the Powder River Indian Expedition.

15. Kidd Diary, July 21, 1865, Kidd Papers, University of Michigan, Bentley Historical Library.

16. Hafen and Hafen, *Powder River,* 165.

17. Kidd Diary, July 23, 1865, Kidd Papers, University of Michigan, Bentley Historical Library.

18. Ibid., July 24, 1865.

19. *OR,* vol. 48, 2:1123; Richard N. Ellis, "Volunteer Soldiers in the West, 1865," *Military Affairs* 34 (1970): 54.

20. Kidd Diary, July 25, 1865, Kidd Papers, University of Michigan, Bentley Historical Library.

21. Ibid., July 26, 1865.

22. *OR,* vol. 48, 2:1127.

23. Hafen and Hafen, *Powder River,* 168.

24. Regimental Order No. 58, July 27, 1865, Regimental Order Books, 6th Michigan Cavalry, RG 94, National Archives.

25. Kidd Diary, July 30, 1865, Kidd Papers, University of Michigan, Bentley Historical Library.

26. Lt. George W. Simonds of Kalamazoo, regimental adjutant of the 6th Michigan Cavalry.

27. Col. Nelson Cole of the 2d Missouri Light Artillery; Col. Samuel Walker, 16th Kansas Cavalry; and Capt. Albert Brown, 2d California Cavalry. Hafen and Hafen, Powder River, 25.

28. One of several attacks by Indians on Federal installations that led to the Powder River Indian Expedition. Ibid., 24.

29. George W. Simonds to James M. Kidd, Aug. 1, 1865, Kidd Papers, University of Michigan, Bentley Historical Library.

30. Hafen and Hafen, *Powder River,* 170.

31. *OR,* vol. 48, 1:356.

32. Kidd Diary, Aug. 2, 1865, Kidd Papers, University of Michigan, Bentley Historical Library.

33. Capt. Frank North.

34. Lts. J. Willard Brown and A. V. Richards. Brown went on to write a prominent history of the role of the Signal Corps during the Civil War.

35. Capt. Nicholas J. O'Brien, commanding the 7th Iowa Battery, attached to the column.

36. Capt. Clement G. Laurant of Louisiana served as Connor's assistant adjutant general.

37. Capt. Sam Robins of the 1st Colorado Cavalry served as chief engineer officer for the expedition; Lt. Oscar Jewett was Connor's aide-de-camp.

38. Capt. Henry E. Palmer of Ohio and the 11th Kansas Infantry served as the quartermaster for the expedition.

39. Dr. Henry Johnson of Jackson, the assistant regimental surgeon of the 6th Michigan Cavalry. Lt. Sessions P. Curtiss of Vergennes; Curtiss was held by the Confederates as a prisoner of war from September 1864 until the end of the war. Upon his release, he returned to duty with the regiment and served the duration of the Powder River Indian Expedition. Lt. Elias B. Stone of Grand Rapids. Lt. John T. Gould of Plainfield.

40. Kidd Diary, Aug. 7, 1865, Kidd Papers, University of Michigan, Bentley Historical Library.

41. Hafen and Hafen, *Powder River*, 115.

42. Ibid., 116.

43. Kidd Diary, Aug. 13, 1865, Kidd Papers, University of Michigan, Bentley Historical Library.

44. Hafen and Hafen, *Powder River*, 117.

45. *OR*, vol. 48, 2:1193.

46. Edgar I. Stewart, *Custer's Luck* (Norman: Univ. of Oklahoma Press, 1955), 37.

47. Ibid., 222–23.

48. Kidd Diary, Aug. 18, 1865, Kidd Papers, University of Michigan, Bentley Historical Library.

49. Hafen and Hafen, *Powder River*, 182.

50. Kidd Diary, Aug. 20, 1865, Kidd Papers, University of Michigan, Bentley Historical Library.

51. Ibid., Aug. 22, 1865.

52. James M. Kidd to James H. Kidd, Aug. 21, 1865, Kidd Papers, University of Michigan, Bentley Historical Library.

53. Kidd Diary, Aug. 25, 1865, Kidd Papers, University of Michigan, Bentley Historical Library.

54. Hafen and Hafen, *Powder River*, 186.

55. At the Battle of the Little Big Horn, fought June 25, 1876, Custer and over two hundred members of his 7th Cavalry Regiment died at the hands of a Sioux war party led by the legendary chiefs Sitting Bull and Crazy Horse. The similarity of the two expeditions is remarkable.

56. Stewart, *Custer's Luck*, 29.

57. Longacre, *Custer and His Wolverines*, 290.

58. *OR*, vol. 48, 1:337.

59. Henry W. Stewart to father, Sept. 21, 1865, Stewart Letters, Waldo Library, Western Michigan University.

60. Longacre, *Custer and His Wolverines*, 291.

61. Hafen and Hafen, *Powder River,* 189.

62. Ibid.

63. Kidd Diary, Aug. 27, 1865, Kidd Papers, University of Michigan, Bentley Historical Library.

64. James H. Kidd, "Reminiscences of a Volunteer," *Ionia (Michigan) Sentinel,* date unknown, Kidd Papers, University of Michigan, Bentley Historical Library.

65. Kidd Diary, Sept. 5, 1865, Kidd Papers, University of Michigan, Bentley Historical Library.

66. Lovell was promoted to major in early July. Perhaps Kidd had not learned of the promotion by the time he wrote this letter.

67. Kidd Diary, Sept. 6, 7, 1865, Kidd Papers, University of Michigan, Bentley Historical Library.

68. Ibid., Sept. 8, 1865.

69. Unidentified.

70. Brig. Gen. James A. Williamson commanded the District of St. Louis. *OR,* vol. 48, 1:10.

71. Hafen and Hafen, *Powder River,* 192.

72. Lee, "Disappointments," in Lee, *Personal and Historical Sketches,* 286.

73. Longacre, *Custer and His Wolverines,* 294.

74. *Ionia (Michigan) Sentinel,* May 15, 1866.

75. Lt. Col. Harvey H. Vinton of Vergennes, Kidd's second in command. Maj. George A. Drew of Detroit, who served as the assistant inspector general of the 2d Brigade, Third Division, Cavalry Corps. He was a special favorite of George Custer and used his influence to advance his own career, to the scorn of Kidd.

76. Kidd Pension Records, RG 15, National Archives.

77. Maj. John W. Barnes of New York, who served as assistant adjutant general to General Dodge. Heitman, *Historical Register,* 1:192.

78. Bvt. Maj. Gen. Frank Wheaton of Rhode Island commanded Federal forces stationed at Fort Laramie.

79. Longacre, *Custer and His Wolverines,* 293.

80. James M. Kidd to James H. Kidd, Nov. 16, 1865, Kidd Papers, University of Michigan, Bentley Historical Library.

81. Longacre, *Custer and His Wolverines,* 294.

Conclusion

1. *In Memoriam: Companion Bvt. Brig. Gen. James Harvey Kidd, Insignia 3744,* Military Order of the Loyal Legion of the United States, Michigan Commandery, Circular No. 5, Series of 1913, 1.

2. *Ionia (Michigan) Sentinel,* June 5, 1866.

3. Ibid., Mar. 20, 1913; James H. Kidd postwar notebook, Kidd Papers, University of Michigan, Bentley Historical Library.

4. *Ionia (Michigan) Sentinel,* unknown date, Kidd Papers.

5. Ferry to Kidd, June 30, 1866, Kidd Papers, University of Michigan, Bentley Historical Library.

6. James A. Hardie to Thomas W. Ferry, June 27, 1866, ibid.

7. E. E. Branch, ed., *History of Ionia County Michigan: Her People, Industries and Institutions* (Indianapolis: B. F. Bowen, 1916), 1:373.

8. *Ionia Souvenir of 1907*, 43.

9. *Ionia (Michigan) Weekly Standard*, Jan. 31, 1868.

10. Certified Record of Marriage, Kidd Pension Records, RG 15, National Archives.

11. *Ionia (Michigan) Sentinel*, Feb. 25, 1871.

12. *Ionia (Michigan) Weekly Standard*, Apr. 28, 1881.

13. Thomas W. Ferry to James H. Kidd, Dec. 27, 1871, Kidd Papers, University of Michigan, Bentley Historical Library.

14. *Ionia (Michigan) Sentinel*, Aug. 19, 1871.

15. Ibid., Dec. 22, 1876.

16. Ibid., June 12, 1866.

17. Ibid., June 25, 1870; *Ionia (Michigan) Weekly Standard*, June 23, 1882.

18. *Ionia (Michigan) Weekly Standard*, June 18, 1870.

19. Ibid., Mar. 20, 1913.

20. "Major Earl R. Stewart: Will Interest Himself in Appropriation for Ionia Armory," *Ionia (Michigan) Sentinel*, date unknown, Kidd Papers, University of Michigan, Bentley Historical Library.

21. *Ionia (Michigan) Sentinel*, Mar. 20, 1913.

22. Ibid., Sept. 18, 1868.

23. "Gen. Kidd's Boom: His Friends Want to Make Him Governor," *Ionia (Michigan) Sentinel*, date unknown, Kidd Papers, University of Michigan, Bentley Historical Library.

24. Ibid., Aug. 7, 1885.

25. *Ionia (Michigan) Weekly Standard*, June 16, 1882.

26. Ibid., Dec. 21, 1888.

27. *Ionia (Michigan) Sentinel*, Apr. 22, 1892.

28. The monument consists of a bronze equestrian figure of Custer, facing the Confederate lines, hat in hand, and charger reined high. It originally stood in Soldier's Park on East Front Street in the City of Monroe, but was later moved to the intersection of Elm and North Monroe Streets, where Custer's home stood. An aluminum marker reads:

Major-General George Armstrong Custer. Born in North Rumley, Ohio, George A. Custer grew up in Monroe in the home of his half-sister, Mrs. David Reed. February 9, 1864, in the Presbyterian Church here, he married Libbie Bacon, only daughter of Judge Daniel S. Bacon. During the Civil War, he received six brevets and was made Major-General before he was 26 years old, a rare distinction. From 1866 until his death at the Battle of the Little Big Horn, General Custer commanded the famous Seventh Cavalry Regiment, leading them in scouting and Indian fighting throughout Kansas and the Dakota Territory. This statue of General Custer, created by Edward C. Potter, was erected by the State of Michigan, unveiled by Mrs. Elizabeth B. Custer and dedicated by President William Howard Taft, June 4, 1910. The statue was rededicated September 3, 1955, by the First Cavalry Division of which Custer's Seventh Cavalry Regiment was a part. George S. May, *Writing on Michigan and the Civil War by Michigan Residents from October 1960 to October 1962* (Lansing: Michigan Civil War Centennial Observance Commission, 1962), 52–53.

29. Kidd, *Historical Sketch*, 2.

30. Elizabeth Bacon Custer to James H. Kidd, undated letter, Kidd Papers, University of Michigan, Bentley Historical Library.

31. Kidd Pension Records, RG 15, National Archives.

32. H. B. Hutchings to James H. Kidd, June 1, 1910, Kidd Papers, University of Michigan, Bentley Historical Library.

33. Otto G. Kirchner to James H. Kidd, June 7, 1910, ibid.

34. H. B. Hutchings to James H. Kidd, June 16, 1910, ibid.

35. *Ionia (Michigan) Sentinel*, Mar. 20, 1913.

36. Lee, *Personal and Historical Sketches*, iii.

37. *Detroit Advertiser and Tribune*, Oct. 19, 1864.

38. Joseph Jessup to brother, Sept. 27, 1864, Jessup Papers, University of Michigan, Bentley Historical Library.

39. The recipients were Cpl. Gabriel Cole, Company I, 5th Michigan Cavalry (Sept. 19, 1864, at Winchester); Pvt. Ulric L. Crocker, Company M, 6th Michigan Cavalry (Oct. 19, 1864, at the Battle of Cedar Creek); 2d Lt. Thomas W. Custer, Company B, 6th Michigan Cavalry (May 10, 1863 at Namozine Church, Virginia; and Apr. 6, 1865, at Sailers Creek, Virginia; Sgt. Henry M. Fox, Company M, 5th Michigan Cavalry (Sept. 19, 1864, at the Battle of Winchester); Capt. Hastings M. Smith, Company M, 5th Michigan Cavalry (July 24, 1863, at Newby's Crossroads, Virginia); Sgt. Charles M. Holton, Company A, 7th Michigan Cavalry (July 14, 1863, at the Battle of Falling Waters); and 2d Lt. Elliott M. Norton, Company H, 6th Michigan Cavalry (Apr. 6, 1865, at the Battle of Sailers Creek, Virginia). Medal of Honor Citation Files, National Archives.

40. The seven officers were Russell A. Alger of the 5th and 6th Michigan Cavalry (Alger served as secretary of war under President William McKinley and oversaw conduct of the Spanish-American War in 1898); Simeon B. Brown of the 6th Michigan Cavalry; Kidd; Allyne Cushing Litchfield of the 5th Michigan Cavalry; Stagg; Kidd's dear friend Henry E. Thompson of the 6th Michigan Cavalry; and Luther S. Trowbridge of the 5th Michigan Cavalry, who also received a brevet to major general in June 1865. In addition, Thornton F. Brodhead, the first commander of the 1st Michigan Cavalry, who was mortally wounded in action at Second Bull Run on August 30, 1862, received his brevet prior to the formation of the Michigan Brigade. For further information, see Roger D. Hunt and Jack R. Brown, *Brevet Brigadier Generals in Blue* (Gaithersburg, Md.: Olde Soldier Books, 1990), 10, 78, 84, 329, 360, 580, 612, 626.

41. Trowbridge to Kidd, Dec. 5, 1889, Kidd Papers, University of Michigan, Bentley Historical Library.

42. Edward Cahill, "History That Has Never Been Told," *Ionia (Michigan) Sentinel*, Apr. 27, 1909.

43. *Ionia (Michigan) Sentinel*, Jan. 13, 1913.

44. Ibid., Mar. 18, 1913.

45. "Gen. James H. Kidd," clipping from unknown newspaper, unknown date, Kidd Papers, University of Michigan, Bentley Historical Library.

46. Ibid.

Appendix B. *James H. Kidd's Report for the Year 1864*

1. Deane's force had operated as an independent command attached to the cavalry division of Brig. Gen. William W. Averell, operating in the western region of Virginia and eastern Tennessee.

2. Lt. Pendill was from Prairieville. The wound he received in The Wilderness forced his discharge from service.

3. Lt. Edie was from Lowell. He had enlisted as his company's first sergeant in 1862 and was commissioned as an officer in June 1863.

4. Brig. Gen. James B. Gordon's Confederate brigade of North Carolina cavalry.

5. Commonly known as Sheridan's Trevilian Raid.

6. This statement is incorrect. The railroad was actually the Virginia Central Railroad.

7. Again, this is incorrect. There was no infantry involved in the Battle of Trevilian Station, the largest all-cavalry battle of the Civil War.

8. Sgt. Marvin E. Avery of Birmingham served as sergeant of Kidd's Company E for the entire term of Avery's service.

9. Lt. Luther G. Kanouse of Cohoctah mustered as first sergeant of Company D in 1862. Commissioned an officer after being wounded in action at Trevilian Station, he was wounded again at the Third Battle of Winchester on September 19, 1864. Despite two serious combat wounds, he served out the term of his service.

10. Capt. James Mathers of Pavilion, who was buried in the National Cemetery in Winchester.

11. Maj. Gen. Joseph Kershaw of South Carolina, commanding a division of infantry under Early.

12. Maj. Harvey H. Vinton of Vergennes. Vinton's commission as major was dated May 19, 1864. He was promoted to lieutenant colonel with commission dated June 6, 1864.

13. The cavalry brigade commanded by Brig. Gen. Williams C. Wickham, a prominent Virginia politician.

14. Although he does not name it, Kidd refers here to the Battle of Cedar Creek.

Bibliography

Primary Sources

NEWSPAPERS

Detroit Advertiser and Tribune
Detroit Free Press
Grand Rapids Daily Eagle
Ionia (Michigan) Sentinel
Ionia (Michigan) Weekly Standard
Mecosta (Michigan) County Pioneer
National Tribune
New York Times
Philadelphia Weekly Times

MANUSCRIPT SOURCES

Eleanor Brockenbrough Library, Museum of the Confederacy, Richmond, Virginia
    Fitzhugh Lee Papers
Clarke Historical Library, Central Michigan University, Mount Pleasant
    Dexter Macomber Diaries
    Hiram Rix Jr. Diary
Gettysburg National Military Park Library, Gettysburg, Pennsylvania
    Luther S. Trowbridge Letters
Historical Society of Pennsylvania, Philadelphia
    Simon Gratz Collection
    Newhall Family Papers
Library of Congress, Manuscripts Division, Washington, D.C.
    Alfred Pleasonton Papers

Allan and Rita Losh Collection, Cedar Falls, Iowa
    George W. Hill Diary
Michigan State Archives, Lansing
    Adjutant General's Reports
Monroe County Library System, Monroe, Michigan
    Robert Frost Collection of Custeriana
National Archives, Washington, D.C.
    James H. Kidd Service Records
    James H. Kidd Pension Records, RG 15
    Medal of Honor Citation Files, RG 94
    Regimental Order Books for 6th Michigan Cavalry, RG 94
Bentley Historical Library, University of Michigan, Ann Arbor
    William Baird Memoirs
    Victor E. Comte Papers
    Franklin P. Grommon Diary
    Edwin R. Havens Papers
    Thomas W. Hill Diary
    Joseph Jessup Papers
    John B. Kay Diaries
    James H. Kidd Papers
    J. W. Monaghan Diary
    Henry E. Thompson Letters
    Victor C. Wattles Letters
Alderman Library, University of Virginia, Charlottesville
    Beverly Whittle Papers
Virginia Historical Society, Richmond
    Robert E. Lee Headquarters Papers
Waldo Library, Western Michigan University, Kalamazoo
    William Ball Papers
    Albert and Byron Fisher Letters
    Joseph Gillett Letters
    Edwin Harvey Letters
    William H. Rockwell Letters
    Henry W. Stewart Letters
    Francis Wright Letters

                          PUBLISHED SOURCES
Agassiz, George R., ed. *Meade's Headquarters 1863–1865: Letters of Colonel Theodore C. Lyman from the Wilderness to Appomattox*. Boston: 1922.
Allen, Stanton P. *Down in Dixie: Life in a Cavalry Regiment in the War Days from the Wilderness to Appomattox*. Boston: D. Lothrop, 1888.
Branch, E. E., ed. *History of Ionia County Michigan: Her People, Industries and Institutions*. Indianapolis: B. F. Bowen and Co., 1916.

Butler, Matthew C. "The Cavalry Fight at Trevilian Station." In *Battles and Leaders of the Civil War*, vol. 4., edited by Robert U. Johnson and Clarence C. Buel. New York: Century Publishing Co., 1904.

Carpenter, Louis H. "Sheridan's Expedition Around Richmond May 9–25, 1864." *Journal of the United States Cavalry Association* 1 (1888): 300–324.

Catalogue of the Officers and Students of the University of Michigan for 1861. Ann Arbor: Univ. of Michigan, 1861.

Catalogue of the Officers and Students of the University of Michigan for 1862. Ann Arbor: Univ. of Michigan, 1862.

Chamberlain, Joshua L. *The Passing of the Armies.* 1903. Reprint. Dayton, Ohio: Morningside, 1989.

Clark, John A. "The Final Push to Appomattox: Captain Clark's Account of the Seventh Michigan Cavalry in Action." Edited by Frances R. Reece. *Michigan History Magazine* 28 (1944): 456–64.

Coburn, J. Osborn. *Hell on Belle Isle: Diary of a Civil War POW.* Edited by Don Allison. Bryan, Ohio: Faded Banner, 1997.

Comstock, Cyrus B. *The Diary of Cyrus B. Comstock.* Compiled by Merlin E. Sumner. Dayton, Ohio: Morningside, 1987.

Connolly, James A. *Three Years in the Army of the Cumberland: The Letters and Diary of Major James A. Connolly.* Bloomington: Indiana Univ. Press, 1959.

Cooper, David M. *Obituary Discourse on Occasion of the Death of Noah Henry Ferry.* New York: John F. Trow, 1863.

Cotton, Burwell Thomas, and George Job Huntley. *The Cry is War, War, War: The Civil War Correspondence of Lts. Burwell Thomas Cotton and George Job Huntley, 34th Regiment North Carolina Troops.* Edited by Michael W. Taylor. Dayton, Ohio: Morningside, 1994

Custer, Elizabeth Bacon. *The Civil War Memoirs of Elizabeth Bacon Custer.* Edited by Arlene Reynolds. Austin: Univ. of Texas Press, 1994.

Custer, George Armstrong. *Custer in the Civil War: His Unfinished Memoirs.* Edited by John M. Carroll. San Rafael, Calif.: Presidio Press, 1977.

Custer, George Armstrong, and Elizabeth Bacon Custer. *The Custer Story: The Life and Letters of General George A. Custer and His Wife Elizabeth.* Edited by Marguerite Merington. New York: Devin-Adair Co., 1950.

Dahlgren, John. *Memoir of Ulric Dahlgren by His Father.* Philadelphia: J. B. Lippincott and Co., 1872.

DePeyster, John Watts. *Decisive Conflicts of the Civil War, or Slaveholders' Rebellion.* New York: MacDonald and Co., 1867.

Dillenback, J. D., comp. *History and Directory of Ionia County, Michigan.* Grand Rapids: J. D. Dillenback, 1872.

Doubleday, Abner. *Chancellorsville and Gettysburg.* New York: Charles Scribner's Sons, 1882.

Douglas, Henry Kyd. *I Rode With Stonewall.* Chapel Hill: Univ. of North Carolina Press, 1940.

Ford, Worthington C., ed. *A Cycle of Adams Letters 1861–1865*. 2 vols. Boston: Houghton-Mifflin, 1920.

Glazier, Willard. *Three Years in the Federal Cavalry*. New York: R. H. Ferguson and Co., 1870.

Grant, Ulysses S. *Personal Memoirs of Ulysses S. Grant*. 2 vols. New York: Charles L. Webster and Co., 1886.

Harris, Moses. "The Union Cavalry." *War Papers Read Before the Commandery of the State of Wisconsin, Military Order of the Loyal Legion of the United States*, Vol. 1 (1891): 340–73.

Harris, Samuel. *A Curious Way of Getting Rid of a Cowardly Captain*. Chicago: Adolph Selz, n.d.

———. *In a Raid With the Fifth Michigan Cavalry*. Chicago: Adolph Selz, n.d.

———. "Major General George A. Custer—Stories Told Around the Campfire of the Michigan Brigade of Cavalry." *Illinois Central Magazine* 3 (Dec. 1914): 14–20.

———. *Michigan Brigade of Cavalry at the Battle of Gettysburg, July 3, 1863, Under Command of Brig.-Gen. Geo. A. Custer*. Cass City, Mich.: privately printed, 1894.

———. *Personal Reminiscences of Samuel Harris*. Chicago: Rogerson, 1897.

———. *On the Picketline, Thankful*. Chicago: Adolph Selz, n.d.

———. *A Story of the War of the Rebellion: Why I Was Not Hung*. Chicago: privately printed, 1895.

History of the Eighteenth Regiment of Cavalry, Pennsylvania Volunteers (163rd Regiment of the Line), 1862–1865. New York: Publication Committee, 18th Pennsylvania Cavalry, 1909.

Hopkins, Luther W. *From Bull Run to Appomattox: A Boy's View*. Baltimore: Fleet-McGinley Co., 1908.

Hudgins, Robert S., II. *Recollections of an Old Dominion Dragoon: The Civil War Experiences of Sgt. Robert S. Hudgins II of Co. B, 3rd Virginia Cavalry*. Edited by Garland C. Hudgins and Richard B. Kleese. Orange, Va.: Publisher's Press, 1993.

Humphreys, Andrew A. *The Virginia Campaign of 1864 and 1865*. 2 vols. New York: Charles Scribner's Sons, 1883.

Ionia Souvenir of 1907. Ionia, Mich.: n.p., 1907.

Isham, Asa B. "The Cavalry of the Army of the Potomac." *Sketches of War History, 1861–1865: Papers Prepared for the Ohio Commandery of the Military Order of the Loyal Legion of the United States* 5 (1903): 301–27.

———. *An Historical Sketch of the Seventh Regiment Michigan Volunteer Cavalry from Its Organization, in 1862, to Its Muster-Out, in 1865*. New York: Town Topics Publishing Co., 1893.

———. "Through the Wilderness to Richmond." *Sketches of War History, 1861–1865: Papers Prepared for the Ohio Commandery of the Military Order of the Loyal Legion of the United States* 1 (1888): 198–217.

Kempster, Walter. "The Cavalry at Gettysburg." *War Papers: Read Before the Commandery of the State of Wisconsin, Military Order of the Loyal Legion of the United States* 4 (1896): 429–43.

Kidd, James H. "Address of General James H. Kidd, at the Dedication of Michigan Monuments on the Battle Field of Gettysburg, June 12, 1889." *Journal of the U.S. Cavalry Association* 4 (1891): 41–63.

———. *Historical Sketch of General Custer.* Monroe, Mich.: Monroe County Library System, 1978.

———. *The Michigan Cavalry Brigade in the Wilderness.* Detroit: Winn and Hammond, 1890.

———. *Personal Recollections of a Cavalryman in Custer's Michigan Brigade in the Civil War.* Ionia, Mich.: Sentinel Printing Co., 1909.

Klement, Frank L., ed. "Edwin B. Bigelow: A Michigan Sergeant in the Civil War." *Michigan History* 38 (Sept. 1954): 193–252.

Lanman, Charles. *The Red Book of Michigan: A Civil, Military and Biographical History.* Detroit: E. B. Smith and Co., 1871.

Lee, William O., comp. *Personal and Historical Sketches and Facial History of and by Members of the Seventh Michigan Volunteer Cavalry, 1862–1865.* Detroit: Ralston-Stroup Printing Co., 1904.

Lyman, Theodore C. *Meade's Headquarters 1863–1865: Letters of Colonel Theodore C. Lyman from the Wilderness to Appomattox.* Edited by George R. Agassiz. 1922. Reprint, Lincoln: Univ. of Nebraska Press, 1992.

McDonald, William N. *A History of the Laurel Brigade.* Baltimore: Sun Job Printing Office, 1907.

In Memoriam: Companion Bvt. Brig. Genl. James Harvey Kidd, Insignia 3744. Military Order of the Loyal Legion of the United States, Michigan Commandery, Circular No. 6, Series of 1913.

In Memoriam: John Hammond. Chicago: P. F. Pettibone and Co., 1890.

Merritt, Wesley. "Sheridan in the Shenandoah Valley." In *Battles and Leaders of the Civil War.* Vol. 4. edited by Robert U. Johnson and Clarence C. Buel. New York: Century Publishing Co., 1904.

Michigan at Gettysburg: Proceedings Incident to the Dedication of the Michigan Monuments Upon the Battlefield at Gettysburg, June 12th, 1889. Detroit: Winn and Hammond, 1889.

Moore, James. *Kilpatrick and Our Cavalry: Comprising a Sketch of the Life of General Kilpatrick.* New York: W. J. Widdleton, 1865.

Mosby, John S. *The Memoirs of Colonel John S. Mosby.* New York: Little, Brown and Co., 1917.

———. *Stuart's Cavalry in the Gettysburg Campaign.* New York: Moffat, Yard and Co., 1908.

Munford, Thomas T. "Operations Under Rosser." *Southern Historical Society Papers* 13 (1896): 133–44.

Neese, George M. *Three Years in the Confederate Horse Artillery.* 1903. Reprint, Dayton, Ohio: Morningside House, 1988.

Opie, John N. *A Rebel Cavalryman with Lee, Stuart, and Jackson.* Chicago: W. B. Conkey Co., 1899.

Pond, George E. *The Shenandoah Valley in 1864.* New York: Charles Scribner's Sons, 1883.

Portraits Biographical Album of Ionia and Montcalm Counties, Michigan. Chicago: Chapman Bros., 1891.

Record Fifth Michigan Cavalry, Civil War, 1861–1865. Kalamazoo, Mich.: Ihling Bros. and Everard, 1905.

Record First Michigan Cavalry, Civil War, 1861–1865. Kalamazoo, Mich.: Ihling Bros. and Everard, 1905.

Record Seventh Michigan Cavalry, Civil War, 1861–1865. Kalamazoo, Mich.: Ihling Bros. and Everard, 1905.

Record Sixth Michigan Cavalry, Civil War, 1861–1865. Kalamazoo, Mich.: Ihling Bros. and Everard, 1905.

Rice, Allan. "A Letter From a Young Michigan Cavalryman." *America's Civil War* 10 (Mar. 1997): 74–79.

Robertson, John, comp. *Michigan in the War.* Lansing: W. S. George and Co., 1882.

Rodenbough, Theophilus F. "Sheridan's Richmond Raid" In *Battles and Leaders of the Civil War.* Vol. 4. Edited by Robert U. Johnson and Clarence C. Buell. New York: Century Publishing Co., 1904.

———. "Sheridan's Trevilian Raid." In *Battles and Leaders of the Civil War.* Vol. 4. Edited by Robert U. Johnson and Clarence C. Buell. New York: Century Publishing Co., 1904.

Rosser, Thomas L. *Riding With Rosser.* Edited by S. Roger Keller. Shippensburg, Pa.: Burd Street Press, 1997.

Sanford, George B. *Fighting Rebels and Redskins: Experiences in Army Life of Colonel George B. Sanford, 1861–1892.* Edited by E. R. Hagemann. Norman: Univ. of Oklahoma Press, 1969.

Schaff, Morris. *The Battle of the Wilderness.* Boston: Houghton-Mifflin, 1910.

Schenck, John S. *History of Ionia and Montcalm Counties, Michigan, with Illustrations and Biographical Sketches of Their Prominent Men and Pioneers.* Philadelphia: J. B. Lippincott and Co., 1881.

———. *Index of Persons in Ionia County Mentioned in History of Ionia and Montcalm Counties.* Lansing, Mich.: W.P.A., 1940.

Schuricht, Hermann. "Jenkins' Brigade in the Gettysburg Campaign." *Richmond Dispatch,* Apr. 5, 1896.

Sheridan, Philip H. *Personal Memoirs of P. H. Sheridan, General, United States Army.* 2 vols. New York: Charles L. Webster, 1888.

Supplement to the Official Records of the Union and Confederate Armies. 100 vols. Wilmington, N.C.: Broadfoot Publishing, 1990.

Swank, Walbrook D., ed. *Confederate Letters and Diaries, 1861–1865.* Shippensburg, Pa.: Burd Street Press, 1992.

Trowbridge, Luther S. "The Operations of the Cavalry in the Gettysburg Campaign." Military Order of the Loyal Legion of the United States, *Michigan War Papers,* Vol. 1 (read October 6, 1888), 7–8.

Wainwright, Charles S. *A Diary of Battle: The Personal Journals of Colonel Charles S. Wainwright, 1861–1865.* Edited by Allan Nevins. 1962. Reprint, Gettysburg, Pa.: Stan Clark Military Books, 1990.

Wallace, Robert C. *A Few Memories of a Long Life.* Fairfield, Wash.: Ye Galleon Press, 1988.

The War of the Rebellion: A Compilation of the Official Records of the Union and Confederate Armies. 128 vols. Washington, D.C.: GPO, 1880–1901.

Wells, Edward L. *Hampton and His Cavalry in '64.* Richmond, Va.: B. F. Johnson Publishing Co., 1899.

Wilson, James Harrison. *Under the Old Flag: Recollections of Military Operations in the War for the Union, the Spanish War, the Boxer Rebellion, Etc.* 2 vols. New York: D. Appleton, 1912.

Secondary Sources

Bearss, Ed, and Chris Calkins. *The Battle of Five Forks.* Lynchburg, Va.: H. E. Howard Co., 1985.

Black, Linda G. "Gettysburg's Preview of War: Early's June 26, 1863 Raid." *Gettysburg: Articles of Lasting Historical Interest* 3 (July 1990): 3–8.

Bush, Garry L. "Sixth Michigan Cavalry at Falling Waters: The End of the Gettysburg Campaign." *Gettysburg: Articles of Lasting Historical Interest* 9 (July 1993): 109–16.

Calkins, Christopher. *The Danville Expedition of May and June 1865.* Danville, Va.: Blue and Gray Education Society, 1998.

Carter, Samuel, 3d. *The Last Cavaliers: Confederate and Union Cavalry in the Civil War.* New York: St. Martins Press, 1979.

Coddington, Edwin B. *The Gettysburg Campaign: A Study in Command.* New York: Charles Scribner's Sons, 1968.

Coffin, Howard. *Full Duty: Vermonters in the Civil War.* Woodstock, Vt.: Countryman Press, 1993.

Ellis, Richard N. "Volunteer Soldiers in the West, 1865." *Military Affairs* 34 (1970): 53–55.

Freeman, Douglas Southall. *R. E. Lee: A Biography.* 4 vols. New York: Charles Scribner's Sons, 1934.

Graham, Martin F., and George F. Skoch. *Mine Run: A Campaign of Lost Opportunities, October 21, 1863–May 1, 1864.* Lynchburg, Va.: H. E. Howard Co., 1987.

Hafen, LeRoy R., and Ann W. Hafen, eds. *Powder River Campaigns of 1865.* Glendale, Calif.: Arthur H. Clarke Co., 1961.

Heatwole, John L. *The Burning: Sheridan in the Shenandoah Valley.* Charlottesville, Va.: Rockbridge Publishing, 1998.

Heitman, Francis E. *Historical Register and Dictionary of the United States Army.* 2 vols. Washington, D.C.: GPO, 1903.

Henderson, William D. *The Road to Bristoe Station: Campaigning With Lee and Meade, August 1–October 20, 1863.* Lynchburg, Va.: H. E. Howard Co., 1987.

Historical Publication Committee. *Prelude to Gettysburg: Encounter at Hanover.* Hanover, Pa.: Hanover Chamber of Commerce, 1963.

Hunt, Roger D., and Jack R. Brown. *Brevet Brigadier Generals in Blue.* Gaithersburg, Md.: Olde Soldier Books, 1990.

Hutton, Andrew Paul, ed. *The Custer Reader.* Lincoln: Univ. of Nebraska Press, 1992.

Jones, Virgil Carrington. *Ranger Mosby.* Chapel Hill: Univ. of North Carolina Press, 1944.

Keen, Hugh C., and Horace Mewborn. *43rd Battalion Virginia Cavalry: Mosby's Command.* 2d ed. Lynchburg, Va.: H. E. Howard Co., 1993.

Kinsley, D. A. *Favor the Bold—Custer, The Civil War Years.* New York: Promontory Press, 1967.

Klingensmith, Harold A. "A Cavalry Regiment's First Campaign: The 18th Pennsylvania at Gettysburg." *Gettysburg: Articles of Lasting Historical Interest* 20 (Dec. 1998): 51–74.

Longacre, Edward G. *The Cavalry at Gettysburg: A Tactical Study of Mounted Operations During the Civil War's Pivotal Campaign, 9 June–14 July 1863.* Lincoln: University of Nebraska Press, 1986.

———. *Custer and His Wolverines: The Michigan Cavalry Brigade 1861–1865.* Conshohocken, Pa.: Combined Books, 1997.

———. "Judson Kilpatrick." *Civil War Times Illustrated* 10 (Apr. 1971): 10–12.

———. "Sir Percy Wyndham." *Civil War Times Illustrated* 8 (Dec. 1968): 12–14.

McKinney, Francis F. "Michigan Cavalry in the Civil War." *Michigan Alumnus Quarterly Review* 43 (1957): 136–46.

Mahr, Theodore C. *The Battle of Cedar Creek: Showdown in the Shenandoah, October 1–30, 1864.* Lynchburg, Va.: H. E. Howard Co., 1992.

Martin, Samuel J. *"Kill-Cavalry": Sherman's Merchant of Terror. The Life of Union General Hugh Judson Kilpatrick.* Madison, N. J.: Fairleigh-Dickinson Univ. Press, 1996.

May, George S. *Writing on Michigan and the Civil War by Michigan Residents from 1960 to October, 1962.* Lansing: Michigan Civil War Centennial Observance Commission, 1962.

Monaghan, Jay. "Custer's 'Last Stand'—Trevilian Station, 1864." *Civil War History* 8 (1962): 245–58.

Morgan, James A., 3d. *Always Ready, Always Willing: Battery M, Second U.S. Artillery.* Gaithersburg, Md.: Olde Soldier Books, n.d.

Morris, Roy B., Jr. *Sheridan: The Life and Wars of General Phil Sheridan.* New York: Crown Publishers, 1992.

Power, J. Tracy. *Lee's Miserables: Life in the Army of Northern Virginia from the Wilderness to Appomattox.* Chapel Hill: Univ. of North Carolina Press, 1998.

Rhea, Gordon C.. *The Battle of the Wilderness, May 5–6, 1864.* Baton Rouge: Louisiana State Univ. Press, 1994.

———. *The Battles for Spotsylvania Court House and the Road to Yellow Tavern, May 7–12, 1864.* Baton Rouge: Louisiana State Univ. Press: 1997.

Shevchuk, Paul. "The Battle of Hunterstown, Pennsylvania, July 2, 1863." *Gettysburg: Articles of Lasting Historical Interest* 1 (July 1989): 93–104.

Stackpole, Edward J. *Sheridan in the Shenandoah*. 2d ed. Harrisburg, Pa.: Stackpole Books, 1992.

Starr, Stephen Z. *The Union Cavalry in the Civil War*. 3 vols. Baton Rouge: Louisiana State Univ. Press, 1979–84.

Stewart, Edgar I. *Custer's Luck*. Norman: Univ. of Oklahoma Press, 1955.

Swank, Walbrook D. *Battle of Trevilian Station: The Civil War's Greatest and Bloodiest All Cavalry Battle*. Shippensburg, Pa.: Burd Street Press, 1994.

Urwin, Gregory J. W. *Custer Victorious: The Civil War Battles of General George Armstrong Custer*. Rutherford, N.J.: Associated Univ. Presses, 1983.

Warner, Ezra J. *Generals in Blue: Lives of the Union Commanders*. Baton Rouge: Louisiana State Univ. Press, 1964.

Wert, Jeffery D. *Custer: The Controversial Life of George Armstrong Custer*. New York: Simon and Schuster, 1996.

———. *Mosby's Rangers: The True Adventures of the Most Famous Command of the Civil War*. New York: Simon and Schuster, 1990.

———. *From Winchester to Cedar Creek: The Shenandoah Campaign of 1864*. Carlisle, Pa.: South Mountain Press, 1987.

Wheeler, Richard. *Witness to Appomattox*. New York: Harper and Row, 1989.

Wittenberg, Eric J. *Gettysburg's Forgotten Cavalry Actions*. Gettysburg, Pa.: Thomas Publications, 1998.

———. "The Midnight Fight in the Monterey Pass, July 4–5, 1863." *North and South* 2.6 (May 1999): 44–54.

Index

One of Custer's Wolverines

was designed and composed in Linotype

Janson by Terry Bain; printed by sheet-fed offset

lithography on 50-pound Glatfelter Supple Opaque Natural

stock (an acid-free paper made with 60% recycled pulp

using 10% post-consumer waste), Smyth

sewn and bound over binder's boards

in Arrestox B cloth with Multicolor endpapers,

and wrapped with dust jackets printed in three colors

on 100-pound enamel stock finished with matte film

lamination by Thomson-Shore, Inc.; and published by

THE KENT STATE UNIVERSITY PRESS

Kent, Ohio 44242